WRITING THE
CHRIS†IAN
ROMANCE

GAIL GAYMER MARTIN

WRITER'S DIGEST BOOKS
Cincinnati, Ohio
www.writersdigest.com

Published by Writer's Digest Books, an imprint of F+W Publications, Inc., 4700 E. Galbraith Road, Cincinnati, Ohio 45236. (800) 289-0963. First edition. For more information, visit us online at www.writersdigest.com or www.fwpublications.com.

12 11 10 09 08   5 4 3 2 1

Distributed in Canada by Fraser Direct, 100 Armstrong Avenue, Georgetown, Ontario, Canada L7G 5S4; Distributed in the U.K. and Europe by David & Charles, Brunel House, Newton Abbot, Devon, TQ12 4PU, England, E-mail: postmaster@davidandcharles.co.uk; Distributed in Australia by Capricorn Link, P.O. Box 704, Windsor, NSW 2756 Australia.

Library of Congress Cataloging-in-Publication Data

Martin, Gail Gaymer
   Writing the Christian romance / by Gail Gaymer Martin. -- 1st ed.
      p. cm.
   ISBN 978-1-58297-477-4 (pbk. : alk. paper)
   1. Love stories--Authorship. 2. Christian fiction--Authorship. I. Title.
   PN3377.5.L68M37 2007
   808.3'85--dc22

                           2007027363

Edited by Michelle Ehrhard and Rachel McDonald
Designed by Eric West and Claudean Wheeler
Production coordinated by Mark Griffin

NOTE: All Bible references use the New International Version (NIV).

Permissions

Permissions for the following excerpts are on file:

Dedication

To my husband, Bob, who provides me with amazing support and love. I couldn't do this without him or the Lord.

Acknowledgments

A couple years ago, I was approached by Lin Johnson, managing editor of the *Christian Communicator, Advanced Christian Writer,* and *Church Libraries* and director of the Write to Publish Conference. She suggested that I propose a book on writing Christian romance based on the numerous articles I'd written on the subject for a monthly column in the *Christian Communicator,* a magazine published by American Christian Writers. This book is the result of Lin's advice, with help from numerous Christian author friends who provided me with quotes and novel excerpts. I can't thank them enough for allowing me to use their words and talent.

* * *

Hannah Alexander (www.hannahalexander.com), Tamera Alexander (www.tamera alexander.com), James Scott Bell (www.jamesscottbell.com), Irene Brand (www. irenebrand.com), Colleen Coble (www.colleencoble.com), Lyn Cote (www.books byLynCote.com), Margaret Daley (www.margaretdaley.com), Athol Dickson (www.atholdickson.com), Robert Elmer (www.robertelmerbooks.com), Louise M. Gouge (www.louisemgouge.com), Valerie Hansen (www.valeriehansen.com), Kristen Heitzmann (www.kristenheitzmann.com), Denise Hunter (www.denise hunterbooks.com), Angela Hunt(www.angelahuntbooks.com), Randall Ingermanson (www.ingermanson.com), Kathi Macias (www.kathimacias.com), Patt Marr (www.pattmarr.com), Cindy Martinusen (www.cindymartinusen.com), Tom Morrisey (www.tommorrisey.com), Catherine Palmer (www.catherinepalmer.com), Marta Perry (www.martaperry.com), Deb Raney (www.deborahraney.blogspot. com), Gayle Roper (www.gayleroper.com), Lisa Samson (www.lisasamson.type pad.com), Marlo Schalesky (www.marloschalesky.com), Janice Thompson (www. janiceathompson.com), Missy Tippens (www.missytippens.com), Lenora Worth (www.lenoraworth.com)Thanks to my editor, Michelle Ehrhard, for her patience, kindness, and help, and to everyone else who worked on this book. Thanks also to my agent, Pam Hopkins, who has been with me from the beginning.

About the Author

Gail Gaymer Martin is an award-winning author of forty romances and romantic suspenses, including *The Christmas Kite*, *Michigan*, and *Finding Christmas*, with more than one million books in print. Her books have appeared on the Christian Booksellers Association best-seller list, and she has received the Romantic Times Reviewers Choice Award for Best Love Inspired and the American Christian Fiction Writers Book of the Year. She is currently a romance fiction columnist for the *Spirit-Led Writer*. Gail was formerly a high school teacher and counselor, and later an adjunct instructor at Davenport University in Warren, Michigan.

TABLE OF CONTENTS

Introduction

Romance has been the top-selling genre in popular fiction for many years. In 2004, romance earned 1.2 billion dollars in sales revenue. Book Industry Trends 2005 predicted a 50 percent increase in religious books sales (including fiction) over the next five years. And though Christian romance is a smaller slice of the romance pie (coming in at 11.4 percent in romance paperback sales), it increased 30 percent in 2004 and continues to grow. Romantic suspense has also gained momentum: Steeple Hill added the genre to its program in 2005, and the line has already doubled.

WHO READS CHRISTIAN ROMANCE?

Christian romance is read by Christian women, men, and teens who read other types of Christian books, as well as secular romance readers who have also discovered Christian romance. Reading romance novels begins in the teen years, drops in the twenties when careers and parenthood fill people's time, and then it rises in the retirement years. The strong interest in romantic fiction has drawn readers into other Christian genres that provide romantic plotlines as well, such as romantic suspense and women's fiction. This has broadened the reader base of Christian fiction in general.

WHY DO CHRISTIAN AUTHORS CHOOSE TO WRITE ROMANCE?

With more romances being sold than any other type of popular fiction, the need for good stories is increasing, opening doors for authors to obtain contracts and reap royalties. However, money and book sales are not the only motivations for many Christian fiction writers. In an informal survey of Christian authors, a variety of motivations were indicated for writing Christian romance; however, a large number expressed a motivation beyond fame and fortune. Almost half write Christian romance because of the opportunity to promote Christian values and share their faith. Janice Thompson, author of *Hurricane* and *Banking on Love*, says it this way, "If I can, through my stories, show the reader the parallel between 'human' romance and 'the sacred' romance, then I've nudged them one step closer to the ultimate 'Romancer.'"

The decision to write Christian romance offers an amazing opportunity to spread God's Word and touch lives through stories that inspire and offer hope. While life can press on hearts and souls, these novels can be a release to readers. They enter into a world of people who, like themselves, are dealing with life's problems, and are shown how God's love and the characters' faith make all the difference. Ministering to readers through a beautiful love story is serving God in a unique way.

I've been asked, as have many Christian authors, if it is necessary to be a Christian to write Christian romance. The answer is easy: Since the message comes from the heart and from a deep understanding of God's Word, laws, and promises, writing believable Christian romance is impossible if the author lacks true depth of faith. Writing Christian fiction is more than having characters utter a prayer or attend church or Sunday school; it is reflected in the language, actions, deeds, thoughts of the characters, and Christian worldview that is difficult to represent if not from the heart. Sincerity, truth, and an abiding love of God are what make Christian romance an emotional, spirit-filled journey of love and commitment.

This book offers detailed explanations on the craft of writing Christian romance, illustrated with examples from published Christian romances. It also provides thoughts and advice from Christian authors about writing while staying authentic and true to your faith.

Writing Christian romance has opened doors for me beyond my wildest dreams, and I know it can open doors for you. I often think of Psalm 21:2: "You have granted him the desire of his heart and have not withheld the request of his lips." Imagine the joy you will feel when God grants you the desire of your heart.

CHAPTER 1

What Is Christian Romance?

According to *The American Heritage Dictionary of the English Language*, romance is an ardent emotional attachment or involvement between people, especially that characterized by a high level of purity and devotion: love.

You've heard the well-known phrase "love makes the world go 'round." Countless clichés have been uttered about love and romance. Songs by the hundreds of thousands express the joy and heartbreak of love; movies extol the pleasure and pain of falling in love. This preoccupation with romance validates its importance to both men and women.

DEFINING CHRISTIAN ROMANCE

With romance permeating all areas of the music, film, and television industries, it's not surprising that the Christian romance novel is a major fiction genre. At its simplest, romance is the story of boy meets girl, boy loses girl, boy finds girl, boy and girl have a happy ending. The element of the happy ending is what truly defines romance.

My personal expanded definition of Christian romance is the story of two people with individual goals and needs, the physical and emotional attraction that holds them together, the conflict that separates them, and their coming together, through a deeper purpose and God's guidance, to embrace in love and commitment.

The main elements of Christian romance are: believable characters, realistic conflicts, a solid faith message, and, as with all romance, a happy ending. Most are written through the eyes of the hero and heroine (two points of view), have few subplots, and run from 45,000 to 80,000 words.

Common Romantic Elements

Phyllis Taylor Pianka, in her book *How to Write Romances*, lists common elements found in all romance fiction, including Christian romance.

- a hero and heroine
- a critical situation
- conflict
- romantic encounters
- a resolution to the conflict
- a happy ending in which the hero and heroine make an emotional commitment to one another

DIFFERENCES BETWEEN SECULAR AND CHRISTIAN ROMANCE

Though Christian romance follows the basic pattern of a secular romance, it differs significantly in a variety of ways. While secular romance develops two story threads (personal growth, which is the characters' struggles to obtain their goals; and romantic growth as they fall in love), the Christian romance applies three threads: personal, romantic, and spiritual growth. Spiritual growth is the characters' deepening relationships with God and greater understanding of their spiritual needs as they work through their problems.

Four other major differences between secular and Christian romance deal with the use of:

- violence
- profanity
- physical sensuality and explicit sexual content
- spiritual elements and a take-away faith message

Violence

Christian publishers are opening the door to forms of violence in some genres; for example, Ted Dekker's thrillers. However, readers have expectations of what is appropriate in Christian romance and will avoid purchasing books that present offensive scenes. Further, they often will be wary of the publishing house's books in the future.

Some violence can be found in most thrillers, suspense, police procedurals, and war stories. Violence is necessary, to a degree, in Christian romantic suspense, and most publishers allow violence if it is needed for the storyline and handled in a nongraphic manner. The difference between secular and Christian novels is the level of detail. Gratuitous violence, explicit descriptions, details of blood and gore, and any scene depicting violence to women and children must be handled with extreme sensitivity. If violence is part of a story, it is important to include the elements of righteous justice for the criminal, meaning punishment for the crime, and justice and redemption for the hero and heroine who may have had violent tendencies in their pasts.

There are ways to handle violence in Christian romantic suspense while avoiding details; for example, begin a scene with the aftermath of the violent action, or focus on the internal struggle of the character as he battles against the impending evil. Let the emotion, rather than the physical description, provide readers with the drama of the scene.

In a scene from my romantic suspense *Finding Christmas*, the impending evil is a former client of Joanne Fuller's murdered husband, an attorney. The scene describes Joanne and her young daughter, Mandy, who have been kidnapped by the villain.

> Angelo pushed Mandy forward. She slipped into a rut and fell. He yanked her up by her coat neck and pushed her ahead of him, his pistol wagging toward the ground as he stalked forward.
>
> Mandy's fear-filled eyes searched Joanne's, and she sent her daughter a fervent look, shifting her gaze toward the road and praying Mandy would understand to run when she could. Joanne sought a diversion, anything to distract Angelo long enough for Mandy to get away.

As he shoved Mandy nearer, Joanne continued to wrestle with her hands bound to the slender tree trunk. She sent up a prayer and, then in desperation, cried out. "I hear them." She didn't know why she'd said it, but she prayed he'd look around. "I knew they'd come."

He faltered a minute, his brutal look aimed at her. His gun swaggered in the air as he marched away from Mandy and stuck his face into hers, his breath assaulting her nostrils, his voice hissing. "You can watch your daughter die now." His arm snapped upward as he grabbed the collar of Joanne's coat.

"Leave her alone," Mandy screamed. "You always hurt people."

"Oh yeah," he said, turning back toward her, his pistol aiming at Mandy.

Tears rolled down Joanne's face from the sting of his hand and from despair.

"Shoot me," Joanne screamed. "Kill me and get it over with."

He pivoted toward her and aimed the pistol.

"Run!" Joanne screamed. "Run."

He swung back toward Mandy, and a shot rang out. Joanne gave way to blackness.

Angelo's violence is dramatized to readers as they witness, through Joanne, her and Mandy's fear and panic. This scene has no profanity or gory violence, only those physical actions necessary to make the point of Angelo's depravity.

Notice the dynamic words that help create the drama of the scene: *yanked, pushed, wagging pistol, stalked, shoved, wrestled, brutal, gun swaggered, assaulting, sting, marched,* and *hissing.* These words, which reflect his violence and emotional instability, play against Joanne's cunning and calmer approach, possible because she is leaning on the Lord. Her *fervent look,* her *prayer,* her *diversion,* and *distraction*—the descriptive words and realistic dialogue portray a mother willing to give her life for her child.

Even in romance, topics such as rape, unfaithfulness, domestic violence, and other acts of immorality are found; but again, details can be communicated without a real-time, play-by-play account. Dialogue, introspection, or nightmares can provide enough information to understand the event's impact on the character. In *Upon a Midnight Clear,* I chose to have a rape in the heroine's past become known through dream scenes. With each dream, the image moves closer to the rape. The final dream provides the rape scene, but without detail: "… she couldn't breathe; she was sinking into some deep swirling ocean of icy black water. She heard her blouse tearing and felt her skirt rising on her thighs, and she died beneath the blackness."

Readers know what has happened without the physical details. They experience the pain, fear, and humiliation of the rape and how it has affected the heroine's life. Dwelling on the emotion and providing only a suggestion of detail allows readers to use their imaginations as much or as little as they want to fill in the blanks.

Profanity

Many people, even some Christians, use swear words out of habit or when angry. In secular fiction, profanity is common in the dialogue of both the average cop and the "bad guy." In Christian fiction, however, the use of profanity is unacceptable. Find a way to work around those words and instead show the anger through action, internal monologue, or acrid dialogue that jumps from the page with bitter sarcasm or caustic comments.

Christian fiction authors should not fall back on common euphemisms—indirect or vague terms used to replace cursing—to suggest profanity. *Gosh, gee, gee whiz, geez,* and *golly* are all words created to replace God and Jesus' name; *dang, drat, heck, shucks, shoot,* and numerous other four-letter words are euphemisms for words like damn, hell, and other offensive phrases, and they are as inappropriate as their original counterparts. Some publishing houses prohibit euphemisms, so avoid their use. Instead, let readers imagine the language by using such lines as *his filthy words filled the air, he bombarded the room with vile language,* or *he cursed under his breath.*

Physical Sensuality and Explicit Sexual Content

Sexual desire is a natural part of human emotion, but the ideal approach is to provide the emotion without exploitation. Christian romance stresses chastity for the unmarried, and married couples close the bedroom door when it comes to sexual intimacy. Allow the writing to be evocative rather than explicit. Handholding, embraces, gentle caresses, and tender kisses can create a touching love story without details of body parts and descriptive scenes of lovemaking. The romance can be tasteful while still recreating the delightful emotion of falling in love. (See chapter five for details of sensuality in Christian romance.)

Award-winning author Gayle Roper says this about sensuality:

> I have a catch phrase I use for Christian romance: chaste but promising. Christian romance need lack nothing in emotional impact. In fact, the restraint on the part of the characters can heighten the tension. In spite of the strong physical and emotional pull of genuine affection, the characters choose to remain chaste because they believe this is right, this is what God asks of them.

Spiritual Elements and a Take-Away Faith Message

Christian fiction is built on the spirituality of the hero and heroine and shows their struggle to remain true to their beliefs while dealing with the life issues and problems that challenge them. The story shows the spiritual growth of characters, whether believers or nonbelievers. Christian characters should present a realistic look at Christians in everyday life so readers can relate and apply the message to their own lives. Basing stories on a scripture lesson will present the theme or focus of the novel; the Bible verse and message become a take-away for the reader. This element will be covered fully in chapter six.

WRITING REAL

Christian romance provides a modern-day parable to assure readers of God's promises and give them hope and comfort. When Christian fiction was new, publishers were guarded. They wanted to be trusted, and offending a reader was the last thing they wanted to do. When books are returned for refund, the publisher loses money and, Christian or not, publishers are in a business to make a profit. So the early stories, while pleasant, were often less than exciting—enjoyable tales of families and stories of love with happy endings, but with predictable plots and conflicts too easily fixed. Die-hard fiction readers couldn't sink their teeth into the stories and stayed with secular fiction, where the subject matter often captured real-life issues. Today, however, Christian fiction has grown into a dynamic force of realistic stories that tackle deep and devastating human problems.

Relevant Plot Topics

A recent survey taken by a group of Christian authors illustrated the topics they considered relevant. The long list included unfaithfulness, divorce, infertility, abuse, domestic violence, physical disabilities, cancer, Alzheimer's, drug addiction, pornography, aging, abortion, isolation, alcoholism, lying, pride, depression, mental illness, racism, promiscuity, prostitution, homosexuality, and many other real-life issues.

Talented Christian romance writers are challenged to dig deep into the world and create stories that touch readers' hearts and souls. They create characters with serious problems and real flaws, present complex emotions based on human experience, delve into major struggles of life and faith, and deal with the heartache that affects thousands and thousands of Christians—all while remembering Christian fiction has a happy ending.

To break into the Christian romance market, it is necessary to understand your audience and the parameters set by the various publishing houses. Read books from several Christian publishers to see the depth of conflicts and characterization that go into Christian romance novels today and learn what works and what doesn't.

The problems in the stories cannot be solved with easy answers or by a miracle from God. Instead, they must challenge the characters to use the gifts God has given them to resolve their own problems and, in so doing, find happiness. Writing books about real-life issues and faith struggles common to all Christians is writing "real."

SINGLE-TITLE VS. CATEGORY CHRISTIAN ROMANCE

More Christian romance novels are published in the category genre (sometimes called series or formula romances) than in Christian single-titles (also called standalone or mainstream romance). A novel written as a category romance might have a greater chance of selling than a single title. Because of this, it is important to understand the differences in these two Christian romance formats. In order for you to decide whether to write a single-title or category romance, you will need to weigh the pros and cons of both.

Single-title romance refers to novels that stand alone and are placed on the bookstore shelves independently, usually by the author's last name. In the Christian Booksellers Association (CBA), these books are usually printed in trade-book size, about 8½ x 5½ inches, and are substantially longer than category romance. A single-title romance remains in the bookstores as long as it is selling. If it sells well, the book may go back for subsequent printings.

While single-title books have a longer shelf life, their success depends on the author's name and established readership. Therefore, single titles are much more difficult to sell because fewer are published each year. Single-title romances are not formula driven, but instead depend solely on the author's ability to consistently create a compelling story that hooks readers.

Category-style romances are mass-market size, 6½ x 4 inches, and are published with a series number and released a month at a time. At the end of the month, any books remaining in the bookstores will normally be removed and returned to the publisher to make room for the next month's category books. These books are found in the bookstores on the category shelves under the publisher's Christian romance line rather than the author's name. They can also be sold directly to readers who order each month's releases in advance from the publisher's direct mailing programs. Direct mailings differ from publisher to publisher, but they can be anywhere from thirty thousand to one hundred thousand copies above and beyond the retail sales.

Category books are not reprinted the way a single title might be. Once the books have sold, they are out of print. If a category book is taken off the shelves but has not yet gone out of print, it may be ordered from the publisher or through online bookstores. Some publishers, such as Steeple Hill, will sometimes reissue the out-of-print books a few years later in either an anthology, a duet (two novels in one volume), or as a special standalone.

Category also differs from single-title romance in that it has a basic formula expected by editors and readers. Novels that do not fall into this formula will likely be rejected by publishers. The formula is as follows:

- The hero and heroine meet within the first couple of pages of the story. Awareness should be immediate, but the romantic journey should be slow and based on Christian attributes as opposed to physical attraction.
- A meaningful need brings the hero and heroine together, something more than being neighbors. Something important connects them so they must work or spend time together.
- Every scene should involve the hero and heroine. If they are not together, the scene includes their thinking or talking about the other.
- Subplots are limited because of the book length. If a subplot is included, it must make a direct impact on the faith or romantic journey of the hero and heroine.
- Lengthy details and flashback scenes are avoided.

The fact that more category romances are published each year than single titles may make it slightly easier to break into the industry. Though the royalty rate to the author is a smaller percentage than for single titles, retail sales and direct orders can result in receiving more money overall.

The success of category romance is based on a book line that is enjoyed by readers, allowing books to sell without the author being well known. But whether writing single-title or category romances, your goal is to write a compelling story that readers will remember.

FINDING A STORY

I am frequently asked where I find my ideas. My imagination is triggered in all kinds of ways. Sometimes song lyrics create word pictures, or newspaper and magazine articles offer a nugget for a plot idea. Life experiences, special occasions, or events can present scenes or a skeleton plot. Listening to scripture in church or reading the Bible can present a theme or central truth that I want to explore in a novel. Sometimes the new settings of vacations have captured my imagination, or my own talents and abilities have evoked a storyline.

Imagination is amazing. You are not limited by boundaries, only by possibility. You've heard that sometimes truth is stranger than fiction;

allow your creativity to turn everyday life situations into meaningful fiction stories. Don't limit your vision to the tried-and-true plotlines, but search those tried-and-true ideas to create the unexpected, then weave them into creative narratives.

Having a unique ability, talent, or hobby can provide fodder for the creative mind and supply details that bring a story to life. My husband's military experiences and background in music, stained glass, catering, and cooking allow me to go beyond my own expertise and extract information and ideas from his background.

The lives and faith struggles of family and friends can also produce new ideas, but their privacy must be respected. This can be done by putting a twist on the true incident or premise and making it new.

When I interviewed Louise Gouge, author of the historical Christian romance trilogy *Hannah Rose*, *Ahab's Bride*, and *Son of Perdition*, she said her idea came from doing a study of Captain Ahab in *Moby-Dick* during graduate school. She formulated her thoughts around what kind of woman Ahab would have married: "What I've done in all of these stories is play off of something already written, first Melville's character and then my own."

Marta Perry, whose novel *Hero in Her Heart*, a finalist for the Romance Writers of America RITA Award, says she found her winning plot reading a short newspaper article on service animals, which included brief mention of seizure alert dogs:

> The article didn't have nearly enough information, but once I started researching I found so much that I wondered why I'd never heard of it before. I even found online diaries kept by people who trained with seizure alert dogs, which provided exactly the sort of information I needed and sparked so many ideas for my characters that I couldn't keep up with them. An initial tidbit plus a lot of research can add up to a winning plot!

Lyn Cote, author of The Women of Ivy Manor series, says, "I always begin with setting, which gives me the type of people (characters) who would live there, which gives me what they would be doing in that area and what challenges they'd be facing, and that leads me to their conflicts and then I have a story."

Christian author Lenora Worth says, "I've gotten several ideas singing in church. My In the Garden series came to me while we were singing that song."

Kathi Mills-Macias, author of *The Ransom* says, "Plots usually come first in the form of a 'niggling' thought, chewing on my poor, overworked brain. When I can no longer ignore it and start actively exploring it, excitement starts to set in." Kathi continues on to say that her niggling thought is often a theme:

> An idea came to me one day as I was walking against a very stiff wind. It was a difficult time in my life, and the wind seemed to symbolize my struggle. The thought expanded to the Christian walk, but instead of symbolizing the struggle, it spoke of the never-changing One who has walked the hard road ahead of us and triumphed. The novel was my very first sale, *Yesterday, Today, and Forever*, published in 1989. I believe all creativity originates from Him.

Stories come in a variety of ways, and research can add to the plot, so let your mind and notebooks collect ideas. One day, these ideas can connect to form wonderful Christian romances that touch readers' lives and spirits.

EXERCISES

1. Review the Christian category romance formula in this chapter and compare it to your own work in progress.

Meeting of the hero and heroine. Do they meet within the first couple pages? Do they show a spark of interest in or curiosity about the other?

The need factor. What brings the hero and heroine together? What elements in the story keep them together? Is being together brought on by a strong "need factor"?

Goals, motivation, and conflicts. Are the characters' goals and motivation sufficiently clear? Do the conflicts stem from opposing goals or needs? Are the conflicts strong enough to keep the story dynamic?

Vivid emotion. Does the conflict create strong emotion? Is the emotion shown rather than simply named?

Spiritual take-away. Does this story offer a Christian worldview? Does the story present a realistic faith or spiritual concern with which the characters must deal? Does it give readers insight about faith that they can take away with them when the novel is finished?

2. Study your last few plotlines or review the past few Christian romances you've read. Identify any real-life issues on which the stories focus. Were they compelling? If not, what could you or the author have done to help readers relate to the problem?

3. List all the fairy tales you can think of, the less familiar the better. Select one, and see how you could develop a contemporary Christian romance from the idea. Then do the same using Bible verses.

4. Use the "what if" method of brainstorming to trigger a story. List your talents and hobbies, unique experiences, travels, and job experience. Select one idea on your list, and then ask yourself a "what if" question: *What if I were a college professor and my student fell in love with me? What if I attended an international conference for my favorite hobby, met a citizen of a foreign country, and sensed God had led me to this person? What if I won a beauty pageant but knew that I was far from beautiful?* Explore your own ideas, ask yourself what the Bible expects in these situations and in our lives. Approach the story from a Christian worldview, then move ahead by adding complications as you develop the romantic plot.

CHAPTER 2

Creating Believable Characters

What's a Christian romance without characters? A story may begin with a plot idea or a setting, but it goes nowhere until characters are placed in the story. Without believable, engaging characters, the best plot will fall flat. A love story provides the reader with a relationship: Two people meet and are curious about, interested in, and then attracted to each other, but something stands in their way of forming a romantic relationship. The conflict between this man and woman, stemming from their backgrounds and life experiences, and the struggle to resolve the tension and conflict between them, are what make a story compelling.

WHAT MAKES CHARACTERS BELIEVABLE?

Compelling, believable characters must be three-dimensional individuals with depth, realistic goals and needs, credible motivation, and complex emotions. Christian characters are not static. They grow and change as they move through the story and are impacted by the events and situations in their lives. While their faith will strengthen or temporarily weaken depending on the events, the eventual growth of the positive qualities and faith of the hero and heroine as they fall in love deepens the plot and makes the story memorable.

Readers want to relate to the characters, to connect with and care about their plight. They relate to their struggles because they have had the same experiences or have seen these problems in the lives of those around them. They identify with the heroine's loss of virginity or heartache in having given up a child for adoption. They know what it is to be impatient or to listen to and participate in gossip. They can understand the hero's vulnerability despite his attempt to be strong.

Since the character's past creates who he is today, it is what formulates the individual's present needs, goals, and weaknesses. Even if the hero or heroine is a Christian, each has flaws, sinful ways, and shames. Christians sin, and so should the characters in your novels, so put something secret or flawed into the character's private world that addresses problems as complex as those real-life people struggle with.

An unflawed hero or heroine is a cartoon character, not a believable, compelling individual to whom readers can relate. Give them events in their lives that they want to forget, deeds they fear others will learn, secrets that smother their growth until love moves into their hearts through the actions of the other and the workings of the Holy Spirit. As this happens, the characters grow—as does their faith.

In *Loving Ways*, I created a hero whose present life is paralyzed by his past.

Ken winced. Annie's attitude jarred his memory. He'd been a drinker, created fear in others, embarrassed his family, and caused them shame. *For better or worse.* Annie's words crept like tendrils through his conscience. His life had been worse, not better. Since running into Gordon, the old days kept niggling at him and brought back fear of discovery. He wished the guy hadn't remembered him.

As in real life, people can't hide from the past. They may try to cover it for others, but the past haunts their behavior, attitudes, and values, and becomes a ghost in their relationships with others. Some people put on false fronts, build their past on lies or twisted truths, and live in fear that they will be found out. This is what Ken has done with his secret—

never a secret to God or himself—and while pretending his past "isn't so," the reality of it ties him in knots.

Not all characters have a deep, dark sin, but in real life most people have, at one time or other, behaved in inappropriate ways or participated in non-Christian behaviors, whether drinking, lusting, cursing, lying, having evil thoughts, gossiping, or stealing. The negative behavior may be only a serious argument with a parent that resulted in distance between them, but if an apology was never given before the parent dies, the individual might allow that one indiscretion to linger on his mind and make him feel unloving or unkind. He might think he would make a terrible parent because of his lack of patience or that he is unworthy of the blessing of children. Even the smallest sin can affect the one who committed it.

Remember, also, that the characters' positive attributes should be foremost in the readers' minds while introducing the flaws and weaknesses. Characters who have a deep desire to change, who are vulnerable, yet still likeable, as they struggle with their weaknesses and imperfections, will elicit the readers' sympathy.

Give all major characters a passion and determination to succeed, even the villain. Remember, even the worst person has a few good qualities. The villain might be evil, but perhaps he loves his mother or his dog. Blending weaknesses and strengths and showing the characters' vulnerability and need for God create compelling characters that can make your novel a winner.

Creating the Opposition Character

To help create flawed yet compelling characters, take this tip from James Scott Bell, author of *Plot & Structure*: "When I teach about writing the opposition character, I tell the writers they must come up with an answer to the question, 'Why do I love this character?' It's a mind-bender, and it keeps them from coming up with the moustache-twirling villain. You must give them [the villain] their due."

CHARACTER, STORY, OR THEME

Which came first, the chicken or the egg? You've heard this old query, and people ask a similar question of writers. How do you begin? Do you have a story idea that needs characters, or do you have characters who need a story?

Christian author Randall Ingermanson, author of *Retribution* and *Double Vision*, offers this tip:

> If you're going to create a convincing character, you first need to create a convincing story world. Your character must fit your story world. You can't put Gandalf in New York City. Gandalf requires Middle Earth. Once you've done that, I recommend that you develop your characters and your plot together. Work a little on the characters, then a little on the storyline. Then repeat as many times as you need. It's more important to know what's inside your character than what she looks like. Who cares if Ashley's eyes are green? I want to know if her heart is green! If you know your characters and what makes them tick, they'll behave realistically. Before I write a novel, I normally write up the storyline for each character as seen from their point of view. Every character is the hero of their own story! Even your villain thinks he's the hero in his story. If you grasp that simple fact, you'll never paint a cardboard character again.

Ingermanson's philosophy summarizes the need to create a character while keeping in mind the world in which he or she will be planted. This refers to both the setting and the storyline. He has also hit upon an important character technique: Each character, good guy or bad, is the hero of his own story.

No matter which comes first—characters, story, or theme—believable characters are vital to enhancing the plot. In Christian romance, the hero and heroine must have a world that provides fodder for the spiritual elements of the plot and allows them to experience tension, conflict, and emotion and allows them to fall in love. No matter which triggers your imagination first, the three elements will work together to create a story with a theme that drives or is driven by a character.

Opposites Attract

Characters affect the plot in a variety of ways, depending on how their individual needs and motivations play off each other. As the old saying goes, "opposites attract," so for the biggest spark, create a hero and heroine who strike a chord with the other's conflicts and aspirations.

If you create a neat and orderly heroine, create a hero who's laid back and messy. If your hero likes to be on time, give him a heroine who is often late. If you have a hero with patience, create a heroine who's impatient. A compassionate heroine who wants to help others can antagonize a hero who expects her full attention.

While fashioning these contrasts, however, make sure to find those things that make them compatible—they both love family, they are both Christians, or they have a shared love of nature. The flaws that can create tension early in the story will improve and change, allowing character growth—the heroine realizes her lateness shows disrespect to the hero; the hero learns that if he's less messy, he's demonstrating his willingness to change for the heroine.

Techniques to Create Characters

In creating a character, start by looking at your own attributes, qualities, values, and degree of faith or scrutinize the properties that comprise the personality and attributes of family and friends. Unless you are writing a biography, the characters you introduce can be a mixture of people you know and people you create, not a singling out of one specific individual.

Once you have a general idea of the characters needed to write a compelling story, apply other techniques to define them and bring them to life. Some authors utilize character sketches of the hero and heroine; others create an outline, while some interview the imaginary individuals to learn of their likes and dislikes, their fears and longings. This activity provides you with a past, present, and future for each character, as well as the characters' dreams, longings, fears, and secrets. The interview or outline questions are motivated by the basic plot idea that you have begun to develop.

Digging into the character's personalities, moral attributes, and belief system helps deepen understanding of the hero or heroine. Once you understand the attributes and personality of the characters you want to create, develop physical descriptions. The expression "you are what you eat," slightly modified, also goes for attire: "You are what you wear." Physical clothing and appearance help define who the characters are. To be true to the character, you are wise to give thought to the physical description and provide physical attributes that trigger the appropriate image for readers. Consideration should be given to Christian values in the appearance and dress of your characters. This will be covered more fully in chapter five.

Having a photograph of the hero and heroine is helpful. I'm the recipient of a number of clothing catalogues each week, which are a great source of research. Catalogues often use the same models in different clothing, hairstyles, and poses. When I find models whose looks appeal to me as a possible hero or heroine, I cut out the photos and glue them to sheets of paper. This gives me hairstyles, expressions, physiques, appearances in various settings, and a wardrobe to describe. While writing the novel, I keep the photographs beside me so I have a vivid picture of each in my mind. The Internet is another viable resource for finding interesting faces to use as models for characters.

Free Online Character, Personality, and Career Tests

The Internet provides numerous sample psychological tests and career assessments that can be used to learn more about your character by answering the test questions as your character might respond.

Character tests and personality sketches can be found online at http://similarminds.com/personality_tests.html, http://chatterbean.com, which also explores romantic qualities, and www.careerexplorer.net, a site that features job descriptions as well as career assessments. Another popular Web site, www.dmoz.org/Science/Social_Sciences/Psychology/Test, provides many links to career, psychological, and personality tests. By using a search engine, you can find a multitude of free online resources. These are useful to helping you make your characters unique.

CHARACTER WORKSHEET

This character worksheet allows you to note physical details of your hero and heroine. But you can record the character's hopes, fears, goals, and dreams as well as details on the character's occupation, family and friends, church, and other information that will be invaluable as the story progresses.

Character name: ....

Age: .... Height: .... Weight: .... Eye color: ....

Hair color and style: ....

Identifying physical characteristics: ....

Idiosyncrasies and mannerisms:..

Greatest strength: ....

Greatest flaw: ....

Greatest need or want (long-term goal):...

Short-term goal:...

Other strengths:...

Other weaknesses: ....

Darkest secret: ....

Greatest fear: ....

Biggest regret: ....

Most powerful dream:..

Character's conflicts with the love interest: ....

Romantic/interpersonal conflict (what keeps them apart?): ....

Danger to falling in love: ....

Darkest moment:..

What about character renews the spirit of other character? ....

How does strength overcome greatest weakness for happy ending?.................

What does character learn by end?..

Place of employment and position:..

Type of car: ....

Parents' and siblings' names and details: ....

Significant friends or other people: ....

Childhood background:..

Naming Characters

Names can spark personality types, trigger memories of people you once knew, or remind you of famous people. No one can name a character Madonna without thinking of the singer or use the last name Shakespeare without thinking of the poet.

In Christian romance, authors sometimes give their characters biblical names, but remember to keep the name realistic to contemporary characters and to the characters' images. Look for names that fit the setting of your story and that really tell readers something about your characters.

The U.S. government's Social Security Web site can be a tremendous resource for selecting character names. At www.ssa.gov/OACT/babynames, you can find information relating to popular names in the United States, for each state, and by the birth year from 1880 to the present.

CREATING THE HERO AND HEROINE

The hero and heroine are the major focus of a Christian romance, and all other characters are there to provide elements such as motivation, conflict, or new information and to move the story toward the happy ending.

Though the hero and heroine are usually appealing to the eye, the emphasis focuses more on their internal qualities than their physical traits. What are the attributes and characteristics that make a Christian hero or heroine? Does he have broad shoulders tapering to a trim waist? Is he tall and dark? Is he blond and witty? Is she curvaceous? Does she have a tender heart or a spunky personality? Though each author has a broad spectrum of choices, it is wise to know the more defined guidelines of most Christian publishing houses. These guidelines can be found on the Internet at the publisher's Web site, or they can be requested by mail. For example, while secular fiction traditionally presents the Alpha male (the driving, domineering, and often wealthy hero), Christian fiction leans toward the Beta male (the more sensitive, sometimes laid-back character who tries to hide his vulnerability beneath a quiet, boyish, or defensive exterior).

Physical Attributes

Though physical attributes are highlighted in most romances, Christian romances tend to avoid sexual references. The hero might have a square jaw, raven black hair, mesmerizing blue eyes, and a broad chest, but references to the lower extremities are avoided by some Christian publishers unless the description is needed for a specific purpose. Some publishers encourage keeping descriptions above the chest on the male hero and above the shoulders on the heroine.

The romance genre implies two people finding each other appealing with growing emotions that lead to a loving commitment. You may want to please readers by making your hero and heroine attractive—the heroine with a beautiful face, trim, shapely body, and amazing hair and eyes, and the hero tall and well-toned, with good looks and broad shoulders tapering to a trim waist. While this isn't reality, some authors want to add a fairy-tale quality to their stories to arouse the readers' imaginations.

Nothing is wrong with a handsome hero and beautiful heroine, but the delight in writing Christian romance is that the stories have a greater purpose than writing about beautiful people. You certainly want the hero and heroine to find each other appealing and attractive, but this genre allows for characters who are not perfect specimens: a hero with glasses, for example, or a heroine whose hips are rounded more than she likes. Christian romance focusses not on the outer person, but on the inner qualities. Though characters are not blind to the other's appearance, they become drawn by something deeper, something time and age cannot change. They fall in love with the person within the body.

Character Attributes

Character attributes are those qualities that help the hero and heroine become distinctive, unique individuals. Everyone has a balance of good and bad traits: Perhaps a person is very generous and compassionate, but lacks patience and organization. The conflicting attributes between the hero and heroine cause tension and cause each an awareness of his or her own flaws. Clashing personalities, attitudes, and values create good romantic conflict.

In Christian fiction, the attributes reflecting faith are of greatest importance. In Colossians 3:12–14, Paul lists those qualities which God expects of all Christians: "Clothe yourselves with compassion, kindness, humility, gentleness, and patience. Bear with each other and forgive whatever grievances you may have against one another. Forgive as the Lord forgave you. And over all these virtues put on love, which binds them all together in perfect unity."

When you begin to develop characterization, make sure to include positive fruits of the spirit, as well as the lack of some qualities, that suit the storyline. This creates believable characters with real human faith struggles, and realism is what causes readers to relate and to care about the characters.

In Christian romance, the hero and heroine are sinners who don't follow God's will to the letter. They must have both weaknesses and strengths. Sin is more distressing in Christian romance than in secular romance because the characters have disappointed not only themselves and others with their wrongdoing, but more important, they have disappointed God. The sin can range from telling a lie to stealing or committing adultery, but remember not to give the hero or heroine any present flaw that would turn off readers. (Also keep the publisher's guidelines in mind and avoid such sins as abusive behavior or cursing.) Sins that may be more offensive can be part of the hero's or heroine's past—an unwed pregnancy, promiscuity, or a felony conviction—but the character must pay the consequences of that sin and be redeemed in the readers' eyes by the end of the book.

In real life, people have quirks, idiosyncrasies, and psychological problems. Adding some of these attributes to your characters makes them believable: for example, a hero who cracks his knuckles, and a heroine who screams when she sees a spider.

Although readers love the handsome hero and heroine, avoid making characters physically perfect and skimming over their imperfections. Imperfections can be physical flaws (too short or tall, too fat or thin, bald or frizzy hair) or character flaws (insecure, cocky, too quiet, or too verbose, too prideful). A more serious physical imperfection creates a touching story in my novel *Loving Feelings*. Jenni, a breast cancer survivor who had a mastectomy, thinks about the hero, Todd's beautiful, deceased wife, and relates it to her own situation.

> Tesha. A model. Body beautiful. Jenni's heart kicked against her chest, overwhelming and disheartening her. She gazed at Todd, terribly aware of his attractive face and well-built physique. What had she expected from a handsome man but a gorgeous wife?
>
> Silence settled over them, and absentmindedly, she ran her hand over her chest, aware of how little she would have to offer a man like Todd. She thanked God she wasn't competing against other women in the hope to find a husband.

If you put yourself in Jenni's place, her fear is understandable. She sees her scarred body and is unable to believe that a man would see her as anything but disfigured and repulsive. Yet Jenni has strengths and loveable qualities that cause the hero to stand by her through their struggles, and Todd has learned that physical beauty is not as important as good character and spiritual strength.

The negative attributes of the hero and heroine can eventually be used to show growth and how they overcome these weaknesses by accepting who they are and learning what is really important. God didn't promise perfection. In fact, the Bible says in 2 Corinthians 12:9, "Therefore I will boast all the more gladly about my weaknesses, so that Christ's power may rest on me." Our weaknesses draw us to the Lord, where he can use his strength to our needs. Keep this verse in mind when creating characters.

Let your imagination fly. Select a character from your novel or work in progress and allow his or her needs and motivation to be influenced by the character attributes, or lack of, that enhance the story's conflicts.

For example, let's analyze my novel *With Christmas in His Heart*, a romance set on an island with a heroine who must take a week's vacation from her dynamic career to care for her ailing grandmother. Upon arrival, she meets her grandmother's laid-back roomer (the hero). With the need for conflict in mind, I brainstormed possible traits for the heroine: career-driven, uptight, highly organized, prepared, neat, confident, impatient, uncompassionate, competitive, untrusting, bitter, unsocial, serious-minded, practical, domineering. Since it's important to have readers like the heroine, I removed the most negative attributes unbecoming a Christian and those that don't fit her lifestyle and career. In this list, uncompassionate, bitter, and unsocial.

I needed to give the hero a personality and attributes that would conflict with the heroine's. He is laid back, compassionate, content, spontaneous, generous, witty, patient, messy, accepting, artistic, and tolerant.

Now notice how each character's attributes play against the other's to create conflict.

HEROINE		HERO	
career-driven	untrusting	content	accepting
well-planned	competitive	spontaneous	nonaggressive
impatient	neat	patient	messy
uptight	serious	laid back	witty

To create further conflict, I used the following story elements:

- Her career is her driving force.
- Her career is in jeopardy.
- Her caregiving skills are weak or nonexistent.
- The short caregiving stint becomes longer
- The hero has better caregiving skills than the heroine.
- The hero is playful and witty.
- The hero isn't just a roomer, but a boarder who eats meals with her grandmother.
- The hero is an unassertive business owner.

Seeing the many differences and sources of conflict, you might wonder what would bring these two characters together. Common factors that proved most important in this novel were: love of the grandmother and concern for her well-being, curiosity, creativity, desire to teach the other about what is important in life, and a shared faith.

To create characters that are both likeable and believable, blend a heavier balance of admirable attributes with a weaker counterweight of imperfections. The result is three-dimensional characters and, that key element of a compelling story, conflict.

IS HE OR SHE A CHRISTIAN?

Is the hero a believer? How about the heroine? At times, novels will present a nonbeliever or a weak Christian, one who believed and allowed his faith to waver, but who is brought back to the Lord through his growth and changes with the blessing of the Holy Spirit. Being repentant and seeking forgiveness is often part of a hero's or heroine's journey.

Conflicts in Christian romance often touch upon those fruits of the spirit listed in Colossians 3:12–14. A weak Christian can lose sight of any one of these. The hero can forget compassion and become prideful over career accomplishments, or allow a hobby to become his total focus—his god, in a sense—spending hours in the garage rebuilding his late-model car while the heroine struggles alone to deal with serious issues in her life. He may resent the heroine's intrusive plans or ideas that affect his time or his feeling of success.

The heroine, in response, may become impatient and unforgiving with the hero and, eventually, with God. She may blame the Lord for the hurt in her life or for not answering her prayers.

Conflicts arising from attributes that are part of the Christian walk are all the more significant because they affect not only the relationship between the hero and heroine, but their relationship with the Lord. As the story progresses, these characters will face their failures; they will ask forgiveness of God and find forgiveness in each other for their failings. This happens in a natural, progressive way as they confront their faults, see the repercussions of their behavior, feel the growing distance between themselves and God, change through their personal experiences and awareness, and draw closer to the Lord.

A main character who is not a Christian must come to faith by the end of the novel, but a full conversion must be through the character's personal struggle and not the result of a dramatic revelation from God or a purposeful attempt on the part of another character to use "missionary" actions to convert. The story should show a natural growth from a nonbeliever or a weak Christian to a stronger one who accepts Jesus as Savior.

As you write, give your characters spiritual gifts that arouse the other's love and respect. In my novella "Better to See You," from the anthology *Once Upon a Time*, the hero's faith is stimulated through the heroine's example of Christian living.

> Was this God's work? He wondered. He'd been such a difficult person back then, not only disbelieving, but scorning those who believed ... except Lucy. She had made her faith so desirable, so sincere that he had a difficult time taunting her.
>
> Still, her happy heart and open arms had instilled a small seed of question, of wonder about her beliefs. And he'd done the rest, fertilized by memories of her joy in living, he'd stumbled along until one day, alone in a motel room, he'd picked up a Bible. That day was only the beginning. Lucy would never believe how much he'd changed.

This excerpt shows one way in which a character can re-experience God. Lucy's example of Christian love and action, particularly her personal joy, stirred the hero's desire to have the same kind of happiness in his life.

CREATING SECONDARY CHARACTERS

Since a romance is focused on the hero and heroine, secondary characters are there basically to move the story forward by creating conflict or motivation, provide an outlet for information, or add reality to the story. Therefore, secondary characters are described less than the hero and heroine. Sometimes these characters create memorable moments, humorous or poignant, that add to readers' pleasure of the story. But don't dwell on the character's physical description if his purpose is only to be a "messenger" who provides information or a catalyst to a coming action.

Secondary characters important to the story can be given more attention when their physical descriptions relay an important trait or attribute significant to the plot, like a friend who meddles with the heroine's romance or a grandmother who plays matchmaker. But focusing too much on a secondary character who has little significance to the story can confuse readers by creating an expectation that this character will somehow have a more significant role later in the story. For prominent secondary characters, use only enough description to make them purposeful and real. The more dynamic the descriptions, the more memorable the characters will be. But remember, they should never be as fleshed out as your main characters.

BACKSTORY AND HOW TO CREATE IT

Developing a character's backstory is vital to creating a three-dimensional hero and heroine. Whether a past romance, a difficult childhood, or a dark secret, backstory provides motivation, goals, and conflict in Christian romance. One or two of the conflicts should be part of the spiritual struggle of the character; for example, a prideful character knows that the Lord asks him to be humble.

In Christian romance, issues within the hero's and heroine's pasts are often the "unwanted baggage" that cause the characters to fear commitment, reject love, distrust individuals, or have a multitude of other problems that create the story's major conflicts. All of this backstory is not meant to be put into the story, rather, it is used to flesh out characterization and motivation for goals that will build conflict.

What Encompasses Backstory?

Backstory is all of the action that occurred in the characters' pasts before the story begins. As in real life, these details mold the characters into an individuals with certain traits and attitudes. Their pasts give them strengths, weaknesses, flaws, fears, talents, idiosyncrasies, and goals that make the story real and compelling. It gives them roots.

When fleshing out a character's past, begin with the character's birth. Was it an easy birth? Was this individual the first child in the family, a middle child, the last child, or perhaps the only child? Birth order is a major contributing factor in creating individual personality and traits, and it affects the character's way of dealing with issues. Use a search engine to locate information on birth order and how it affects individuals. Often birth order traits can be used to create conflict between the hero and heroine.

Does the individual come from a dysfunctional family? Dysfunction comes in many forms—the long-term illness or severe disability of a family member; drug, alcohol, or physical abuse; being raised in a home where the focus is on one family member rather than the entire family.

Character Traits That Can Create Conflict

Dysfunctional family members have common symptoms and behavior patterns as a result of their common experiences within the family structure. This tends to reinforce the dysfunctional behavior, either through enabling or perpetuating it. According to Steven Farmer, author of *Adult Children of Abusive Parents*, there are several symptoms of family dysfunction. Notice how these attributes can create hero-and-heroine conflicts in Christian romance.

- denial (refusal to acknowledge a given problem)
- inconsistency and unpredictability
- lack of empathy toward family members
- lack of clear boundaries (throwing away others' possessions; inappropriate touching)
- role reversals (children forced to take over parental role)
- mixed messages
- extremes in conflict (either too much or too little fighting)
- social dysfunction or isolation

Other factors—some positive, some negative—influence people in real life. Consider using some of these to affect your hero and heroine: family faith base (liberal, conservative, or an extreme), family structure (one or two parents, lenient or strict), economic status, divorce, abuse, friendships, health and illnesses, physical attributes, talents, educational background, challenges, failures, successes, work experiences, ethics, romantic experiences, and religious background.

Because the past shapes the characters' present and future, backstory will help create the characters' credible actions and reactions that make them compatible or create conflict.

Backstory Samples

Once the hero's and heroine's backstories are established, it becomes clear how the characters' pasts will create conflicts between them. The following two sample sketches of backstory from my novel *In His Eyes*, help demonstrate this.

Ellene Bordini, 29, grew up in a Christian household with a sister and an older brother who was killed in Bosnia. Her father, Syl Bordini, grieved the loss of his son, the heir to his construction business. Ellene enjoyed contracting and studied building construction in college, then offered her services to the family business. She worked hard and earned her father's respect as a contractor. She was not as successful in romance. Ellene and her high school flame, Connor Faraday, became engaged on their high school graduation day, but in the second year in college, Ellene caught him cheating on her. Though he begged her forgiveness, she ended their relationship and, feeling betrayed, refused Connor's attempts to mend it. Ellene finished her degree and put her energies into her father's business. After dating a variety of men, Ellene finally trusted one and gave herself to him, and he walked away. Filled with shame, she never fully trusted a man again. Until someone comes along with God's stamp of approval, Ellene is content with her work.

Connor Faraday, 30, was raised in a blue-collar home with a father who struggled to make ends meet. Even though Ellene's family was what he considered higher class, Connor knew he was accepted by them, but it didn't stop him from questioning his own self-worth. Raised with no religious upbringing, Connor admired Ellene and her strong faith. When given the come-on by a young woman in college, Connor's male urges led him astray, resulting in the termination of his and Ellene's engagement. Though he hoped to make amends and regain Ellene's trust and love, he learned the other woman was pregnant. Knowing he'd made the woman promises he didn't think he'd have to keep, with guilt and a sense of moral obligation, he married her. Despite their bad start, his greatest joy is his daughter, Caitlin. Four years after their marriage, his wife died, and now Connor raises his six-year-old daughter alone. His life often seems out of harmony, and he longs for the day he feels in tune with the Lord.

Conflicts between the hero and heroine are easily seen in these two sketches. While the story will delve even deeper into these and other problems, creating greater conflict, I established obvious external and internal conflicts using backstory:

- white-collar vs. blue-collar background
- raised with a religious faith vs. raised without
- broken past relationship with lack of forgiveness
- sexual transgressions causing guilt and unsuccessful relationship
- lack of trust and self-worth

How to Use Backstory

Backstory is the subtle seasoning of a novel. It brings out the nuances and flavors that help to create a delicious blend of action-packed motivation and conflict between the hero and heroine. Dumping all of the characters' pasts into the novel in the first pages is like emptying a saltshaker into soup. Instead, decide what information from the characters' pasts is vital to the plot, and in what order the pertinent information should be presented. Always avoid giving too much too soon. Filling the first pages of a novel with backstory can destroy a good story, because it:

- gives readers more information than they need
- creates boredom—backstory is passive, not active
- limits opportunities to surprise readers and create a page-turner
- loses the punch because readers don't care about the characters yet

Once the vital elements of the hero's and heroine's pasts are determined, then it can be decided how and when to add this information. Present backstory in the most active method possible. Flashbacks work if the author is experienced and has the know-how, but a new author is safest providing small pieces of information in introspection or dialogue, as shown in this opening scene from Gayle Roper's novel *Winter Winds,* where the heroine reveals her internal struggle:

"Come on, Trudy, baby. Do it for Mommy?"

Do it for Mommy? Gag! Dori had promised herself when she spent way too much money to buy Trudy that she'd never become one of those weird ladies who talked to their animals like they were mentally impaired babies. And here she was, talking to the little beige terrier as if she were a canine Rain Man.

Dori cleared her throat. "Stand tall, Trudy," she ordered in the sternest voice she could muster.

Trudy immediately went up on her hind legs.

Dori blinked. That was all there was to it? She thought of all the time and money she'd spent on dog obedience classes and the mixed results. Trudy always performed wonderfully before everyone there, but at home she only obeyed when she felt like it.

Dori pictured herself in class. She had always spoken firmly there, and Trudy did as she asked. It was only at home she made a fool of herself with baby talk. With a sigh of disgust, she got to her feet. Just another proof that she needed a life.

The phone rang, and she stared at it for a moment. What if it was Bill Fralinger asking again for a date? Couldn't the man take a hint? Five refusals ought to make him realize her disinterest, or so one would think.

In this opening of Roper's novel, readers know immediately that Dori is discontent. She's bored and has been unwilling to step beyond her safety zone. You see her dog as a companion. You learn pertinent information about Bill's persistent requests for a date and Dori's refusals. But you don't know why, and that's the hook that keeps readers moving forward.

As you experiment with techniques to provide backstory in a subtle yet compelling way, you will learn how to create believable Christian characters that come to life on the page and grasp the readers' hearts. Some techniques to remember:

- Use worksheets or character sketches as an aid to creating characters.
- Give characters true-to-life qualities, both positive and negative.
- Use the qualities to show that the characters are likeable and vulnerable.
- Place the hero and heroine in a story world with conflicts from opposing attributes.
- Use backstory shown in introspection or dialogue to give realistic motivation for character needs and conflicts.

EXERCISES

1. Read the following backstory sketches of the hero and heroine in my novel *A Love for Safekeeping*, noting the characters' motivations, goals, and the conflicts created.

Petite, red-haired Jane Conroy, 29, leaves a "going-nowhere" teaching position in northern Michigan for her hometown of Redmond, Michigan, to take over the family home and a teaching position at Jackson Elementary. Jane's relationship with her father, a police officer killed in the line of duty, has left her with emotional scars. A volatile man, he took his job frustrations out on the family, and as Jane defended her gentle mother, she dishonored her father. Feeling that God has given believers an impossible task of following His commandments, necessitating breaking one to keep another, Jane drifts from her active childhood faith. She is not close to God and loathes police careers.

Strapping, good-looking Kyle Manning, 32, works as a police officer in Redmond, without his father's blessing. Kyle's father, pastor of Redmond Community Church, lost his oldest son during an army training accident and does not want his youngest son involved in a career that perpetuates danger and killing. Though wanting to be a good son, Kyle follows his heart, despite the guilt it creates. He is a gentle man and sees the positive side of his career, protecting people in danger and distress.

From the characters' upbringing or past experiences, list the following for both characters:

- needs/goals
- motivation
- conflicts

2. Reviewing your work in progress or the last four books you've read, list the admirable attributes and the flaws with which the characters struggle. Place an asterisk beside those based on biblical qualities; place a check besides those that go against God's commandments or the Bible's directions for a good Christian. Study how these qualities balance to create a likeable person despite the imperfections.

3. Take a blend of the positive and negative attributes from your list from exercise two and create a Christian hero and heroine character sketch, showing how these attributes can draw them together or create conflict and keep them apart.

4. Using a character worksheet like the one shown on page 22, create a list of interview questions for one of your heroes or heroines. Now, select a character from your work in progress, and interview him or her, using these questions. Answer the questions through the eyes of the character.

CHAPTER 3

The Hero and Heroine: How We Get to Know Them

What characters say isn't always what they mean. What characters feel or believe is often hidden beneath their avoidance or self-protection. Your challenge, then, is to find the most effective ways to let readers become acquainted with the hero and heroine as they get to know each other.

GETTING TO KNOW YOUR CHARACTERS

Readers get to know your characters in five basic ways: physical description, mannerisms, action/reaction, dialogue, and introspection, or the characters' thoughts (this is covered more fully in chapter nine). Use the Getting to Know Your Characters Worksheet (on page 38) to keep track of the five elements in your work and, after writing, to evaluate your story's strengths and weaknesses. Take note of where an element is lacking and develop this section more fully to provide greater characterization of the hero and heroine, making them unique and bringing them to life.

Getting to Know Your Characters Worksheet

Using a worksheet for both your hero and heroine, note the details that will help your readers know them better, inside and out. How do these behaviors make them unique?

Physical description: physical attributes like height, facial features, build, and striking features, clothing and how it is worn...
....
....
....

Mannerisms: traits, habits, idiosyncrasies, eccentricities, movements, gestures, eye contact ....
....
....
....

Action/reaction: physical response to stimuli—anger, needs, compassion, thoughtfulness, conflict, success ....
....
....
....

Dialogue: attitudes, education, occupation, age, dialects, repetitions, hesitations, vocal style, volume, speed ....
....
....
....

Introspection: thoughts that show real inner conflicts, goals, and motivation, which readers see through attitudes, beliefs, values, fears, insecurities, etc............
....
....
....

Use the five techniques to build characterization by first establishing the characters of your hero and heroine and determining their personalities, faith levels, careers, and outlooks on life. Knowing these things will give you guidelines to follow as you determine their appearance—size, physical prowess, vocal tone, and clothing style—and mannerisms and traits, all of which will enhance characterization. A businesswoman might wear reading glasses. Does she hang them around her neck on a chain or store them in a case? Does she misplace them? Does she put them on and take them off to emphasize a point or to betray agitation or nervousness? Remember that her actions and reactions would be influenced by her personality. Is she a private person who hides her feelings? Does she tell it like it is? Is she tactful? Also be sure her dialogue fits the person she is. Can the readers tell when she's upset (by her hesitation) or when she's happy (by her bubbling prattle)?

Avoid Stereotypes

When creating mannerisms and idiosyncrasies to enhance characterization, avoid over-using the traits as you develop your characters. Over-use will create stereotyped characters rather than realistic ones. By layering these traits throughout the story to reflect an emotion and by being consistent, the mannerisms and idiosyncrasies will provide readers with useful information. For example, if the heroine taps her toe when she's nervous, readers will be alerted to her emotion when any toe-tapping begins. By altering these mannerisms and idiosyncrasies as the character learns, grows, and changes, readers will accept the individual as believable and realistic.

Since chapters eight and nine are devoted to dialogue and introspection, this chapter will cover the other three elements: physical description, mannerisms, and action/reaction. In Christian romance, a hero and heroine do not describe themselves to the readers. You will provide descriptions as they arise from the opposite character's introspection or dialogue; the hero will think about the heroine's physical appearance and attributes while the heroine will provide the same information about the hero.

Insightful Descriptions of the Hero and Heroine

Think about your hero's and heroine's personalities and character. Ask yourself how these individuals can be described to enhance the attributes each possesses. Though the Christian romance publisher's guidelines of decorum and modesty must be observed, you still have leeway to use description that will provide readers with a discerning understanding of the characters.

Description not only shows readers what a character looks like, it also helps define the character's personality type—eccentric, casual, uptight, prim, belligerent, obnoxious, flamboyant, unorthodox, or controlled.

Clothing and colors worn are important in expressing who your character is. A quiet, demure young woman wouldn't wear a tight red dress. A baseball cap on the heroine gives the image of a tomboy, while a blouse buttoned to the neck with a navy suit suggests someone uptight and in control. A professional businessman wouldn't wear white socks with his dress shoes, but instead, he would be stylish and polished in a three-piece suit, white shirt, pocket-handkerchief, and tie. Using characters' apparel to reflect their personalities is an excellent technique.

Body posture and eye contact also reflect characterization. A heroine who slumps or avoids someone's eyes might be shy, feel unworthy, or be hiding something. Direct eye contact and a straight back, on the other hand, usually express confidence. A character's growth and change can be illustrated by changing the slumped shoulders to straight, or lack of eye contact to a direct look. Physical mannerisms can also allow the reader to see a character's mood. Those slumped shoulders might show disappointment, while a straight back could show surprise or irritation.

Physical Description Can Create Out-of-the-Ordinary Characters

Physical description can make readers aware of physical or emotional disabilities, unique personalities, or shortcomings that make the hero or heroine unique and memorable. If you create a hero or heroine with a shortcoming or disability, your treatment of the problem must still make him or her appealing and loveable. I recently read a novel with a hero who stuttered. His stuttering was triggered mainly when he was uneasy, so his first meeting with the heroine, a blind date, was poignant.

In Randall Ingermanson's romantic suspense *Double Vision*, Dillon Richard, the hero, is portrayed with a high-function form of autism called Asperger syndrome. Though his disability is not named until later in the book, readers have no doubt that something is amiss from his vivid idiosyncrasies. For example, when Dillon notices that his co-worker hasn't locked his car, readers see Dillon's obsession with detail.

> Dillon put a hand on Clifton's SUV. "Last year 23,378 cars were stolen in San Diego County. The most popular makes among thieves are Toyotas and Hondas. Eighty percent of all cars stolen were left unlocked. You should lock your car."
>
> Clifton studied him, and the grin left his face. "Twenty-three thousand!"
>
> "No, 23,378," Dillon said. "That works out to approximately 8.3 stolen cars per thousand residences."

Dillon's need for preciseness, his preoccupation with exact numbers, and his distress with things being out of the ordinary in "his" world make him real to readers. As his characterization develops, readers are captivated by his relationship with people and his ability to solve a mystery.

A blind hero, an overweight heroine, a reclusive hero, a clumsy heroine, a wheelchair-bound hero or heroine—any of these could make a memorable character if handled correctly.

Sometimes even a small physical problem becomes a conflict in the mind of the character dealing with the shortcoming. Being overweight or short-sighted, having a large nose or two different color eyes, or being shorter or taller than average can cause a character to find herself unappealing. But the Bible reminds us in 1 Peter 3:3–4: "Your beauty should not come from outward adornment, such as braided hair and the wearing of gold jewelry and fine clothes. Instead, it should be that of your inner self, the unfading beauty of a gentle and quiet spirit, which is of great worth in God's sight."

Any disability, shortcoming, or physical uniqueness can be made right through God's love and the love of a person who sees beyond the flaw. "Beauty is in the eye of the beholder" rings true in Christian romance.

Description Shows the Romantic Growth
of the Hero and Heroine

In romance, description is often used to show the growing attraction between the hero and heroine. Readers can watch the growth of the romantic feelings of the hero through his description of the heroine or the heroine's description of the hero. In the following excerpt from my novel *In His Eyes*, Ellene sees Connor again after years of separation following their ended romance. Her thoughts betray the first glimmer of a renewed attraction.

> Still she had to admit, before she'd met him for lunch, she'd often thought about an older Connor. Would he look the same? Would he be bald or paunchy? Their meeting had answered her curiosity. Connor had become a handsome man. Maturity had broadened his chest and toned his muscles so that his trim frame looked well toned and healthy. His smile hadn't changed, and only the small crinkles around his eyes added something new to his character.

In the case of a previous romance between them, the hero and heroine can be drawn more quickly into attraction because it rekindles the old flame; in novels involving a new relationship, however, it is approached with question and distrust, so the growing relationship will be much slower. (See chapter five for more in-depth information about the growth of the romantic relationship and how to create it.)

Descriptions of Vocal Qualities in the Hero and Heroine

Tone affects any words spoken. The words *I love you* spit out in a caustic manner mean something far different from those same words whispered in the heroine's ear. Vocal quality, tone, and inflection—strident, glib, smooth, raspy, caustic, lulling—not only allow the hero and heroine to gauge the truth of what the other says, but also give readers another insight into character. *Her intense whisper slit through the noise* evokes a scene of tension or peril. Perhaps she's being watched or she doesn't trust others around her. The word *intense* seems in contradiction with *whisper*, and the word *slit* adds a sense of danger.

Although vocal qualities aren't easy to show in a novel, the sound can be suggested—*the raspy sound; her silky voice; his words slurred; her pitch raised; his words faded; his stifled voice; his cool, calm words*—and readers can gain a clearer picture of the style of the character or the emotion of the scene. *Her scream pierced the darkness. His words hissed in her ears. Words rolled form his lips like a balm.* These vivid descriptions evoke the emotion of the scene.

Vocal description can serve more than one purpose. Readers hear the voices of the hero and heroine, but just as important, they benefit from getting a deeper look at the internal struggles, the current mood, or the emotion of a character through that description, so allow word choice and reference to vocal tone to enhance what the character is saying.

Distinct Mannerisms

Readers get to know characters through their mannerisms, traits, habits, idiosyncrasies, eccentricities, and gestures. Introduce them early in a novel and repeat them periodically throughout the story to add realism to the characterization.

Mannerisms (inborn behaviors) can also be used as a signal to mood or emotion. They can be as simple as the heroine wringing her hands when she's nervous or biting her lip when she's thoughtful. The hero might use big gestures and talk with his hands he's nervous or cross his arms when he's confident.

Habits (learned behaviors) can involve the hero straightening pictures on the wall or the heroine picking lint off someone else's clothing or smoothing her skirt, all of which could signify the character is precise and orderly. Fiddling with the beads of a necklace or tapping a heel is often a sign of nervousness in a heroine. The hero spreading his arms out as if stretching or rubbing the back of his neck might reflect uneasiness. If he drums his fingers or taps his foot, he's bored or antsy. These mannerisms can help you show emotions without naming them.

Remember, never over-use a mannerism. Better too little than too much. Always be original and avoid stereotypes. And, as in real life, no one is perfect. Give the characters irritating and charming mannerisms, bad and good habits, and flaws and weaknesses as well as strengths.

In Deborah Raney's *Playing by Heart*, Maddie, the heroine, displays a habit that signals her emotional state:

> Footsteps sounded on the stairway not ten feet from where she sat. *Ah, he was awake.* She was finally going to meet the elusive Arthur Tyler. She sat up straighter in her chair. Quickly slipping off her glasses, she moistened her lips and tucked her hair behind her ears.

The readers soon learn that the heroine removes her reading glasses when she's curious and tucks her hair behind her ear when she's nervous or excited. Mannerisms are active, so they provide interest for readers while developing characterization and providing an emotional signal to them. Use them occasionally to enhance the personality or mood of your character.

Action/Reaction

Action refers to an external event—something happens, motivated by a need or goal of a character. Reaction is the physical and emotional response of the character to the action in that particular situation. Action is purposeful, moving the story forward as the character attempts to fulfill his goal or need. Reaction is also purposeful and shows emotion, establishes mood, or provides deeper understanding of the character and his purpose.

For believable characterization, action and reaction must be consistent with the character's personality and style. If the heroine is distrustful of men, she must be wary of most men, perhaps not even fully trusting her father or brother.

Actions and reactions should stem naturally from the characterization you've created for the hero and heroine, and Christian characters should behave in ways expected of a Christian. Realistically, you know this is not always true, so if you write a Christian character who acts or reacts in a sinful or unkind manner, make sure that he seeks forgiveness or that retribution is paid for his misbehavior.

Once you establish your characters' personalities, you will begin to see them as real people who respond in ways appropriate to their upbringing and behavioral style. If the hero is a quiet, thinking man, his action, when upset, would be less volatile than a hero who is outgoing or quick to act. A heroine who dislikes confrontation might react to an angry friend by agreeing with her or leaving the scene of the argument rather than enter into a battle of words.

In the following excerpt from my novel *In His Eyes,* readers witness dialogue and interaction between the heroine and her father in his construction business office. The scene provides insight into the heroine's attitude, her past with the hero, and her present emotion.

Ellene stood close to the door, hoping he'd give her a speedy lecture for snarling at him, but when he lowered the receiver, he motioned toward a chair, his look more tender than she expected. She closed the door behind her and settled across from him.

"I'm sorry, Dad, for—"

He waved his hand to brush away her words. "Ellene, this is our livelihood. Sometimes we must deal with people we'd rather not, but if they're honest and need our services, then you work with them. You wanted a position with the company, and I trusted that you could do the job."

He looked at her above his reading glasses, and she squirmed. "I can, Dad. Have I ever disappointed you?"

"Not at all, I'm pleased with your work. Very pleased." A faraway look filled his eyes, and Ellene figured his thoughts had drifted to her brother who'd died in Bosnia.

His focus returned, and he shook his head. "Today I'm disappointed that you let the past influence your judgment. Business is business."

"I know business is business," she said. "But this is different, Dad. It's Connor. We were engaged, and it ended badly. We have other employees who could do the job."

"He asked for you."

The words jarred her. Why? Though she tried to find a logical reason, none came.

Her father leaned closer, his voice softer. "He said he trusts your judgment." But she didn't trust Connor's. She sat speechless, her mind sorting out her father's words.

Ellene stood at the entrance to her father's office doorway, anticipating his lecture, but his tender look (his action) causes Ellene to apologize (her reaction). Her father's steady stare over his glasses (his action) causes Ellene to react with a squirm and an attempt to defend herself (her reaction). He compliments her (his action), but gets a faraway look in his eyes, remembering (his reaction to his own action), and Ellene remembers her brother's death in Bosnia and that her position at the construction company should have been his (her reaction). Through this, readers begin to see Ellene's motivation to be the best contractor she can be to prove that she can do a "man's" job. The final action is her father's comment that Connor trusts her. Her reaction is she doesn't trust him.

The readers gain much insight into Ellene's motivation, goals, and conflict. Through dialogue that shows action and reaction, the readers see Ellene's spiritual struggle with the commandment to honor her father as well as her struggle with her attitude toward Connor. The Bible teaches forgiveness, and Ellene isn't ready to do that, which gives further insight.

By balancing the five methods of showing characterization—physical description, mannerisms, action/reaction, dialogue, and introspection—you can create well-rounded, compelling characters who induce laughter and tears in readers. By being consistent with their characterizations, you can provide readers with new information using the simplest vocal undertone to a dynamic reaction and enable them to watch the characters' growth through the changes in these qualities over the course of the novel. Following the characters' emotional, romantic, and spiritual growth and learning from the process turns a good story into great one.

If you want to show the heroine's concern over meeting an old boyfriend who'll be attending a friend's wedding, show her anxious behavior. She may grimace at his name or try to think of reasons not to attend. She may begin to feel physically ill. If the hero is up for a promotion and fears he's been overlooked, you can have the employer ask the hero to stop by the office in ten minutes, then demonstrate his nervous reaction by pulling his collar away from his throat or clutching his briefcase more tightly.

EXERCISES

1. Study your work in progress or a scene from another author's work, and find two or three examples of characterization being shown to readers.

2. Review your work in progress and identify the hero's or heroine's strengths and weaknesses. Are any of these strengths or weakness found in Colossians 3:12–14? If you've listed the hero's positive and negative attributes, does the heroine make reference to these? Which attribute does she admire?

3. Make a list of characters in your own current work or a novel you are reading and identify mannerisms given to each. Do the mannerisms provide a clue to the characters' characterizations, moods, or emotions?

4. Write a short scene using this scenario and characterization: *The hero has forgotten the heroine's dinner party and stops, completely oblivious, to see her the next day.* Choose two of the below characteristics for each character that will be important to the scene:

Hero: quick to speak, business-oriented, considerate, rugged
Heroine: introverted, a bad cook, compassionate, a good listener

5. Write a short scene using the storyline that the hero or heroine has told a lie to the other and now faces what he or she has done. You can write this as dialogue with action/reaction between the two characters, or as the offending character dealing with this issue with a friend. You might want to use a mannerism to add deeper characterization to the scene.

CHAPTER 4

The Power of Emotions and the Senses

Emotions turn fictional characters into real people. Compelling characters, plot, and setting are all necessary for fiction, but believable emotions also help to make the difference between a good and a great Christian romance. What brings readers to laughter and tears, drawing them into the story and causing them to care about the hero and heroine, is the rich blend of realistic feelings. Readers relate to the emotions given to characters because they have lived through similar experiences, or they desire to experience the same kind of happiness, joy, or security that the characters enjoy.

EMOTION

Emotion is the intense mental reaction to stimulus of the senses. It is the crux of a good story and it is subjective, meaning each person experiences a stimulus differently, depending on past events. While one person may react to a given situation with anger or frustration, another will ignore it or laugh.

Determining a Character's Emotional Response

How can you determine your characters' emotional responses? The first step is to devise a credible backstory for the hero and heroine. In chapter two, you learned the details of creating backstory using a worksheet or devising a character sketch. The story synopsis of my novel *Loving Feelings* demonstrates how the characters' pasts affect their present emotional responses.

> Jennifer (Jenni) Anderson, 33, grew up in a stable Christian home with an older sister, Kris. After their mother died from breast cancer, the stability crumbled when their father settled into a relationship with a woman neither daughter could tolerate. Rebelling, Kris became wild and became pregnant from a short-term relationship. The child's father vanished from the picture with Kris's blessing and she had a son, Cory. Jenni's life took a sadder turn three years later when she was diagnosed with breast cancer and her sister died during a skiing accident. At 28, while Jenni was recuperating from a mastectomy, she willingly accepted the guardianship of Cory designated in her sister's will. Jenni had always doted on her nephew. Due to the circumstances, she had been overprotective of Cory, and now at age eight, he's become a handful and causes her concern. Along with her worries about Cory, Jenni wants to expand her rapidly growing home chocolate candy-making business. Needing financial backing, Jenni realizes she must take on a partner, which goes against her strong will and independence.

This study of Jenni shows how many of her past experiences could affect her response to present events in her life. She would fear her cancer could return and would worry about her life expectancy. Her sister's and mother's early deaths would make her concern about dying even stronger, and as the guardian of her nephew, an early death would hurt even more knowing this wounded child would be abandoned again.

With a father who seemed to have turned his back on his family for another woman and a sister who'd been abandoned by the father of her child, Jenni would not have a great deal of confidence in men or their ability to make a commitment. She would feel distrust toward men and barricade her emotions from becoming entangled in a relationship.

Her nephew's misbehavior also sets her up for anxiety. While overly protective, she also must be a disciplinarian, and with the job of raising a child thrust upon her, a certain amount of resentment, frustration, and feelings of inadequacy or even hopelessness would be expected.

Finally, considering her scarred body—the result of her mastectomy—Jenni would approach a romantic relationship or marriage as impossible. She would fret over telling the hero about her disease because he might pity or reject her.

The hero's backstory adds to the emotional conflict:

Todd Bronski, 35, grew up in a tough neighborhood with well-meaning parents. He was sent to a Christian school, but his parents did not attend church or provide an example of a good Christian life. Todd's younger brother was a problem child and was killed committing armed robbery when he was seventeen. Todd believed he should have been a more thoughtful, caring brother, providing guidance and direction for him. Instead, he had been too busy overcoming his background and working his way through a local college. He covers his feelings of guilt with arrogance. Working in promotion for stage shows and events, Todd met a model at the Detroit Auto Show. After a quick courtship, they married, but their relationship had serious problems, and Todd soon learned that physical beauty doesn't make a beautiful person. His marriage ended tragically when his wife was killed in a small plane crash, causing Todd to question the Lord's faithfulness. Realizing he's made some bad choices, Todd decides to leave the area and settle in the resort town of Loving, Michigan, with hopes of finding meaning in his life and reconnecting with the Lord.

A look at Todd's background makes it easy to guess his emotional responses to a variety of situations. First, he carries the baggage of emotional guilt, wishing he had done more to save his younger brother. To look at this situation in terms of Jenni's story, it becomes clear how Todd's need to help someone (such as Jenni's nephew) could result in emotional reactions from both Todd and Jenni. Todd might feel determination, even responsibility, to help change this child's direction; Jenni, with her distrust of men and their judgment, would struggle accepting Todd's help, or she might block his efforts. Resultant emotions could be frustration from both characters, even irritation or anger, and intimidation by the other's tenacity. Both would feel confused by each other's reactions, and by their own individual needs to stick with what each thinks is best for the child.

Looking at these two from a romantic angle, Todd and Jenni could deal with the distrust factor. Jenni distrusts men, and Todd distrusts his ability to make wise choices. Drawn to each other, both might question their motivations. Todd might ask himself if he is really drawn to Jenni or whether their relationship is an opportunity to have a second chance to help a boy stay out of trouble. Jenni might feel drawn to Todd but question whether the attraction is to him or to his ability to help her with her nephew—which, though she resents it, she must admit he has done. She would also face her cancer, thinking Todd would eventually see her scarred body and not love her anymore. Why allow herself to fall in love?

A single paragraph of backstory characterization can help you create a three-dimensional character with real emotions based on motivation, conflicts, and goals. Knowing the character's experiences, hurts, successes, and failures can help develop genuine reactions to stimulus by using the flaws, fears, and drives of the individual to fit his or her characterization.

To accomplish real-life emotional responses, study the people around you. Take note of what triggers various reactions to life situations. If you know the person, then you have some idea of past successes and failures, past reactions to a variety of situations, and the most likely future actions. As you create characters, develop backstories that will help arouse the emotions best suited to your story.

Understanding Male and Female Emotions

Christian romance focuses on the hero and heroine. Normally, the story is split equally between the two main characters since each has a stake in the romance and how it will affect their lives.

Men and women handle their emotions differently, which can often create misunderstandings or hurt feelings. While most men consider themselves the breadwinner, the stability of a family, and the person in control, they also consider female feelings and behaviors beyond their comprehension. All this can be a source of story conflict.

These differences are based on long-term cultural and family experiences. Boys don't cry. Boys don't back away from an argument. Boys don't reveal intense emotions. Instead, men cover their feelings with learned traits. They make jokes, get quiet, walk away, deny the feelings, get angry, or show emotion through action rather than words.

In this scene from Deborah Raney's Christian romance *A Nest of Sparrows*, the hero comes upon his fiancée, a widow with three small children, lying on her back on the floor.

> He bent over her. "Starr? Hey ... wake up." The minute he touched her shoulder, he knew something was wrong. Terribly, eternally wrong.
>
> He dropped to his knees beside her and gently lifted her head, turning her face toward him. Her face was drained of color. Her eyes were half open, but their vibrant blue had faded into a cloudy gray, and there was no flicker of life in them, nor in the pulse points he frantically sought for some sparks of hope that she was still with him.
>
> She was gone. He knew it as sure as he knew he loved her. His breath came in short gasps as he eased Starr's body back to the floor and brushed his palm over her eyelids, closing them. The blood pounded in his ears as he stood and whirled around the room, looking for some clue to what had happened. She wasn't lying close enough to the ladder to have fallen.

The hero acts. He does not give way to emotion. There are no tears or sobs—yet. He does what he must, but the emotion is evident in the tender, desperate way he functions. As the scene continues, the hero prays as he expresses his disbelief, then calls 911. He sits beside her, unable to breathe, and finally allows emotion to sweep over him.

Men feel emotion, but they act first. They are often unable or unwilling to show emotion in the same way a woman might with her tears, her words, her need to touch and be touched. While men have the same primary need for a sense of connection, for friendship, for community, even for nurturing and love, they handle the emotion in their own learned way.

Men avoid sharing their emotions, expressing how they feel about personal things, admitting their fears or weaknesses, expressing sympathy, and other emotions they attribute to females. While most women face their emotions and deal with them, men tend to cover their feelings with silence or jokes. Most men avoid tears. When problems become serious, such as depression, a woman feels the pain and often asks for help, but men will do anything to ward off their feelings—sleep, watch TV, become violent or irritable, sometimes drink or cheat on their partners—and cover the pain.

What emotions do men allow to surface in everyday life? Pleasure, anger, disappointment, and courage. Men are more comfortable slapping each other on the back or giving a playful punch to show community than expressing their feelings of friendship with words. In anger, they pound their fists, even stifle a curse word (for a Christian, these outbursts can add silent emotional guilt). When disappointed, they can become withdrawn. In an emergency, men usually jump to action.

A male's emotional expression of love can be largely nonverbal. Reluctant to show vulnerability, a man will often use nontraditional means to deal with his emotion. Rather than say the love words, he will show them in subtler ways—again, action. He will buy the heroine flowers or a CD of her favorite music. He will touch the woman in the form of playful pokes or pats. Some will even miss the more romantic actions—an embrace, a kiss, the words *I love you*—that the female would prefer, instead doing things for her: filling her gas tank, checking her tires' air pressure, sweeping the garage, plowing snow, or bringing home a pizza.

Men often think of practical gifts rather than romantic ones. A bread-making machine or a new food mixer seems as appropriate a gift as diamond earrings. Men use acts of kindness as an expression of love. An ultimate sacrifice can be giving up watching a big football game to take a woman out for dinner. They believe this is a greater way to show love than by buying her a bottle of perfume or a box of candy.

In Christian romance, passion is usually covered beneath tenderness or kindness rather than shown through explicit actions beyond a kiss—though the hero may hint at his sexual arousal by suggesting he go home to take a cold shower or reminding himself in introspection that he's stepping over the line of appropriate Christian behavior.

Women, on the other hand, tend to be talkers more than doers. They like to share feelings; they want to talk about theirs, and they want a man to talk about his. However unrealistic, women often do expect men to read their minds. They hint at their needs and preferences rather than state them, then when a man does not understand the hint or misses it altogether, the woman is usually upset. "What's wrong?" the man asks. "If you don't know, then you don't love me," might be the woman's response. Although this is an exaggeration, it is the essence of how a woman thinks. She wants the man in her life to understand her needs and wants without being told.

Crying is the response of many women to disappointment, sadness, or pain. They are not embarrassed to shed tears over sad news or even touching movies. It provides an outlet for heartache but can make many men feel helpless or uncomfortable. During times like this, women want to be held quietly, allowing the free flow of sadness that helps wash away the pain.

Women want to be appreciated. Whether a homemaker or a career woman who arrives home and throws dinner on the table, women appreciate a thank-you for the meal and for folding laundry. As much as a thank-you is appreciated, the greatest form of thanks is a man who helps with the household chores because he understands that it is hard work.

A look at the advertisements in women's magazines shows many women's romantic preferences: a woman in a candlelight bubble bath sprinkled with rose petals; being fed a cherry dipped in whipped cream; dining in a posh restaurant with soft lights, romantic music, and her man in a suit and tie (which many men dislike). Many women also view gifts of candy, jewelry, and perfume as a far deeper expression of love than a night at the pizza parlor. These difference can add conflict to your story.

Yet in Christian romance, readers want to see and feel love and emotion, so it is necessary to break the male mold of expressing emotion and soften it as part of the character's growth and change. Create men who can show small expressions of love—a tender touch, a sweep of his finger to brush her hair from her cheek, a quick embrace. Those simple expressions early in the story can allow the emotion to grow realistically and provide a wonderful dynamic in Christian romance.

Understanding Complex Emotions

No reaction is pure and distinctive. Real-life emotions are complex, usually a blend of feelings, because people bring past experiences into every emotion. Sometimes a wonderful time of life can fall apart with a telephone call, or the joy of making the last payment on a car ends the next day when the family teenager totals it.

People with optimistic personalities will look beyond "what if this happens?" to the belief that everything will be fine. Others approach life with the expectation that things will fail. Each personality affects how a person copes with and accepts what life has to offer. So, as you create your characters, analyze the personalities you've created with all of the shades of emotion to make it realistic. Search your own reactions to stress, joy, fear, or grief, and you will begin to have a handle on the complexity of emotions.

Even joy, which arouses feelings of happiness, delight, or triumph, can bring undertones of disbelief or anxiety. Disbelief often follows unexpected blessings, such as winning a contest: *They will view the contest records again and find a mistake.* Making reservations for a much-anticipated vacation can be marred by anxiety: You anticipate that something will go wrong—someone will become ill and you'll have to cancel the trip. These responses are typical for everyone who carries emotional baggage into every life situation.

Let's take a look at the emotion of grief, a typical emotion in Christian romance. Grief doesn't only involve death; it comes with a job loss, personal loss such as a house fire, or the loss of reputation. But two forms of grief significant in Christian fiction are loss of a loving commitment and loss of faith. God has expectations and when people fail in these areas, they not only fail themselves, they also fail the Lord. Since Christian romance is based on both the relationship of a man and woman and their relationship to God, these two losses can effect the heaviest grief in the story.

Grief comes in stages, and the length of each stage differs for each individual. One person's grief cannot be compared to another's. Each is private and personal. When dealing with any form of grief, match the stages of grief against your character's backstory. How has he handled loss in the past? How has she learned to compensate for emotional weakness in the present? How has he dealt with his faith in terms of the loss?

In Christian romance, behaving as a Christian means having faith in God. When forms of loss, expressed as grief, come into play, look at the various choices of reaction. While the common stages of grief—denial, anger, bargaining, depression, and, finally, acceptance—are accepted by most authorities, other emotional reactions have also been noted by those who work in grief groups. When creating a character who is coping with grief based on loss, you can also include: shock (sometimes even the loss of memory), numbness, guilt (believing something could have been done to prevent the loss), rage (especially with an illness such as cancer), irritability and emotional outbursts, or powerlessness (feeling vulnerable, frightened, or pessimistic).

The bargaining stage is significant for Christians because it is an outreach to God to prevent the death and to make the person well again, or to bring love back. When His answer is not yes, a person may feel abandoned by God. Abandonment creates emotional scars. It causes the person to question why she is unworthy of God's love or what she has done for God to turn his back on her. Feelings of doubt creep in regarding self-worth, judgment, and the ability to be loved.

Christian romance is about falling in love, but in real life, romance is impacted by the struggles people face in their daily lives. When loss and other stresses weaken a character's faith, the problems can affect his or her romantic relationship. These emotions can cause greater turmoil for a Christian who knows she should trust the Lord, yet is stuck in the grief stages or in unresolved issues. Deeper conflict and tension can ensue when a hero or heroine is not aware of the complexity of his or her own emotions, just as you are not always aware of why you feel the way you do.

Creating Complex Emotions

In the same way grief and joy were dissected, it is necessary to look at the nuances of all emotion so that genuine reactions and feelings can be given to the characters. Emotions are three-dimensional and filled with nuances, usually a blend of feelings. For example, anger can also include disappointment and frustration.

To give a character realistic, complex emotions, decide how that particular individual will respond to a certain stimulus. Consider, for example, the emotions of the heroine going out for the first time with the man of her dreams. She might feel a mixture of excitement, anxiety, happiness, adventure, or inadequacy, depending on her past experience, present goals and motivation, or expectations.

A heroine who has had success in dating would enjoy herself and have no assumptions of a long-term relationship. Her response to the dream date would likely be one of excitement and happiness, perhaps even a sense of adventure. On the other hand, a young woman recently out of a bad relationship—her fiancé having rejected her for someone else, perhaps—would feel unworthy and hopeless. She would perhaps approach this dream date with anxiety and a sense of inadequacy and unworthiness.

In the same way, a hero who asks the heroine to join him for dinner and is refused may feel any combination of frustration, irritation, temporary defeat, depression, embarrassment, or determination. In this scenario, you would need to understand the hero's sense of worth, his past relationships, and his expectations. If the hero's invitation meant only a dinner date for the evening, he might slough off the incident with little concern. If he likes her but senses she wants little to do with him, he could feel frustrated or embarrassed that he'd asked.

If he really cares about the heroine, and senses that her rejection has little to do with him and mostly to do with her own immediate problems—or if he needs to form a relationship with this woman for selfish reasons—he might become even more determined to pursue her.

Revealing Physical and Emotional Responses

The secret to revealing emotion is to *show* instead of *tell*. Telling is describing the emotion; showing is bringing it to life, dramatizing it through action and reaction and mood of the scene. Since action is what powers a novel, showing is the most effective method to reveal emotions because it involves the readers by dramatizing the story events. To say someone is sad or lonely does not tug at the heartstrings. To show loneliness arouses feelings from the readers' own life experiences.

Telling: She was lonely. Loneliness filled her.
Showing: Outside the window, a lone gray cloud floated against the blue sky. She sank into the chair surrounded by an empty silence that pressed against her heart.

In the example above, the words *gray, sank, empty silence,* and *pressed* trigger a sense of loneliness in the readers' minds. Even nature—the lone cloud—reflects the character's feeling of isolation and loneliness.

Although showing is the most important technique to create emotion, you can also bring a scene to life through word choice. A scene from my novel *Upon a Midnight Clear* shows the hero's love for his child through internal monologue and action. The character has been quiet and aloof, at times even abrasive with the heroine, and readers need to see his more tender side, the part he cannot show the heroine.

> A soft night light glowed a warm pink. Natalie's slender frame lay curled under a quilt, and the rise and fall of the delicate floral print marked her deep sleep. He moved lightly across the pink carpeting and stood, looking at her buttercup hair and her flushed, rosy cheeks. His heart lurched at the sight of his child—their child, fulfilling their hopes and completing their lives.

To create this gentle scene, notice the use of pink, rosy, and buttercup colors—pastels that give readers a sense of calm and also of youth. Along with colors, listen for the alliteration; the soft-sounding consonant *f* adds to the language of romance, heard in *soft, frame, fall, floral, flushed,* and *fulfilling.* Word selection is vital to creating a mood, so when writing a tender scene, stay with the softer-sounding consonants and the vowel tones:

Along with the feeling of love, this narration arouses tenderness and awe, giving the hero a much deeper characterization. Each scene must help readers become more acquainted with the main characters through their reactions and emotional responses to life events.

Emotion draws readers into the story and anchors them there by showing rather than telling, using word pictures and word sounds, and creating layers of physical response and reactions that relate to the readers' experiences.

Physical Responses

Emotions are revealed in a variety of ways. Physical reactions are visible signs shown in body movement, posture, and facial expression, but emotion can also be revealed through dialogue (see chapter eight), introspection (see chapter nine) and imagery (see the senses section on page 65). Physical reactions are the first clue to a character's feelings.

The physiological changes that emotions arouse are usually involuntary and vary from person to person. Outward reactions to emotions include shaking or trembling, knots forming in the shoulders, a nervous tic developing in the jaw, or constriction of vocal cords, causing the voice to raise pitch or trigger a scream.

Emotions also cause internal reactions: an increase of adrenaline, which causes a rise in heart rate and blood pressure and stimulates blood glucose levels causing a dizzy sensation or even nausea. Adrenaline will cause blood to rush to the face, making it look flushed, and body temperature to rise, which can result in sweaty palms or a perspiring brow. These outward reactions can be a clue to readers as to what emotions a character is feeling.

Delight and fear can produce some of the same physical responses: a flush, perspiration, or a tremor. Only the mental response, and often the facial expression, will delineate between the two. Picture a young wife, shocked by her military husband's surprise return home. Her heart would pound; she might flush, scream, tremble, cry, or faint. The same young woman attacked in a dark parking lot might experience the same physical reactions. Her mental state, facial response, or movements (toward her husband; away from the attacker) would show her true internal emotion.

Dialogue Reveals Emotion

Words have power, and their meaning is even stronger with inflection and volume. When we read certain words, we can envision the vocal tone without seeing them in action. As you read these unrelated lines of dialogue, note that they can be very clear even without introspection or action.

"Stay away from me."
"Don't touch me again."
"You thrill me."

"I will not put up with this."

"Wow."

"You're so beautiful."

"Help!"

"You're breaking my heart."

"I can't deal with this anymore."

"I love you."

These lines of dialogue, even without physical description, convey an emotional message. You can envision stress, a clenched fist, a tender smile, flexed hands, a blush, arms opening wide, gritted teeth, a tensed jaw, or a rigid body. The list could go on and on.

Not all emotion is that clear cut and dramatic; subtler emotion can be created through word choice. When selecting words for the characters' dialogue, recall their connotative meanings and pay attention to the sound of the word. If the hero says, "You must come to the party" as opposed to "You ought to come to the party," the difference is clear. The first sounds more demanding because the connotative meaning of *must. Ought* sounds more like encouragement. Similarly, some consonants have sharper tones. Notice the difference between the comment *put that down* and *lay that down*. The word *put* has a harder sound, which makes it more demanding than the gentler sound of *lay*. Say the words aloud and hear the difference.

Adding vocal hesitation, dodging an issue, or cutting off the speaker by using an em dash or ellipses can also be a method of showing emotion. Notice the subtler emotion in this dialogue from Christian author Tom Morrisey's novel *High Places*. Set in West Virginia in 1976, Patrick, age seventeen, is trying to arrange a date with Rachel, the pastor's daughter, who is sixteen. Patrick broaches the subject while Rachel is washing dishes from the food the church ladies have sent over.

"Do you ever go to the movies, or concerts or stuff?"

She cocked her head as she placed the strip of masking tape marked "Hooper" back on the baking dish.

"Do you mean, do I go out on dates?"

"Uhm, well … yeah, I guess."

She shook her head.

"Folks in our church don't go to Hollywood movies, Patrick."

That was how she phrased it: *Hollywood* movies.

"Why? Do you think they're—what …? Sinful?"

"Some people do." She set a dish aside and began replacing the masking-tape label on another. "And in some cases, they're right. But even if they're not …" She glanced at the living room before continuing in a whisper. "I've seen a Hollywood movie … or two … and they make it seem as if what you do, that everything will come out perfect in the end, and people see that and then they wonder why their lives don't match that, and it's not that their lives are wrong. It's that the movies have it wrong."

In this wonderful excerpt about young love, you can see the emotional struggle of both Patrick and Rachel as they have their first discussion about dating. The emotion is subtle, yet clear. Patrick is nervous. You see this in his hesitations and low-key approach. To portray his surprise when he realizes she thinks movies are sinful, the author uses the technique of an em dash then ellipses before his final question—*Sinful?* You can almost hear the disbelief in his voice.

Rachel opens with quiet acceptance. According to her head shake, she doesn't date. While it's unclear whether that is her parents' decision or her own, it's obvious that not seeing movies is her parents' rule, because she admits to Patrick in a whisper that she's seen a few. Yet Rachel has given thought to movies, and the dialogue shows her struggle balancing her faith against the worldview of what's right and wrong. The author accomplishes this by changing the terse responses and head nods to a lengthy explanation that appears to have been given much thought.

Words themselves carry emotion, but the emotion can be augmented by using the techniques of changing dialogue style and adding punctuation signals (although you don't want to overdo the em dash and ellipses).

Imagery Reveals Emotion

Emotions are both physical and psychological, but they can also be presented in images. Word pictures arouse emotions and broaden the impact for readers. The first ride on a roller coaster, the first look at your newborn child, the first touch of a man's hand, the first look at the Grand Canyon—all of these images arouse emotions that stay with you. Using these familiar images, word pictures can be an effective way to elicit feelings from readers while bringing the emotion to life for the character.

The images must be selected to fit the storyline and to be true to the character. A heroine, for example, expects to be asked on a second date since the evening went so well. When she meets the hero again, however, he's friendly but makes no overture. Her reaction could be feeling rejected. This emotion can be brought to life by using a word picture in the form of poetic devices, such as similes (showing a comparison by using the word *like*) or metaphors (an implicit comparison that uses a more interesting or colorful word or phrase as a substitute for another). For example, *She felt like a telephone number tossed thoughtlessly into a trash can* or *She was a dewy rose tossed to the ground, wilted and forgotten* arouse much more emotion in the reader than "She felt abandoned."

Poetic language is appropriate not only for romantic scenes, it can be just as dramatic in scenes depicting fear and violence, as a way to avoid the gory details. In this excerpt from Colleen Coble's Christian romantic suspense *Fire Dancer*, Coble's use of word pictures and poetic language catches readers in the mind of the villain:

> My heart dances with the leaping flames of the campfire. Mom never cared much for poetry, said she had no use for it in what she faced every day, but the cadence of words speaks to me. Kind of stupid when you consider who I am and what I do. There is more to a soul than what others see.
>
> The flames mesmerize me. I hold my hands over the flickering light and breathe deep. Close my eyes. We used to roast hot dogs over a fire in our yard, just me and Mom, in fall when the stars were clear and close and the air was a blade in my throat.

The Navajo witch settles beside me. I'm not afraid, even if my breath sounds in my ears. Shrouded by wolf skins, he seems to be growing bigger. People have told me there's no such thing as a skinwalker. They are wrong. The hair on the back of my neck rises, almost as if it's saluting the magic radiating from the imposing figure. The heat he radiates is as bewitching as the flames, almost as if we're twin souls.

Coble blends a combination of dynamic words that create pictures and arouse the senses. *The air was a blade in my throat* is pure metaphor, while the words *my heart dances with the leaping flames of the campfire* creates a distinct picture as she compares the fiery excitement in the villain to the campfire. In the gripping image *the hair rising on my neck … as if it's saluting the magic*, the captivating excitement, the heat, the sense the danger, evil, and fear, are evident in every word. To create this kind of exciting journey for readers, select words that capture the essence of emotion.

Avoiding Timeworn Emotional Language

The secret to writing effective emotion that captures readers' hearts is to make the descriptive language fresh and unique and to avoid emotional clichés.

Sometimes you can fall into the practice of using clichés or timeworn phrases because it's easy. The descriptions slip past readers because they are no longer emotional language. *Green with envy, angry as a wet hen, rigid as a poker,* and *hot under the collar* are all trite and overused. If you want to use a comparison, be creative and come up with something original—*angry as a matador's bull* or *rigid as a schooner mast.*

Look for emotions that emphasize the romance. Vivid, fresh imagery in the form of an analogy (a comparison between two things with common elements) is a creative way to bring life to a jaded romantic. How often have you read "her heart fluttered"? An example from my novel *Loving Treasures* shows the emotion of a heart fluttering in a different way when Jemma Dupre, a young widow, and the hero experience their first meeting.

A summer pinwheel whirled in Jemma's chest, taking her breath away. No one gave her that much kind attention, not even Lyle. She murmured her thanks and sat nailed to her seat while Claire followed him toward the side door. His rich, genial voice drifted from the hallway.

The pinwheel analogy is fresh and unique, and even more important, the comparison of a flutter in the chest to the twirling sensation of a pinwheel is one readers can feel and relate to.

Be as original as possible so that your language and word pictures stimulate wonderful new images for readers. These impressions will cause them to remember the story long after they've read it.

Searching for Real-Life Emotional Responses

How can you find words to express a specific emotion? It's a common question. The first place to look is inside yourself. You live daily with emotional experiences—bored with the status quo of your job, excited about an upcoming event, anxious about a presentation, or ecstatic about a special romantic evening. Think of one of these moments when you experienced a strong emotion. Now relive that emotional experience in your mind. How did you respond physically and react outwardly? By recreating the emotion, you can feel the impact on your physical and mental state. If you can feel the emotion, you can more effectively recreate that emotion for readers because your writing is more authentic. The readers must be able to feel and relate to the emotion to make the book a satisfying read.

Become an actor. Stand in front of a full-length mirror and return to that moment in time. Recall the sensations in your body. Did your stomach churn? Did your heart thump so violently that you thought your breastbone would break? Did your hands tremble? Did you laugh so hard that your jaw and stomach ached?

Look at your facial expressions as you feel the emotion. Are your eyes wide or narrowed? Are your brows knitted or arched? Where are your hands? Are they propped on your hips, knotted on your lap, waving madly at the air?

Though you may never have been estranged from your spouse, you have felt alienated or unloved in other situations. You have been lonely, frightened, worried, or anxious. Finding an experience as close as possible to the one in your story and reliving that emotion will allow you to create real physical and emotional responses in the scene.

Two Techniques to Create Emotional Responses

To create real-life emotional responses in your story, try these methods. At the top of a sheet of paper, name a number of emotions you might expect to witness in a film or TV drama. Now watch a program and jot down what physical and verbal reactions you witness with various emotions. Notice that each character will have his or her own way of responding to a similar emotional stimulus (and keep in mind that men and women often react differently when dealing with the same emotion). When the program is completed, refine your notes so that you can use them as you write.

A similar technique is observing people. Spend a few hours in a café or wandering through a shopping mall, noting the body and facial reactions of the individuals as they converse. Can you detect the emotion being expressed? Look for emotional clues such as leaning closer to the other individual or pulling away, widened eyes, furrowed brow, knotted hands. Watch parents with their children. You may observe a range of emotion, from deep love to deep frustration or anger. No matter which method you use, prepare your notes so they are useful when you need them.

THE SENSES

Your senses are the means by which you experience and perceive everything around you. They heighten emotion by arousing readers' sense memories and drawing them into the story. When you show emotions by giving details and reactions, you can see the hero's flexing biceps, hear his tender voice, taste the peppermint on his lips, smell his musky aftershave, and feel his prickly whiskers.

Readers need to enjoy the romantic experience of the hero and heroine through the full use of the five senses—sight, sound, smell, touch, and taste. Heightening the use of senses means more than including all of them in the novel. It defines the method of delving more deeply into the senses in a creative way. The senses are more than stating what the hero or heroine sees, hears, touches, tastes, or smells; it includes the characters' reactions to the stimulus, the way in which the senses impact them and create an emotion. Consider this example: *The woman shimmered behind the windowpane and through him like a flutter of fine silk.* You not only picture the scene, but you know how it makes the hero feel.

Because of the restriction of graphic sexual intimacy often portrayed in secular fiction, Christian romance depends on emotional sense imagery when dealing with the love relationship between the hero and heroine. Christian romance is open to the beauty of poetic devices and the tenderness of the romantic experience. When you include as many of the senses as possible in a dynamic and fresh way, you have found the secret of creating dynamic emotion.

Heightening the Senses of Sight and Sound

Since sight and sound are the most common senses used in Christian romance, bring these senses to life and make them fresh by creating interesting analogies to describe the romantic sensation. Analogies taken from nature create a vivid picture for readers because they are things almost everyone can relate to, things with which we're all familiar.

Sight

When creating sight images, use texture and color while adding the nuances of the scene. This is what makes the description vivid and encourages the emotional impact. This opening scene from my contemporary gothic romance "Then Came Darkness" (in the anthology *Hidden Motives*) focuses on sight imagery and demonstrates how the use of analogies, along with carefully selected word pictures, creates a mood that arouses the readers' emotions. Gerri arrives at a house that she prays can clear her deceased grandfather of murder.

> The sprawling mansion stood before her like a weight pressing on her spirit.
>
> Gerri Ward paused in the shadow of a towering oak and studied the brooding building. Like the ivy clinging to the gray stone, the dark secret had choked the life from those who lived inside. That's what she had heard from her father over the years.
>
> Gripping the vinyl handles of her luggage, she willed her feet to climb the concrete steps, moved across the broad portico, and paused at the impressive front door. She lowered her suitcases to the drab cement and, with a trembling finger, pushed the doorbell. A deep dolorous chime echoed through the closed door.
>
> Waiting, she pivoted her head as her gaze traveled the length of the porch. Paint, yellowed with age, peeled from the window trim, door frames, and porch roof. The building was blemished with disrepair—like a beautiful woman whose powder and adornment could no longer hide her age. But Gerri perceived more than that. A sense of misery ... deep sorrow blanketed the surroundings as if the sun could not penetrate the encircling gloom.

Reading this example, you can see a number of techniques that help to create the sense of foreboding and misery that I wanted to create. First, look at the literary devices—similes, metaphors, and analogies:

- The mansion is compared to a weight around her spirit.
- The ivy chokes and clings to the gray stone like secrets strangle her life.
- The mansion's blemished paint is compared to a woman who cannot hide her age with powder and adornment.

The word choice also adds to the somberness of the mansion. Words and phrases that create the dire emotions are *sprawling, shadow of a towering oak, brooding building, clinging, choked, strangled, driven, gripping, willed, concrete, drab cement, trembling fingers, deep dolorous chime, yellowed with age, peeled, blemished with disrepair, misery, deep sorrow blanketed,* and *encircling gloom.*

All of these words spark the imagination and add weight to the solemnity of the scene. When creating an emotion or mood, search for the most vivid language to create the picture you want to paint.

Sound

Christian romance uses sound to bring the setting to life: the sounds of the school bus passing, a rooster crowing, or cooing of mourning doves, dogs barking, traffic from a nearby highway, the furnace or air conditioner turning on in the afternoon, the muted sounds of an owl, the wind rattling in the shingles, a garage door opening as a husband arrives home from work, or the howl of a coyote in the mountains.

The sense of sound combines with an emotional response, similar to how sight combines with an emotion. Sounds can range from pleasant to cacophonic. You can compare the tinkle of a bell to the clatter of kitchen pans falling to the floor or the gentle lull of a breeze in contrast to the roaring blast of a gale wind. Listen to the sounds of the words *lull* and *blast*. *Lull* has a soothing, gentle sound that rolls off the tongue, but *blast* has the harder sounds of the *bl* and *st* combinations that add a more raucous tone. For realism, you will want to include sounds that are both pleasant and unpleasant depending on the scene.

One of the most effective ways to recreate sound is by using words that are onomatopoeic. *Zap, crackle, bang, pop, boom, sputter, sizzle, whisk, tinkle,* and *murmur* are onomatopoeias—words that imitate the sounds or objects they are describing.

For example, *Kate put the apple between her lips, near enough for Scott to hear the snap of the skin and to see a fine juicy mist spray into the air.* The word *snap* is onomatopoeic. Say the word aloud and feel the pop effect of the *p* as it leaves your lips. This sentence not only lets you hear the snap of the apple, but you can almost taste it and feel its misty spray. These "sound" words bring paragraphs to life. Use onomatopoeic words to strengthen your description of sound, but remember, never overwork any writing technique. Too much is as bad as not enough.

Adding these types of sounds to scenes, even in the background, lend authenticity and can also enhance the emotion of the characters.

Making Use of Other Senses

In Christian romance, touch, smell, and taste are important because they create additional sense imagery that heightens the readers' romantic response. These senses are used less commonly, probably because they seem harder to recreate than sight and sound. But in the sentence *As she fingered the velvety softness of the rose petal, the nostalgic aroma drifted upward* we are able to evoke both the sense of touch and the sense of smell.

Touch

The sense of touch means describing texture, as in the above vivid comparison of the feel of velvet to the texture of the petal. The body responds physically to the description of touch as it does in other senses, because it arouses emotion by relating the sensation to a past experience. Two techniques that help bring the sense of touch to life are using similes (*the kiss settled on her mouth like a feather*) and describing internal responses to the feeling (*his gentle touch rushed through her with the same sweet tenderness as his kisses*).

Touch is one form of intimacy allowed in Christian fiction as long as it is tasteful and within the publisher's guidelines. Brushing a strand of hair from the heroine's cheek can be as sensual as the secular counterpart of touching a more intimate part of the body. Create sensuality by showing the hero's reaction to the gentle action by highlighting the softness of the heroine's cheek, the silkiness of her hair, and the feel of her breath on his fingers.

Smell

You grimace at an unpleasant odor and breathe deeply at a pleasant scent. Adding various smells helps to create realism in Christian romance; they spark memories of past events and cause characters to relive those moments: *He drew in a breath, recapturing the alluring scent that filled him when he met Molly*, or *The antiseptic odor caught in her throat, causing her to relive the anguish of Bill's near-death experience.*

Some synonyms for smell, such as aroma and fragrance, tend to be positive, while others can be either neutral (scent, whiff) or negative (reek, stench, odor). Focus the description by adding distinguishing adjectives. The pungent odor of a skunk is not easily forgotten, nor is the choking odor of ammonia. A metallic scent of a hot iron can trigger nostalgia for the days Grandma ironed everything from Grandpa's shirts to the bedsheets. These scents can be brought to life even more with verbs that add to the imagery: *the stench churned his stomach* or *her perfume stirred him.*

In Christian romance, the sense of smell can enhance the tender emotion of the growing relationship. Many women wear a signature perfume, which the hero recognizes when she walks into a room and connects to a romantic evening. The new-leather smell of the hero's sports car reminds the heroine not only of the hero, but also of their first kiss that took place in that vehicle.

The sense of smell can be as simple as *She could smell the heat of the sun on his skin* to a more elaborate emotional experiences: *A sweet scent wrapped around him like spring rain in a flower garden. He drew in the pleasant aroma, remembering it was the familiar fragrance that she always wore.*

These phrases present familiar experiences or vivid comparisons to arouse readers' senses. Remember that imagery can come in a mix of senses, as in *Jeff brushed his lips against hers, tasting the sweetness of her mouth and drawing in the scent of her fragrance.*

Taste

Taste is another neglected sense, and since in Christian romance some publishers discourage typical dating activities such as going to pubs, movies, and dancing, scenes sometimes revolve around food: a romantic dinner, a picnic in the woods, a long talk over hot chocolate and cookies, or an evening walk to the ice cream shop. Food is a socially accepted way to entertain, so it is no surprise that food is part of the dating process, and the familiar form of taste can stimulate readers' memories: *With the first sip, her cheeks puckered at the zesty, tart tang that rolled on her tongue.*

Sometimes a taste twist on a kiss can add an original element: *Her mouth tasted sweet and cool like the cola she'd been drinking.* While descriptions of kisses must be tasteful in Christian romance, a reference like this would not be a problem for Christian publishers.

Whether a twinge of passion or a fit of frustration, readers understand the extremes of human emotion by relating to their own experiences and senses. When they see the hero's and heroine's vulnerability, they become empathetic and are drawn to them. Christian romance is enhanced by making the characters' lives real through the senses. Applying these vital elements in your novel will help create a story that lingers in the readers' minds and encourages them to buy your next book.

EXERCISES

1. Locate an emotional scene in your latest work. Read the scene, then go back and ask yourself these questions:

- Have I layered the emotion to show its three-dimensional attributes?
- Is the scene the result of motivation and goals realistic to the character?
- Have I *shown* the emotion, rather than stated it, by using physical motion, facial expressions, and dynamic dialogue?

If the answer to any of these questions is no, then rewrite the scene, incorporating all you have learned about emotion and the senses.

2. Read the following excerpt and identify the senses. Then, go back and find all the colorful, descriptive words that add to the emotion of the scene. Finally, list any words you would consider onomatopoeic.

Silent, Jemma stood with her hands clasped to the handrail until the first colorful shower lit the sky. She gasped, and he saw her face light as brilliantly as the heavens.

One after another, the colors burst into the darkness, spiraling hissing tendrils and dazzling strands blossoming into shapes like red and orange chrysanthemums. Sprays of gold dust sprinkled from the sky. But Philip's hearing and sight were mesmerized by the petite woman in front of him.

3. Using the scenarios below, create the conflicting emotions that could result and write a scene between the character and a friend or relative who provides the role of "devil's advocate."

Sam was a faithful Christian who trusted in God's love and mercy. When the woman he loves is injured in another state, he misses work to care for her and learns that his position in the company has been undermined.

Anna loves God with all her heart, but she has fallen in love with a man who is not a believer. She knows what God expects of her, yet she believes this man is her soul mate.

4. Write a paragraph using one of these settings to create an emotional mood of your choice. Enhance the emotion by including as many of the senses as possible.

- hiking on a mountain trail
- riding on a crowded bus
- looking out an airplane window
- watching a snowfall
- standing in a barn
- sitting in a flower garden

CHAPTER 5

Sexuality in Christian Romance

The romantic relationship is the core of the romance novel, and along with romance comes sexuality. But in Christian romance, the elements that encompass sexuality and how it is expressed differ greatly from secular fiction, and they also vary from one Christian publisher to another. How much is too much must be decided through a blend of Christian morals, biblical direction, and publishing guidelines.

As I said, it's important to study the guidelines of individual Christian publishers. New Christian romance lines are being created because of the growing popularity of the genre, but each line has different standards. Some are more lenient with sexual content and some more conservative. Your decision to publish with any line must be guided by you: Follow your heart and conscience while you write, and then choose the publisher right for you.

THE BIBLICAL GUIDELINES FOR CHRISTIAN ROMANCE

In real-life relationships, what makes a marriage last? Good looks fade. Sexy bodies give way to gravity. Physical attributes wane, as does energy. Marriages are based on attributes that linger and deepen through life experiences and a loving commitment. These make up the virtues of Christian romance. Rather than including romantic elements for the purpose of arousing the readers' feelings of passion and sexual desire, Christian romance strives to touch the heart with human needs of companionship, thoughtfulness, kindness, concern, support, and, the major emphasis, lasting love.

Two Bible verses help the Christian romance author to direct the relationship in a God-pleasing direction. The first, Colossians 2:12–15 (quoted in chapter three), describes qualities the Christian hero and heroine admire—compassion, kindness, humility, gentleness, patience, forgiveness, peacefulness, thankfulness, and love—that can be the major focus of a Christian romantic relationship. The second important scripture, 1 Corinthians 13:4–7, focuses on those enduring qualities from Bible teachings and is God's directions for humankind in terms of love: "Love is patient, love is kind. It does not envy, it does not boast, it is not proud. It is not rude, it is not self-seeking, it is not easily angered, it keeps no record of wrongs. Love does not delight in evil but rejoices with the truth. It always protects, always trusts, always hopes, always perseveres."

These two scripture selections describe character traits and take precedence over physical qualities when forming committed relationships in Christian romance. The verses guide the hero and heroine, just as they guide the lives of real Christians, to reflect on God's direction for their behavior in the world as well as in romantic relationships and marriage. Although this is not always an overt message in Christian romance, it is an underlying concern for the hero and heroine. They want to form a meaningful relationship that will outlast physical attractiveness. Following the verses' teachings, the hero and heroine are drawn to qualities and characteristics that fill the other's needs or expectations in a soul mate.

You can develop the attraction by admiring the hero's or heroine's good looks while focusing on a admirable characteristic: *Although his broad shoulders had caught her attention, his kind eyes captured her heart,* or *He couldn't forget her beautiful face, but her tenderness to the elderly woman was what lingered in his mind.* Whether woven into the introspection or acknowledged in dialogue—*You're not only lovely, you're amazingly thoughtful*—these work well to place the focus on what's most important in the eyes of the character.

These two Bible quotations describe enduring qualities that can become points of conflict in the novel when the characters lack these traits.

The hero struggles with pride, for example, or the heroine lacks trust in men because of a past experience. The flaws result in excellent opportunities for tension and story conflicts.

While the word *love* is found hundreds of times in the Bible and there are many verses that describe the duties of a husband and wife, no verse speaks specifically about romance. Still, there are verses that serve as an excellent guideline for romance, such as Ecclesiastes 4:9–12: "Two are better than one, because they have a good return for their work: If one falls down, his friend can help him up. But pity the man who falls and has no one to help him up! Also, if two lie down together, they will keep warm. But how can one keep warm alone? Though one may be overpowered, two can defend themselves. A cord of three strands is not quickly broken."

In these verses, there are references to intimacy, support, compassion, and security—all elements of a committed relationship—but the last line is the one that makes Christian romance differ from secular. While secular fiction is a two-strand story of the hero and heroine, the Christian romance is strengthened by the three-strand cord—the hero, the heroine, and the Lord. This spiritual connection is ultimate in Christian romance.

Sexual Tension

To delineate the differences in attraction between secular and Christian romance, Lyn Cote, author of The Women of Ivy Manor series, has subdivided secular sexual tension into two parts: the physical and the romantic quality. She says:

> Romantic quality is everything—outside the physical realm—that draws a hero to the heroine, and vice versa, in a powerful attraction. Every hero and heroine—even though he/she might not be consciously aware of it—is searching for certain qualities in another person. When they meet, they are aware that this person is special—disturbing in more than just a physical way. They fight the special awareness, but it draws them irresistibly. Romantic quality emanates from the character, from setting and plot. In the area of character, romantic quality points up: What has the hero/heroine lacked in the past? What does the hero/heroine value?

SEXUALITY VS. SENSUALITY

Sexuality refers to the physical presence of the hero and heroine, the descriptions triggered by awareness of gender; sensuality most often refers to the sexual desire that is not absent from Christian romance, but handled as a spiritual intimacy, binding the hero and heroine in committed love with God as the third strand. In Christian romance, both sexuality and sensuality are presented in appropriate measure to biblical and publishers' guidelines.

While Christian romance focuses on sexuality rather than sensuality, sensuality remains a part of the novel in a more subtle manner. In brief, sensuality refers to an awareness of gender, the physical, emotional, and spiritual difference between the hero and heroine. It deals more with the characters' actions, thoughts, and emotional impact on other characters than with their bodies.

Sensuality is also important in Christian romance in terms of the senses. As mentioned before, the senses of sight, sound, touch, smell, and taste are needed to bring the romance to life; they provide pleasure and are significant in all romance, secular or Christian. The gentle touch of the hero, the heroine's fragrance, the raspy voice of emotion, the lilt of laughter—all are important in creating a story filled with sensual elements appropriate to Christian romance.

Sexuality and Physical Descriptions

Sexuality leads to physical descriptions of characters, especially the hero and heroine, as discussed in chapter three. Physical description is important because it provides readers with a mental picture, and certainly, characters in Christian romance admire the appearance of the hero or heroine, the same as people do in real life. The heroine loves the hero's broad shoulders and the strength of his embrace, while the hero admires the heroine's sparkling eyes and flowing hair. Although references can be made to the heroine's figure or the hero's muscular frame, descriptions should also provide insights into the characterization and qualities of the hero and heroine. Overemphasizing physical endowments for the sake of arousing readers is to be avoided; instead, focus on those traits in the hero's and heroine's characters that interest and attract them to each other.

Although some publishers allow more provocative descriptions, a number of Christian publishers are more conservative. Some ask you to keep the mode of dress demure, avoiding gratuitous descriptions of sexy clothing, sleepwear, or the heroine's bathing suit from the hero's point of view. The desired focus of these houses is on the character's appealing inner attributes. Most editors will weigh the importance of the description to the overall theme and plot of the story. Err on the side of caution and, within reason, avoid provocative details unless they are vital to the plot.

The Bible provides guidelines for Christian standards of romance. The first romance appears in Genesis when God created Adam and then created woman. Before sin, Adam and Eve were naked in the garden, but after sin, they were ashamed. The Lord made garments of skins to cover them, and throughout the Bible, verses provide similar guidance. Later in Genesis, when Rebekah meets Isaac, she covers her face with a veil. As I quoted earlier, 1 Peter 3:3–4 says, "Your beauty should not come from outward adornment, such as braided hair and the wearing of gold jewelry and fine clothes. Instead, it should be that of your inner self, the unfading beauty of a gentle and quiet spirit, which is of great worth in God's sight." You can use these as examples of what Christian readers and publishers expect in Christian romances—modesty and self-control.

Look at the following examples and notice how the descriptions strengthen characterization while avoiding sexual references. Notice how most stay above the waist on the hero and the shoulders on the heroine, and most also emphasis a talent or attribute—singing, energy, cuteness, a college education—but the lack of sexuality does not detract from the appeal of the characters. The characters are interesting and believable, even without extensive physical details.

> Michael Gold was a gentleman, not to mention his proverbial tall, dark, and handsome good looks. When Grace had first met Michael, he'd reminded her of Adam Cartwright from the television reruns of her mother's favorite show, *Bonanza*. She'd quickly learned that comments about his good looks embarrassed him. And Michael didn't need to coast on his looks, for he was richly endowed with a vocal talent. (*Note of Peril*, Hannah Alexander)

Gage Farrell's face came up in her mind. Thoughts of him—hair the color of black walnuts, eyes the color of evergreen needles—had intruded on her business all week. How could she hold her own against a college-educated business partner—a man who'd handled commercial real estate for nearly six years? (*Hope's Garden*, Lyn Cote)

He pictured Rona, the woman at the restaurant. Now that was energy. She darted from one station to the next, pouring coffee, bussing tables, and taking orders without a hitch—a bundle of the cutest energy he'd ever seen. He envisioned her long, straight hair bouncing against her shoulders, the sweep of the wave that tucked beneath her chin when she tilted her head. And those eyes, as gray as a stormy sky but with a hint of sunshine behind the clouds. (*Family in His Heart*, Gail Gaymer Martin)

The man was as masculine as his voice. A strong jawline rescued his face from mediocrity, and his body looked as if it had been chiseled from Petzoldt Ridge. (*Mending Places*, Denise Hunter)

THE ROMANTIC PROCESS AND SENSUALITY

In real life, romance has a pattern. Two people meet and become better acquainted as their paths continue to cross; next, they find themselves thinking and dreaming of the other until the relationship moves into a romance and they begin to fall in love. These stages vary depending on the situation. A romantic relationship between old friends might blossom more quickly than that of two strangers, while people with previous relationships that left emotional scars might take more time in moving from stage to stage.

In Christian romance, the relationship progresses in the same four basic steps: awareness, interest, attraction, and falling in love.

While these stages do not lead to the bedroom before marriage, they lead to passion and desire to be together in a committed relationship.

Awareness

Awareness in Christian romance has to do with curiosity. When the hero and heroine first meet, they notice each other beyond mere acknowledgment of the other's presence. They are aware of the other person; something in the personality or manner arouses their curiosity. Intrigued, they ask questions, wonder about the person, wonder why they care.

Emotional Aspects of the Awareness Stage

This curiosity is sometimes accompanied by hesitation. The heroine may know that curiosity leads to interest, which leads to attraction, and that gives her pause. Perhaps she prefers to focus on her career, or enjoys her singleness and doesn't want a relationship, or fears love will bring disappointment as it has in the past. A Christian hero may realize a relationship means being honest, which means revealing a sin that he's kept hidden from everyone.

Awareness can be a positive experience, with qualities of the hero or heroine eliciting good feelings and encouraging them to get to know one another better. The heroine is impressed when a new man at the office holds the door open for her or pulls out her chair at a board meeting. Perhaps the hero comes into the heroine's life when she's trying to retrieve a kitten from a tree or when pleading a worthy cause at a church meeting. She admires his politeness while he admires her concern for others.

Sometimes it's the opposite: The first awareness is triggered by a negative reaction, the result of clashing personalities or a character who appears to be a threat to the status or the well-being of the other. Perhaps a heroine finds the hero too much like someone who failed her in the past. The tension created as her romantic awareness grows adds extra conflict to the story and keeps readers intrigued.

Christian author Irene Brand provides an excellent example of a negative reaction leading to an interest-generating first meeting in her romantic suspense *Yuletide Peril*:

> Janice swung quickly toward the store just as a tall tawny-haired man opened the door and bumped into her. Janice staggered backward. The man's strong arm suddenly wrapped around her waist and kept her from falling.
>
> "That was a close call," he said sternly. As if reprimanding a child, he added, "You should look where you're going."

Janice's face flamed. Although she knew the man was right, she motioned toward her sister and quipped, "I preferred looking at what was behind me, rather than what was in front of me."

Realizing that she was still in his embrace, Janice squirmed free, as with a pleasing grin, the man said, "Touché. Thanks for reminding me I wasn't being careful, either."

Janice lowered her gaze, deeply humiliated and irritated that she'd given way to one of her failings—a tendency to lash out at people when they criticized her. That wasn't the way to start life in a new town.

"That was rude of me. Thanks for saving me from a fall. I should have been more alert." Taking a deep, unsteady breath, she stepped away from him.

The man's short, wavy hair flowed backward from his high forehead, and his warm dark blue eyes clung to her heavily-lashed green ones for a moment. His face reddened slightly, and he said, "No problem." He strode purposely toward a black van parked at one of the pumps.

It took a lot to fluster Janice, but she realized that her pulse was racing. Surely it must be from the near fall, rather than the thrill she'd experienced when the man had embraced her.

This scene reflects a common occurrence. Out shopping, you get bumped by a person or tripped by a door, causing you to stagger backward. You cling to your packages or handbag trying to retrieve your decorum and your balance—and possibly your temper. Now add another element. The person who bumps into you catches you in his arms. How does that make you feel? Protected? Safe? Upset? Confused? All of the above?

In Brand's excerpt, the embrace befuddles the heroine, causing first embarrassment and then a racing pulse. Notice the pattern that moves from negative feelings, to apology followed by forgiveness, to denial of the emotion. Yet, beneath it all, readers see the opportunity for romance.

A hero and heroine who have known each other and then become romantically aware can add a different dynamic to the story. Once comfortable and natural with each other, they can become uncomfortable and confused at their growing feelings, questioning their motivation and good sense.

No matter how the hero and heroine have come upon each other, awareness is the gentle stage of a romance when a stealthy second look or an unexpected smile connects them in a special way. Sometimes the main feeling is pleasure; other times irritation is in the forefront. The obvious conclusion is they are confused by the first stage of a romance, romance often being the last thing on the hero or heroine's mind—but sometimes God has a plan in his mind.

Physical Aspects of the Awareness Stage

Within the stages of romance, the outward expression of the hero and heroine's blossoming relationship grows in proportion to the emotional commitment they have for each other. They may not reach this stage at the same time. Physical demonstration of awareness is limited. Some personalities are vibrant and touch people more than others, so the more outgoing character could lay a hand on an arm or shoulder to draw attention or when talking. In most cases, however, physical actions are limited to a playful pat, the accidental brush of hands, or a simple touch.

Emotion triggers physical response, and while the outward physical reactions may be hidden, the internal reactions can be more overt. The heroine may feel her pulse skip or stomach tighten when she connects with the hero. Both may feel flustered at the first meeting; giddiness is also a realistic response. Think of the day you met your spouse or a special person in your life. Recall how you felt internally, what physical responses you felt, and then use those realistic feelings in your novel.

Spiritual Aspects of the Awareness Stage

Christians trust the verse in Proverbs 16:9: "In his heart a man plans his course, but the Lord determines his steps." When things happen to Christians, they tend to look to this verse and connect the event to what God has in store for them. When the Christian hero and heroine feel drawn to each other, they question if this is someone special sent by God.

During the awareness stage, the spiritual concerns are not as strong as when the relationship begins to build, but the Christian hero and heroine will both be questioning whether this person is a Christian and looking for clues to his or her beliefs. Some characters will come out and ask, while others may use more subtle approaches, such as talking about a church activity and weighing the other's response.

Christians form friendships with nonbelievers at work for some social activities, but when it comes to dating—especially when they feel the pull of strong emotion—knowing the other party is a Christian is vital.

Awareness-stage dating styles are often different than in secular books. While going out for a drink and ending up in bed is not uncommon in secular romance, a one-night stand is never a consideration in Christian fiction. Each step forward is slower and more thoughtful because of the biblical commitment that involves love and marriage.

With this spiritual element in mind, create characters who weigh their head and heart feelings as they build a relationship and struggle to understand if the awareness they feel is their own will or the Lord's. This conflict is an important part of Christian romance—share it with the readers through the characters' thoughts or actions, indicated by dialogue reflecting beliefs, morals, and values, and the lack of physical interplay.

Interest

Interest is a step beyond awareness in Christian romance. It is a subtle change readers will sense through the character's actions and introspection—a self-admission allowing emotions to grow, beginning when the hero or heroine feels drawn to the other. This can occur shortly after their meeting, especially if they have known each other in the past. A good technique is to have the interest rise over the next couple of chapters after meeting. The hero and heroine connect in a special way by sharing mutual values, interests, and goals as well as introducing conflicting goals.

Emotional Aspects of the Interest Stage

The interest is a known factor in moving along with the relationship, and it can be expressed through introspection—for example, the hero thinking he'd like to know the heroine better, or that she has attributes with which he feels kinship—or conversation with another character. The hero and heroine will look forward to seeing each other. They might connive ways of bumping into each other, and they could experience physical reactions such as sweaty palms or an escalating pulse.

The interest phase can still involve denial and the struggle to stay uninvolved. What triggers this denial is often found in the characters' needs and motivations. A sin or flaw may have to be revealed, or a need might seem threatened by a relationship. The interest step in the romance is also a time when trust is questionable and fear of rejection is prevalent.

Again, emotion is the key to tension that moves readers forward. As mentioned earlier, when a relationship rebuilds from a couple who were once engaged or who dated years earlier, the new interest arouses concern and suspicion. Why would this relationship work now when it didn't before? Why should either of them set themselves up for hurt again? Though the love they once shared is drawing them together, fear and distrust is keeping them apart.

A friendship romance can be effected by bringing the hero and heroine into close proximity, and then having them become aware of each other as a single man and woman who could be more than friends.

When both characters let down their guards, reality, wisdom, or obstinance can cause one or both to withdraw. This backward motion is to reset boundaries for the protection of their hearts, the truth about the past, or just pure determination not to give in to the romance.

But as the hero and heroine give in to their hearts, readers have a chance to observe the changes in them. To do this, show the attributes that once separated them now fading and having less effect on their lives. Because biblical love is giving, not self-centered, you can demonstrate their concern for each other by giving them opportunities to overlook their own needs in order to meet the needs of the other person.

It's important to make these changes believable to readers. Characters can't hate each other one minute and fall in love the next. The shift must be gradual and subtle as you delve into their introspection and show what new feelings are sprouting up in their thoughts. These changes in character growth, romantic elements, and faith are what allow the relationship to move from awareness and interest to attraction, and what lead to believable commitment.

Physical Aspects of the Interest Stage

As awareness grows, the hero's causal touch might trigger a sensation along the heroine's arm. The hero may have the desire to brush a curl from the heroine's cheek but holds back, uncertain of her feelings and possible reaction. Each approaches the other with caution.

Because each reaches the interest stage at a different time and with a different degree of certainty, the hero might kiss the heroine on the cheek as a thank-you, but if she isn't ready for the familiarity, her response may be to draw back with a look of confusion or dismay instead of a smile.

During the interest stage, when the characters have admitted—at least to the readers—that they are drawn to the other, there can be more outward signs of a growing relationship. Keep the expressions simple—lingering looks that cause a change in heart rate, an admiring glance at the heroine's slender neck, or tracing a line along the hero's arm.

The romance moves, for example, from a playful pat to his hand on her shoulder, to brushing a leaf from her hair, to her thank-you hug, to holding her hand longer than necessary, to hand-holding, to his arm around her shoulder, then to her waist, and finally to an embrace.

The internal physical reactions during this stage would be stronger than in awareness. Seeing or anticipating the hero or heroine might result in an escalated heart rate or lightheadedness. His touch or her smile can trigger nervousness, flutters, or breathlessness. These are brought about by the uncertainty of a possible relationship and the stress of making the right moves and saying the right thing.

The intimacy grows in proportion to the certainty that God approves of the relationship; as that certainty grows, each is more willing to take a step forward.

Spiritual Aspects of the Interest Stage

In Christian romance, God's will is an ever-present element, and romance itself is not taken lightly. Decisions are made with prayerful consideration. Chastity or lifelong commitment are the only options for most Christians, and divorce is often avoided because of differences in biblical interpretation; therefore, the hero and heroine move slowly and often hold back their true feelings rather than rush the relationship. They will test it as they consider biblical expectations and struggle with their own physical arousal, to be sure their feelings are not only the fire of passion but God's leading to the special someone with whom they can share a committed love.

At the interest stage, while the characters attempt to follow what they believe is God's will, their emotional struggles can lead to confusion and even more distance from forming a relationship, which in turn adds to the growing conflict. This struggle often takes place when the characters fight the Lord's leading, when there's a clash between what God wants and what the characters want, or when there are fears of being unforgiven for a past deed or feelings of being unworthy. In my novel *Loving Ways*, Ken wrestles with his feelings for Annie and his feelings of unworthiness.

> Maybe he cared about Annie because in her he saw his mother, a woman so controlled by her environment she let her life fly past without even tasting it. Maybe he cared because …
>
> No. He stopped that line of thinking. A woman like Annie needed a good wholesome man. A solid Christian. Not someone like him. Not with his background … his past. If Annie knew, she'd not only refuse him entrance into her house, but send him packing and find a new landscaper.

Attraction

Attraction occurs when the hero and heroine dream of being together, when their every thought drifts to the other, and when they begin to weigh the pros and cons of a relationship. During the attraction stage, tension between the head and heart is an important element, and both internal and external conflict are often a clash between logic and emotion. This occurs when distrust, fear, doubt, or overanalysis battle against the characters' senses and feelings.

Emotional Aspects of the Attraction Stage

Conflict creates dynamic, romantic tension between the hero and heroine. It exemplifies natural human difficulties in weighing what is important and what is right or what is safe but will bring happiness—the dynamic between reasoning and gut-wrenching feelings. This tension causes readers to become involved and to cheer the characters toward a happy ending. The attraction scenes involve the senses, and it is at this point that the relationship becomes more physical, especially in terms of touch.

When the heroine or hero fights the romantic feelings for fear of making a mistake or that it's not God's will, feelings of being empty, incomplete, and lonely depict the struggle, and such words are used in introspection or dialogue to show the character's incomplete feelings. The reverse is also true: When a marriage proposal and lifelong commitment is accepted, the characters feel whole and complete, fulfilled, vital, and ready to forge ahead with their promises.

Physical Aspects of the Attraction Stage

In the early stages of attraction in Christian romance, the first physical demonstration is often on the cheek, hand, nose, or eyes. The outward expressions of romance move gradually, but as the relationship grows and blossoms, the door is opened for more outward demonstration of romantic feelings: an intimate face-to-face embrace, using more of the senses; and, finally, the kiss with more urgency. While secular romances may have elements of passion much earlier in the story, most Christian editors look for evidence of a deepening relationship before the characters heighten the romance. This deepening relationship often appears near the middle of the book, although you can bring these actions into the story sooner if the hero and heroine are rekindling an old romance.

The physical internal responses can be expressed in a variety of ways to show a growing desire for one another: The hero's stomach may tighten, the heroine's knees grow weak, and the characters may become breathless in the kiss.

As the relationship grows, the kisses and emotions deepen as they struggle to follow their Christian morals, but kissing scenes never describe the use of the tongue or other titillating details. The description usually deals more with the inner response—the feelings and emotions of the characters—than a depiction of the action of the kiss.

A Kiss in Christian Romance

This excerpt from Valerie Hansen's *Deadly Payoff*, book five of The Secrets of Stoneley series, provides an example of a kiss appropriate to Christian romance. In this story, Shaun and Delia were once briefly married, but Delia's father broke them up and they've been separated for years. In the middle of the book, Shaun asks Delia for a kiss. She knows she's crazy to respond to his request, but she's tired of fighting her feelings and of insisting that he doesn't matter to her when he does. Delia gives up and accepts his kiss.

She closed her eyes and tilted her face up to him. His breath was warm and sweet on her skin. Her lashes fluttered. Her heart sped. What was taking him so long? In the past, he'd always been quick to act. Now, he seemed to be operating in slow motion.

Delia's hands had been pressed flat to his chest. She pushed them up and threaded her fingers into Shaun's thick hair, relishing the opportunity to touch the man who had, for a short, lovely time, belonged to her. And she, to him.

When she heard Shaun moan and felt him tighten his hold she realized she'd made a tactical error. He hadn't been hesitant to kiss her, he'd been struggling to control himself.

Something inside Delia flared like a campfire on a starlit beach. It was as if her whole being had been waiting twelve long years for Shaun's kiss. And what a kiss it was!

He didn't crush her lips awkwardly, the way he used to when she was seventeen. Instead, his mouth barely grazed hers, exploring, claiming, then finally settling as though it knew exactly where it belonged. A more perfect, heartwarming, inspiring kiss would have been impossible.

Although the kiss shows passion, it's presented it in a non-graphic way that is gentle and tasteful. The scene deals more with emotion and memories than sexual desire.

While human emotions are important in the outward expressions of love, keep in mind your Christian readers and publishers. Keep the embraces appropriate to your characters' beliefs and faith.

Spiritual Aspects of the Attraction Stage

The closer the hero and heroine are to admitting they are falling in love, the more serious the faith issue grows. Although both the hero and heroine are often Christian, if they are not on equal planes in terms of their faith, this will be a major conflict. The Bible says that Christians should be equally yoked, meaning their partner should also be a Christian, so true love cannot come to fruition without both hero and heroine having embraced faith in Christ as their Savior.

It is important that the hero and heroine each arrive at his or her own acceptance of Christ and God's Word, rather than having it thrust upon them by the other character. This journey must be one of learning for the nonbeliever through the examples of the other character, searching scripture, and prayer.

Falling in Love

The Bible mandates that marriage be a forever relationship, so falling in love is a serious step in Christian romance. Awareness, interest, and attraction are the three typical stages of romance, but the Christian romance will go beyond those stages to an admitted love by each party. This expression of love is usually not spoken until the end of the book because what readers look for is the final acknowledgment of a committed love with God's blessing. If it comes earlier, then the story has ended, unless a new conflict arises.

Your challenge in the attraction stage is to keep the characters' love and faith growing while creating realistic blockades in the form of issues, secrets, or problems that hinder the hero and heroine from expressing the strong feelings of love they have acknowledged to themselves.

Emotional and Physical Aspects of the Falling-in-Love Stage

Romantic intensity is a part of falling in love, and in Christian fiction it is an intensity with God's blessing. While secular romances allow the hero and heroine to indulge in sexual intimacy, Christian romance doesn't. Still, the feelings are real, and if you are to write a book that represents real life and real Christian struggles, sexual desire can be addressed.

While some publishers ask authors to avoid using words to suggest the feelings of passion such as *desire, sexy, heat, hot, sexual longing,* and *arousal,* to want to write "real," you must find a way to show the struggle of the hero and heroine to remain chaste in their relationship.

This can be done playfully—the hero saying that he needs to step outside to cool off—or more dramatically. Gayle Roper, in her book *Summer Shadows,* creates a vivid picture of an intense sexual struggle between the hero and heroine, a widow who once enjoyed the freedom of showing her love to her husband. The action, reaction, and dialogue portray the reality Christians must face as love deepens and commitment is near.

> When a trio of meteors flared and died in the southern sky, Abby turned her head to Marsh. "Did you see?"
>
> He grinned his slow grin. "I did. Beautiful." But he wasn't looking at the sky. That's when she realized that they were definitely touching, shoulders pressed tightly together and hands linked.
>
> Marsh raised himself on his elbow and leaned over her, and her mouth went dry. Slowly he lowered his head, giving her plenty of time to pull away. But she didn't move. She wanted his kiss.
>
> His lips were soft and warm, and her blood began to sing. She wrapped her arms around his neck and kissed him back, pulling him down to her. Tears pooled behind her closed lids. She'd forgotten how wonderful a kiss from a man you loved could be.
>
> She'd also forgotten how intense the longings could be, longings she had soothed regularly during her marriage. Appetites once sanctified now coursed through her without God's blessing on their appeasement. In the words of the old King James, she burned and with an intensity that scared her.
>
> Her hands moved from Marsh's neck to his chest and she gave a gentle shake. "Marsh! Marsh!"
>
> "Um?" He kissed her nose, her eyes. His hands held her face.

It felt so good! "Marsh, we have to stop." She turned her face, burying it in his neck.

He stilled abruptly, dropped his hands and sat up, his back to her. She could hear his labored breathing. "I'm sorry," he mumbled. "I—I'm sorry."

She sat up and rested a hand on his back. "I'm not upset. It's all right. It wasn't you who scared me. It was me."

He turned to her. "What?"

She wrapped her arms about her knees. "I was married, Marsh. I know what it's like to love a man and be loved. It's like nothing else, and your kiss reminded me of how wonderful it can be. Should be. Would be." She laid her head on her knees. "I wanted us to continue too much."

They sat silently as meteors continued to rain above.

Explosions, fireworks, and meteors are often used to symbolize sexual release during intimacy. In this scene, Roper provides the same symbol of passion, but she does it in a manner appropriate to Christian romance. You see the heroine's tremendous longing to be loved intimately. You see her honesty about her feelings, and the hero's restraint as they control this natural urge. This scene is not subtle, yet it allows Roper to show real passion in a way acceptable to Christian readers and most publishers.

Spiritual Aspects of the Falling-in-Love Stage

The falling-in-love stage allows a full sweep of emotion—the intensity of making a commitment, the struggle to remain morally true to God's Word, and the belief that the relationship will last forever in a world that follows its own rules.

While sexual desire is one form of struggle, the intensity can also come from the confession of a dark secret and the release found in forgiveness. You can make the intensity arise by opening a new door to the character's life, a door that releases him or her, for example, from the bonds of distrust or self-loathing. It is a time of forgiveness, compassion, and love winning out over sin and fear. Allow the characters to show the release of pain or the discovery of joy so that the growth is connected to the character's relationship with the Lord.

Sexual Intimacy

Gratuitous and explicit sexual scenes are not allowed in Christian romance, so the kiss is the most intimate physical expression of love between the hero and heroine. Normally, sexual intimacy between married couples in Christian romances will be implied rather than explicit. Your writer's voice can influence a publisher regarding whether a scene is appropriate. If the scene is written with beauty and purpose, most editors will approve many romantic elements needed to create the best story possible.

In my novel *Loving Feelings*, the heroine has had a mastectomy, and her fear of intimacy is understandable. She felt unlovable and unworthy of a man, so after falling in love and marrying, the final bedroom scene is necessary to show the reaction of the hero when he sees her scars for the first time. The scene is in the heroine's point of view.

> "I'm honored and blessed to be your wife." Though hushed, her words were sure.
>
> He sought her gaze again, asking permission without words. She answered with her eyes.
>
> Gently, Todd moved his hand to her shoulder and drew down the slender strap of her gown. She didn't look at him, afraid of what she would see on his face.
>
> A warm tear struck her skin as Todd bent to kiss her scar. When his gaze met hers, tears rimmed his eyes. "Thank you," he whispered, his finger brushing her wound. "Thank you for trusting me."
>
> The tenderness in his voice lifted Jenni's heart and spirit. "Thank you for loving me."

This gentle scene, though not graphic, does imply the intimacy of the hero touching her breast, normally avoided in Christian romance, but the scene is necessary to assure readers that Todd not only accepts Jenni's scar, but is stirred by her wound and understands the depth of trust it took for her to be intimate with him. Without this scene, the impact of the conclusion would leave readers wondering.

When dealing with sexual intimacy in Christian romance, you must weigh what is absolutely vital to your story and what isn't. You will learn that the publisher's guidelines are only that—a guide. Common sense and an understanding of Christian worldview can help make wise decisions. Remember, the example above is not graphic. There is no description of her breast or details of any sexual feelings aroused with the kiss, only tears and tenderness.

As you write your novel, remember the importance of sexual tension that results from the internal and external conflicts of the hero and heroine as they fall in love, but remember, too, that in Christian romance, sexuality does not refer to detailed body descriptions or promiscuity. Christian romance is based on character attributes as described in the Bible and depicts a chaste relationship that focuses on tenderness and thoughtfulness, keeping a focus on God's will. It is evocative, not provocative.

And They Lived Happily Ever After

Christian romance has the well-loved, happily-ever-after ending that readers love, as well as a conclusion that is the culmination of emotion, senses, and romance. Rather than a titillating bedroom scene, Christian romance must pull out all the stops in providing readers with a dynamic ending filled with romance and emotion. As I said earlier, the romance is based on the three-fold cord—a man, a woman, and God—so the ending is the time to heighten that aspect of the romance and give readers a happy ending they won't forget.

This final scene from Patt Marr's Christian romance *Promise of Forever* perfectly illustrates the technique of strengthening the end of the story with emotion, faith, and the commitment of love between a man and woman.

"Watching you love the Lord made me want to have Him back in my life."

That made her love him even more. There was contentment in his eyes that she'd never seen before, but she recognized it. It came with knowing the Lord.

"I don't know how you can forgive me for being so rude the other night. You didn't deserve any of that attitude or those awful words. I'm so sorry, Beth."

"But wasn't that a different man talking?" She smiled to let him know he needn't worry.

"Very different," he agreed. His eyes moved over every inch of her face and stopped on her mouth.

Hope exploded in her heart. He loved her. It wasn't over if he could look at her like that.

He took a step closer. "Beth, if you'll give me another chance, I'll—"

She'd heard all she needed to hear. It only took one spectacular effort to get out of her chair and into his arms, the best place on earth. He held her high, her feet off the floor, and claimed kisses that were long overdue. The feel of his mouth on hers and his arms around her ... it was all she had hoped for.

He buried his face in her neck and murmured, "I love you, Beth, and I need you."

She leaned back to look in his eyes, his beautiful eyes, so filled with love.

"I've never said that before, Beth, not to anyone."

"I need you, too," she said, caressing his face. "I know you said you would only stay until—"

"I'm not going anywhere," he said, his mouth next to hers. "If you'll have me, I'm yours for life."

That meant jillions of kisses to come, but none would be better than these. With no more practice than they'd had, it was amazing how good they were at loving with kisses.

In this excerpt, the hero's faith is acknowledged and rejoiced over by the heroine, their love is given full sway, and the senses are aroused with tender touches, lingering kisses, and the feel of his arms around her. Every element of the three-fold cord has been addressed.

Each part of the romance plot provides the hero and heroine an opportunity to address their faith and decide if their relationship is God-pleasing. The beauty of Christian romance is the ability to travel the journey with the hero and heroine as they conclude that, indeed, the relationship was God's desire as much as their own.

EXERCISES

1. Study your descriptions of the hero and heroine in your latest work to see if you've followed the guidelines to focus less on physical descriptions and instead stressed the character's attributes. If you've missed this element, rewrite these scenes so that your emphasis is more on Christian traits than on any part of the body that might be offensive to the more conservative Christian.

2. Now that you have reviewed your characters' descriptions, examine the trait descriptors you have used. Do they receive less attention than the physical? Review the Bible references earlier in this chapter, Colossians 2 and 1 Corinthians 13. Have you depicted how these qualities enhance the characters, or how the lack of them cause romantic tension? If you find a lack of Christian attributes, rewrite these sections to show that those elements are what have attracted the hero and heroine as much as good looks.

3. Review your plotline and decide if you've followed the four steps of romance: awareness, interest, attraction, and falling in love. Where in the plot does the first kiss occur? Is it on the cheek or the lips? Review the buildup you've created to the first romantic kiss. Does it follow the progress of resolved conflict and take place at a point of change and growth of the characters? If not, move the kiss scene to a plot location where readers can accept the kiss as believable and appropriate in Christian romance.

Writing the Christian Romance

CHAPTER 6

Spirituality and Romance

What truly sets Christian romance apart from other romances is the faith message woven throughout the story. The purpose of Christian romance is not to evangelize; it is first to entertain and second to present life and romance through a Christian worldview. Like a fine tapestry, the spiritual elements are entwined in the story threads, creating a vivid theme inseparable from the plotline.

Though Christian publishing houses vary from a conservative to a more liberal approach to the amount of faith content in their romances, all publishers look for scenes built around believers doing everyday things—going to work, grocery shopping, folding laundry, going on a picnic, talking over coffee, facing problems, falling in love—and evaluating their relationships with the Lord. Faith is shown in action and introspection as much as in dialogue, so readers see how the character grows in faith during the novel. The faith message is integrated into the plot and demonstrated through the everyday actions and reactions of characters in their life, both in church and in the world.

Although every story, in a sense, holds a salvation message, this is not the only worthy theme for Christian romance. Stories revolving around trust, honesty, forgiveness, fear, weakness, shame, pride, sin, guilt, and self-centeredness—to name only a few—create realistic, everyday struggles of believers and nonbelievers alike.

The spiritual message rises naturally from the developing conflicts based on the characters' attempts to deal with their flaws or faith issues while they turn to God for guidance in solving their own difficulties. This means the storyline does not necessarily revolve around church activities and fellowship or contain Bible quotes or prayers spoken in detail throughout the novel.

Think of how your faith is expressed in your own life. Many Christians don't necessarily walk around quoting scripture, but they do have knowledge of the Bible. Christians know the commandments and what God expects. They feel close to Jesus as he walks beside them daily. They send up prayers of thanks and prayers of need. They avoid swearing. They chastise themselves for not behaving in a Christian manner, often feeling regretful or disappointed when they are envious or impatient. Most Christians understand that bad things happen to good people, even though they don't like it.

These same elements are what you should weave through your stories, showing your characters dealing with life as Christians, stumbling in their faith walks, and pulling themselves up again. They face the fear of failing in the relationship, they question their feelings and their partner's feelings, and wonder if this is the person the Lord has in mind for them. They are tempted sexually but know to stay true to God's Word and remain chaste.

CHARACTERS AND THEIR FAITH

In Christian romance, the hero and heroine may meet at the same level of faith, but often they come to the story at different levels. One may be a nonbeliever who will find the Lord during his spiritual journey. If both are believers, you may have a character who is more secure in his or her faith while the other is troubled by a personal attribute that goes against God's Word. The romance is also a faith journey, and as the characters travel along this road, readers will see the ups and downs of their strengths and weaknesses as real people in a world that doesn't always follow biblical principles.

Consider the characterization of your hero and heroine and where they are in their faith journey as you develop their behavior and personalities. Is the hero a believer but dealing with pride and self-centeredness? Is the heroine caught up in the material world, ignoring God's instruction to show compassion? The spiritual flaws of each character can become the center of their internal conflict, especially if one's strength clashes with the other's weakness. For example, the hero supports a charity that involves his time, and the heroine wants him to be with her. Perhaps a charity drive clashes with one of her glitzy social events. You can see how this impacts both internal and external conflict.

Leave room for growth as you open the story, and allow the characters to make mistakes and stumble. If the behavior is important to the plot conflict, the hero or heroine might have had devious or sinful pasts before accepting the Lord. The baggage a hero and heroine drag into the story adds to the characters' conflicts.

Along with past experiences, the faith level of each character will determine how each responds to successes and failures. Through the characters' attributes, you can show where they begin on the spiritual journey and how much they grow by the end of the book. Think back to the hero who supports a charity, and the heroine who wants his total focus. What would happen if the hero refuses to attend the heroine's social event and spends the entire evening at the charity event? As they grow and change, they might be more open to compromise: attend part of the fund-raiser and then proceed to the party. As the heroine becomes more aware of her worldly focus on couture fashion designs, she would likely give up a glamorous gathering to attend a charity event, eventually becoming as active in the charity as the hero.

How characters live out their faith is the key to weaving faith into your book. Just as in real life, words and deeds reflect what is in the heart. Reveal the characters' flaws, then strengthen them by aligning them more closely with what God expects—but remember that we are all sinners. Your characters should never be perfect.

Questions to Flesh Out Spirituality

Christian author Margaret Daley uses a series of questions to flesh out her characters' spiritual strengths and weaknesses as she develops her story.

Does he/she believe?

Has he/she ever believed?

Why doesn't he/she believe?

What made him/her lose faith in the Lord?

What makes him/her turn to God for help?

When did he/she accept Christ? Why?

How does he/she practice his/her faith?

Does he/she have doubts about his/her faith? Why?

How does his/her faith help him/her when he/she falters?

What kind of temptations has he/she dealt with?

What kind of questions does he/she have about God?

What kind of faith does his/her family have?

By answering these questions from the beginning of your plotting, you will have a good feel for your characters' faith journey that will allow it to grow naturally as they are affected by the issues, needs, experiences, and blessings in their lives.

FOCUSING ON THE FAITH MESSAGE

The struggle between the world's view and the Christian's view in your characters is what helps create spiritual conflicts, which are the heart of your story. Guilt, shame, distrust, and lack of forgiveness, especially in their own misdeeds, rear their heads like dragons and breathe the fire of self-loathing or unworthiness on the characters as they confront their inability to follow God's Word.

Conflict, both external and internal, is vital to a Christian romance. While external conflict deals with the outward problems the hero and heroine face, the internal conflict shows the characters' self-doubts and concerns, as well as their spiritual struggles. These conflicts hinder the relationship and cause deep emotions that make the story compelling.

As the story begins to grow in your mind and heart, the spiritual struggle of the characters will come alive. Sometimes a spiritual issue arises to trigger the story idea, and you can identify the theme immediately with a Bible verse. When searching the Bible, focus on what the Lord expects of you in terms of spiritual attributes, and you can be guided to faith issues that are worthy of addressing in your fiction.

As Christians read the Bible verses that guide their lives, they understand what the Lord expects of them. When they fail, they know they have disappointed God and must ask for forgiveness. Some people can forgive others more easily than themselves, and depiction of this in a novel deepens a character's spiritual struggle. Seed the Word in your writing, and allow the Lord to direct you in the story's message.

The Faith Journey

Characters can't end up the same as they were at the beginning of the novel. As they learn and experience life, they will gain new qualities and hone the good ones they reveal at the beginning of the novel. If the heroine is usually patient, she can learn greater patience during the long illness of a loved one. If the hero is self-centered at the beginning, he can learn compassion and concern for others. The readers must see growth in the characters and the romance.

Before the end of the book, if either the hero or heroine has been a weak Christian or nonbeliever, he or she must come to the acceptance that Jesus is the Savior and that God's promises are sure. Growth of character and faith is as vital to the novel as the culmination of the romance and the last kiss. This can be accomplished in dialogue or introspection, but having the character show depth of conviction and growth by acting or reacting in the new "improved" manner is very effective.

Make the Spiritual Message Natural

Making the spiritual message natural means avoiding the preachiness that was a criticism of Christian fiction, including romance, for years. You have learned that the first purpose of Christian romance is to entertain, and approaching a novel with an agenda detracts from its entertainment value. You may want people to know that Jesus is the way or that God is the Father Almighty or that the Holy Spirit brings people to the Lord, but if these messages are delivered overtly and repeated over and over in a story filled with Bible verses and prayers, most readers will turn away and find a book that entertains as well as touches their hearts.

Using Bible Verses in Characterization

Below are a few areas in which the hero and heroine can exhibit Christian attributes reflecting their faith and their ability to follow God's Word. By showing opposite behavior, they will have failed and, in God's eyes, sinned and need to repent and be forgiven.

BIBLICAL ATTRIBUTES

Colossians 3:12–14	Show compassion, kindness, humility, gentleness, patience, forgiveness, and love.
Luke 8:14–16	Be honest and patient.
Matthew 6:25–27	Do not worry about eating, drinking, or clothing.
Matthew 6:14–16	Show forgiveness and store up treasures in heaven.
Exodus 12:3–17	Follow the Ten Commandments.
Matthew 15:18–20	Refrain from evil thoughts, murder, adultery, sexual immorality, theft, false testimony, and slander.
Philippians 1:3–4	Avoid selfishness and conceit.
1 Peter 2:1	Detest malice, deceit, hypocrisy, envy, and slander of every kind.

Luke 12:2–3	Overcome secrets that control your life.
Matthew 11:28–30	Ask God to carry your burdens.
2 Corinthians 12:20–21	Resist quarreling, jealousy, outbursts of anger, factions, slander, gossip, arrogance, disorder, impurity, sexual sin, and debauchery.

Read these biblical references in full, and make note of others as you read your Bible so you can benefit from the teachings and know what God expects.

By allowing characters to ignore God's command, the hero and heroine will falter in their faith and pay the consequences of sorrow and sin. These make excellent conflicts because they are real-life issues with which all Christians must struggle.

As I said earlier, the spiritual message must be woven through the story like a fine thread, adding color and design to the finished product of your novel. This means making faith a natural extension of the characters and their values and beliefs. When a message is pushed into the story, it becomes preachy and loses readers who immediately realize that the discussion has been included for their benefit. The conversation doesn't move the story forward or connect with previous discussions; it's as if the author decided it was time to add a salvation message and popped it in. Though you want to share the comfort of faith and the promise of salvation through the death and resurrection of Jesus Christ, the challenge is to present a strong spiritual theme or truth without overshadowing the story.

How can this be done? By sharing your Christian views and message while remembering entertainment is the main thrust of Christian romance. Present a story filled with external and internal conflicts, then weave in the spiritual theme or biblical truth that is the story's focus. Let the message flow from the characters' need to explain a value or to respond to an issue in the realistic way in which Christians would react in everyday life.

In Hannah Alexander's romantic suspense *Safe Haven*, the heroine, Karah Lee, has been estranged from the Lord following disappointments in her life, particularly her divorce. The faith of the hero, Taylor, has also suffered the pangs of losing loved ones—a son, a wife, and a partner—but he continues to hold on to his beliefs. He understands that God is in control, but not always the way a believer wants. Karah Lee's aunt has been a steadfast voice in her ear to bring her back to the Lord, which the hero considers wise. Notice how the dialogue moves from a discussion about bitterness to a lesson in faith. This scene in the hero's point of view opens with Karah Lee speaking first.

"I guess it could be possible that I've tried to use my father as a scapegoat all these years to explain why I've been avoiding God." Her words sounded casual, as if she were repeating something she didn't necessarily believe—even as if someone had said those words to her sometime in the past, or that maybe she'd read them in a book.

"So why have you really been avoiding Him?" Taylor asked.

She tested the gate, then pushed it open and walked through. "I guess you would probably think it was because I've wanted to hold on to my bitterness all these years, and I know that in order to have a good relationship with God, I'd have to release that bitterness." Again the casualness, but this time he caught a thread of tension underlying the words, as if the casualness was feigned.

"Sounds like you've been doing a lot of thinking about it."

"I have an aunt who calls me every few weeks from California." She glanced over her shoulder at him. "She's my mother's older sister. She's quadriplegic, and she has a lot of time to interfere in family problems."

"It sounds as if she also has a lot of time to pray. And to think. Do you ever listen to her when she interferes?"

"Usually I can keep her off the subject, but lately she's been harping on me a lot."

"She sounds like a wise lady." Taylor followed her through the gate. *Oh Lord, is that what I've been doing all this time? Hiding beneath my bitterness?*

Blaming You for something someone else did? Please forgive me. "You know, it's possible God's always been there, always waited patiently for us."

"Waited for what?" Karah Lee asked. "I'm a believer."

"You're estranged from God, you said so yourself. What kind of relationship is that? Maybe He's just waiting for you to admit you want to restore the relationship. Maybe He's just giving us both a chance to get over ourselves and realize that what matters in life is really how we handle all our baggage."

Both the hero and heroine have struggled in their faith journeys, but readers see that the hero has a more solid grip on what God expects. Their discussion, which stems from each character's issues of coping with life's hurts and disappointments, fits into the actions of their daily lives as they amble through an old church cemetery.

When life issues enter a conversation, it is not unnatural for people of faith to include God and their beliefs in the discussion. The cemetery setting in the excerpt has triggered a discussion of family, which led to disappointments and sorrow, but the scene could just as easily have occurred while washing dishes or walking in a park, as long as a conversation about family triggers the new discussion.

A look into your own family background will reveal similar emotional memories that may have caused you to question where God was when you needed Him. So remember, as you weave faith into dialogue and action of your story, make it stem from realistic situations in the characters' lives.

USING SCRIPTURE

Scripture can certainly be included in Christian romance. How it's handled makes the difference between a "preachy" romance and one that both entertains and witnesses to God's promises. Whether direct Bible quotes or paraphrases, you can make the greatest impact by allowing the scripture to work naturally into conversation or introspection.

Direct Bible Quotes

Quoting the Bible is not something most people do in general conversation, so it is important to find realistic purposes when quoting scripture.

Relate to your own relationship with the Lord and note how God's Word is part of your life. A typical technique is to have the hero or heroine in a worship service, listening to the preacher; for example, "Take to heart the words from Psalm 37:7: 'Be still before the Lord and wait patiently for him; do not fret when men succeed in their ways, when they carry out their wicked schemes.'" The clergy might quote the verse with or without the biblical reference—most publishers do not require the verse notations. Another method is to have the hero or heroine search the Bible for a passage that speaks to a personal problem.

Many Christians don't retain long Bible passages to memory nor do they use them when talking to others about their faith. When a direct Bible passage is quoted, it is usually a special verse that has been laid on their hearts. These verses are usually familiar to most Christians, such as "with God all things are possible," or "forgive, and you will be forgiven." You can see how they might easily be included in a conversation: "Don't worry, Jane. With God all things are possible." Or "John, you can't hold a grudge forever. The Bible says, 'Forgive, and you will be forgiven.'"

When you use Bible quotes, remember to work them into dialogue and introspection in a real-life way, and keep them short. When a quotation is lengthy, readers sometimes feel preached at rather than ministered to.

Paraphrasing Scripture

Christians share their faith through paraphrasing God's Word more often than with direct quotes. In Christian romance, paraphrasing is often the most natural way to share Bible truths with readers while still making the scene realistic, not "preachy." The paraphrasing must be accurate, and the words should naturally fit into the flow of the conversation, as they do in this scene between Karen and her grandfather from my novel *Out on a Limb*.

"Grandpa, please. You're a Christian, and you know better. What does God say you should do when you're upset with a neighbor?"

"Park my car in front of his roadside stand. That's if he had one."

She faltered at his comment. "That's not what God says."

"Sure does. An eye for an eye. A tooth for a tooth. So why not a parked car for a parked car."

Karen shook her head. "Grandpa, you know why." She took a step backward. "Should I get my Bible?"

He lowered his gaze, and her heart softened. She sensed God's urging. Instead of huffing and puffing, she calmed herself and sat in the chair beside him. "An eye for an eye is in the Old Testament. When Jesus came to earth, he gave us some new commands to follow. I know you've read them. Jesus said, 'I know you've heard eye for eye and tooth for tooth, but I'm telling you that if someone strikes you on the right cheek, turn the other cheek.' "

Her grandfather shifted his gaze from the floor as if he wanted to counter her comment, but he couldn't debate with the Lord.

Karen stared at him until he looked at her. "And you know what else the Bible says?"

He shrugged.

"Love your enemy and pray for him."

She watched him bristle. "I can pray for him," he sputtered, "but I can't love him."

Make sure the verses relate to the primary issues on the hero or heroine's mind, then weave them into the conversation or introspection in a natural way. Test your paraphrase by reading it aloud to determine whether it sounds like something you would hear in everyday conversation. If not, reword it so that it fits naturally into the dialogue or introspection.

USING PRAYER

The Lord's Prayer is the finest biblical example of a formal prayer. Jesus told us to pray in this manner: beginning with *Heavenly Father, Almighty God, Dearest Lord*, or another phrase to address God. The body of a prayer follows with praise, petitions, and conclusion, including *amen*. You hear this type of prayer in church, at church meetings, and in family prayers.

In most people's lives, however, prayers are short petitions and brief thank-yous without formal structure. In Christian romance, prayer is more natural when it is spoken in the same manner a Christian prays in his own life: a conversation with God using everyday words he might use with family and friends.

Christians often have traditional prayers at meals and bedtime, but prayers can occur throughout the day in joyful praise or a time of need. It's natural to ask God for help when dealing with a family crisis or when a friend is ill. A mother might utter a prayer that her child is safe if he is late coming home, and when he arrives home, the mother will send up a thank-you before dealing with the reason the child was late. As you write your story, use prayer at natural moments, just as you do in your own life.

Prayer can provide an insight into characterization and be used to demonstrate the growth of a character. If the hero has lost his faith and utters a prayer in desperation, readers will realize he has made a step toward strengthened faith.

In this scene from Marta Perry's Christian romantic suspense *Tangled Memories*, Corrie deals with her dilemma in her introspection. She speaks to God as if he were a friend sitting beside her. Notice also how a specific Bible verse is mentioned and then paraphrased in her informal prayer.

> Corrie touched the photo of her parents, her fingertips lingering on the young faces. She'd done her best, hadn't she? At least she'd proved to her own satisfaction that her mother was an honest woman. That she was the child of Trey and Gracie's marriage.
>
> *That should be enough, Lord. Why do I still feel so empty?*
>
> She'd put the photo in her Bible at Psalm 139 for a reason. She smoothed the page, reading the words that she could say by heart.
>
> *You know me inside and out, you know every bone in my body; You know exactly how I was made, bit by bit, how I was sculpted from nothing into something.*
>
> God knew her, as God knew all things. God understood what had brought Trey and Gracie together and what had split them apart. Maybe she never would. She closed the Bible and laid it gently into her open suitcase.

The naturalness of this prayer provides readers with a look into the character's struggle to find love and sense of family she's longed for, as well as her relationship with God.

Sometimes characters pray without readers hearing the prayer, but you can indicate the essence of it: *He sent up a prayer*, or *She looked toward heaven and thanked the Lord*, or *He bowed his head and asked God for help*.

Prayer—whether formal, conversational, or unspoken, a full paragraph or a single word gasped for God's help—is as natural to a Christian as breathing, and it is an essential element of Christian romance. .

PUBLISHERS' PREFERENCES

Though Christian publishing houses vary on certain elements of Christian romance, they all want to see the spiritual thread woven through the story and follow accepted standards based on a Christian expectations and worldview. The variations from publisher to publisher are most often based on denominational tradition and the preferences of their readership.

Some publishing houses prefer that you avoid naming the specific denomination or religion of your hero and heroine unless it is necessary for the plotline. This is done so as to not bias readers. A mention of the Baptist church on the other side of town or the Roman Catholic church around the corner is acceptable, as long as the comments are not derogatory. In the same way, conservative publishers prefer you to avoid a specific denominational name (for example, United Methodist of Middletown or St. Paul's Lutheran), and instead give churches a generic name: First Church of Middletown, Community Christian Church, First United Church, Cornerstone, Trinity, or Hope Church. These do not specify the church denomination.

As always, there are exceptions. Certainly a novel set in biblical times might require elements of the Jewish faith, and stories revolving around Amish characters will require Amish faith traditions. An Italian family saga would most likely require Roman Catholic traditions. This makes the story believable and is necessary.

Check a publisher's guidelines when writing scenes that involve Holy Baptism or the Eucharist, because these sacraments vary widely from one religious denomination to another. Some faiths baptize babies, some only adults; some sprinkle, some immerse. In the same manner, communion is passed to the worshipers' seats in some faith traditions; others kneel at an altar. Some use only grape juice; others use wine. Some use bread, while others use wafers. Some Christian readers are disturbed by scenes that go against their faith traditions.

All publishers agree you should avoid doctrinal issues, violence, foul language, and cursing. Dancing, smoking, and playing cards or games of chance, and the use of wine, beer, or alcohol varies with each publishing house, so again, check the guidelines. If it is important to the characterization or plot and presented tastefully, these activities may be acceptable to the publisher; for example, if you're writing a wedding scene, you could mention a toast without naming the drink and listen to the music without dancing.

In some publishing houses, divorce is avoided, so the hero and heroine must be single or widowed. If you can find a believable reason for the character to have remained single, this helps the realism of the novel. With being chaste a concern of many publishers, some editors require authors to include another adult character in the mix when the hero and heroine are living or sleeping in the same residence. Your challenge is to work through these restrictions so that you can still present a realistic story that is believable to readers while staying within the acceptable boundaries of the publisher's guidelines.

THE ULTIMATE PURPOSE

All Christian publishers want a story that reflects the way believers deal with life. Christian publishers want to provide readers with a Christian perspective. They expect you to provide readers with believable characters struggling against compelling, real-life problems that are entertaining and yet have a meaningful ministerial value. Your goal is this: Beneath your entertaining story, readers will be emotionally touched, identify with the struggles and growth of your characters, and changed by the message and led to seek the Lord's will in their own lives.

EXERCISES

1. Considering your work in progress or latest work, write a two-sentence answer to this question: Besides wanting to entertain, what is my purpose for writing this novel?

2. Read the Bible verses from Colossians 3:12–14, Matthew 6:25–27, and Luke 8:14–16 (found on pages 100–101). Select other verses at random. Make a list of spiritual elements that God expects. Now ask yourself how people often fail the Lord's request to follow his expectations. Allow these topics to stimulate your thought in terms of story ideas and plotlines. Make a list of those that trigger a plot idea.

3. Locate a scene that deals with a faith issue in your most recent novel or your work in progress. Read the scene and ask yourself if the scene flows naturally into the plot. Is the discussion natural? Does the dialogue sound the way people would talk in real life?

4. Review how you have used scripture and prayer in your novel. Is the scripture quoted or paraphrased? Does the quoted scripture appear in a natural way? If not, rewrite the scene so that it sounds realistic. Read your quoted scripture, and then paraphrase the verses to decide if that sounds more natural.

CHAPTER 7

Understanding Point of View in Christian Romance

Point of view (POV) is one of the most troublesome elements of fiction because it is necessary to know not only the kinds of POV available, but which one serves the story best. Using point of view improperly can signal a "beginning author" to an editor.

Readers see and experience the story through the senses—sight, sound, taste, smell, and touch—of the character who owns the scene. "Owning the scene" means the POV character is the central focus of that scene, and it is through his or her eyes that readers experience the scene. In Christian romance, it is important to decide whether the hero or heroine will be the focal character of the scene so that readers can experience exactly what he or she is feeling, sensing, comprehending, and living through all of the sense perceptions that occur in everyday life.

CHOOSING THE BEST POINT OF VIEW FOR CHRISTIAN ROMANCE

The most common point of view for Christian romance is third person limited (he and she), alternating the hero or heroine's POVs by scene or chapters. The hero's scenes are totally through his eyes, the heroine's are totally through hers. In Christian romance, this method allows readers to enjoy getting to know both the hero and heroine intimately by seeing their relationship through both characters' eyes and thoughts. The story is theirs, and the readers care about them, so only the two POVs are typical in a romance. An occasional third POV might be part of a story; for example, the criminal in a romantic suspense or a secondary character whose POV makes a significant difference to the hero and heroine's relationship.

Which Character Has the Most to Lose?

Although we know the hero and heroine are central to a love story, you must decide which of the two will serve best as the POV character for each scene. This is done by deciding which character has the most at stake in the scene; give the scene to the one who has the most to lose.

In romance, both characters lose if the relationship falls apart, but even if it's blossoming, one character will be the most vulnerable by confessing a secret, sharing a fear, or opening the door to the relationship. Another way to determine this "stake" is by deciding which character needs to share his or her true feelings with readers more fully through introspection.

In my novel *Secrets of the Heart*, the heroine became pregnant in her early teens and gave up her child for adoption. Now, years later, she has fallen in love with a man who values chastity above all things. It is clearly the heroine who has the most at stake in this scene—the most to lose—so the confession scene comes from the heroine's POV.

"Don't stop me," she said and rattled on about the hurt and shame she'd felt after she'd ruined her life.

"It's okay, Kate. I'm shocked but—"

"And that's not all, I had a baby daughter given for adoption when I was fifteen. She was born at ... Madonna House." The last word faded into her sobs.

"I'm soiled, Scott," she said, pulling herself together. "I'm dirty linen, unfit for a decent Christian man like you."

Scott reached out to hold her, but she pushed him away, sensing his shock and knowing he was repulsed.

Before she could stop herself, before she could catch her breath and realize what she'd done, Scott rose and stumbled away from her.

"I can't fight you any longer," he said. "This is the last thing I thought would happen tonight. I'm sorry, but I can't handle this." He spun on his heel and tore across the grass out of sight.

Although we agree that the scene belongs to Kate, we can also see that the news has devastated the hero. He's walked away from Kate, leaving her tangled in the aftermath of her confession. Still, we realize from Scott's reaction that the confession is also crucial to Scott's relationship with Kate.

The next scene is in Scott's POV, which is also called a sequel, and it helps readers understand Scott's reaction:

During the night shift at County General, Scott's distraction concerned him. He struggled to concentrate on the patients and push his own desperation aside. He'd spent a couple of sleepless nights plodding through the horrible memory of Kate's disclosure, overwhelmed by the outcome.

Yet, her confession was the least devastating. What hurt him to the core was her lack of faith in him. After knowing him for a year, sharing untold hours together, why hadn't she told him sooner? He'd done everything under heaven to let her know that his life was empty without her, and still, she didn't trust him to share her doleful secret.

Kate's scene ended with a hook—Scott walked away when she needed him most. Readers might initially be angry at him for his reaction. He could at least have said something calming or kind, and then told her he had to think; instead, he charged away. But Scott's scene makes it clear that it was not Kate's confession that upset him, it was her lack of trust in him. Since trust is the basis of any good relationship, Scott sees this lack of trust as a barrier between them and their chance for a successful marriage. Readers can now lean back with a sigh and relax, confident that Scott will do the right thing; there is a renewed hope for the happily-ever-after ending romance promises.

If the confession scene had come from Scott's POV, readers would have known immediately why he was upset, which would have taken the zing out of the scene. Making the best POV decision possible is important to deepen characterization and is also necessary to provide a satisfying, page-turner novel. Before writing a scene, picture it from both the hero's and heroine's POV, then decide who owns the scene.

Change the POV Character

When a scene between the hero and heroine doesn't seem to work or lacks the purpose or excitement it needs, changing the POV character can often solve the problem. Take the same scene and rewrite it from the other character's POV. This allows you to see and hear the information with a new perspective, and the stronger emotion or new hook provided by the change in POV will allow the scene to make a greater impact on readers.

Using POV for Character Insight and Emotion

Much can be learned about a character through dialogue or action: hearing a conversation or seeing a character tremble, turn away, flush, quake, shake a fist, or kick a rock. But without the ability to look inside the character's mind, readers cannot totally understand the stress or drama of the moment. Inside the POV character's head, readers can hear the truth of his present struggle or the anguish from past or present turmoil. The POV character's introspection reveals what's in his heart and mind, thus helping readers to know the real feelings and attitudes of the characters.

DEFINING POV TYPES

The types of POV available to you for popular fiction, which includes Christian romance, are third person (limited and multiple), first person, and multiple first person. Other POVs not as popular in Christian romance are omniscient (sometimes called detached observer) and a combination of POV types.

Third Person in Christian Romance

Third person is the most common POV and is probably the easiest to write and the most popular among fiction writers. Third person, most often written in past tense, is accomplished by showing the life experiences, thoughts, and actions of a character, rather than the character telling the story directly.

Third person multiple refers to showing scenes from the POV of one character at a time and is the main form of third person for writing Christian romance. In Christian romance, the hero and heroine own different scenes within the story to show their attitudes and emotions and share their thoughts with the readers.

The details will differ in a scene depending on whether the hero or heroine is the POV character of that scene. Using the heroine's POV in this sample, notice how everything is viewed through her eyes:

> Alice Greene stood beside the old barn and watched the sun rise. The cows' contented moo echoed behind her as if they were happy to have been milked and fed. She turned toward the sound and grinned, knowing she'd been the one to make them happy.

The next example demonstrates what the scene would look like if the author chose to use the POV of the hero, Chip, a ranch hand:

> From the bunkhouse, Chip's gaze settled on the pretty little filly who paused in front of the barn. Through the open window, he heard the cows lowing and noticed the woman turn toward the sound, her brown hair knotted in a ponytail, flicking behind her like an old Dobbin whacking flies from his flank.

Using this POV gives readers a different dimension of Alice Greene while also introducing the hero, Chip, with his sense of humor and interest in the young woman. When choosing whose POV to use in a story with multiple viewpoints, you must decide which character would be most suited to presenting the scene to the readers.

Advantages and Disadvantages of Third-Person POV

As I mentioned, third person is the most common POV style and is the easiest to learn. The story is told totally through the eyes of either the hero or heroine, one scene at a time. One character can reflect his or her feelings about another and unintentionally lead readers astray with a bad deduction. Characters can keep secrets from other characters and share inward struggles with life and faith through introspection. A successful technique is having a different voice for each character, with enough distinction between dialogue style, mannerisms, and thought processes to leave readers with no doubt about who is speaking, even without a character tag. Third person puts readers into the heart and soul of the character, making it a good choice for Christian romance (although first person can be more powerful in this regard).

Technique for Testing Third Person Limited

An effective way to ensure you are writing quality third-person POV is to replace the proper nouns and pronouns of the character who owns that scene with your own first-person POV. Write it as if you are the POV character who is experiencing the event. When you hear it this way, you will know if the POV is clear and if everything you are seeing and hearing is possible in the real world.

For example, read this line: *"This is unacceptable," Jane yelled, her eyes snapping with fire and her face as red as neon.*

Did you spot the error? Test it by replacing the name Jane with "I" and the pronoun her with "my." Now it's easy to see the problem. Unless you were looking in a mirror, you would not see your own eyes snapping with fire or your neon red face. To write with quality, the author's visual description can be changed to something the speaker would know and feel.

"This is unacceptable," Jane yelled, her fingers coiled in a fist and her face burning.

In real life, while you can't see your snapping eyes or red face, you can feel your hands balling into fists and the heat of an angry flush.

The disadvantages of third person are few. First, while in the heroine's POV, she cannot know what the hero is doing or thinking—which means neither can the readers—she can only surmise: *She assumed from the look in his eyes he was angry;* or in the hero's POV, *She turned away, afraid, he assumed, to let him see how she really felt*. The same problem lies with interpreting what a character means in dialogue. The undertone message is only speculation. Second, while writing, you must be totally focused on the single viewpoint at a time and not slip into another character's POV. "Head-hopping," discussed more fully later in this chapter, is a sure sign to editors of an inexperienced writer.

Once you master the multiple-third-person POV, you will find it an effective way to give equal treatment to the hero and heroine as you share their thoughts and words or show their love, faith, and character growth.

First Person in Christian Romance

In first-person POV, the story is viewed through one person's eyes only. This is the "I" voice, where readers become intimately involved with the character because it is only through that character's limited vision that they can experience all of the senses. Through the character's thoughts and actions, the readers can interpret, learn, sense, and know only what the character experiences. The readers have no opportunity to know another character as well. It is through the POV voice that we learn the character's ups and downs as she struggles with the spiritual workings in her life.

First person is usually told in past tense, but is sometimes told in present tense. Although past tense is most common, it sounds as if it is a retelling of a story. Present-tense POV provides immediacy as well as action and excitement without distancing readers. Things are happening now, as if readers are there with the main character, experiencing the events along with her. Either tense works for Christian romance, but readers tend to be more comfortable with the story written in past tense because it is more familiar to them. Also, present tense is difficult to maintain, and it is easy for the writer to slip into past tense without realizing it. So be aware of this if you choose to write in first-person present tense.

Although it is not as common, multiple-first-person POV can be used in Christian romance with the hero and heroine each alternating scenes from the first-person perspective. This will be discussed in more detail later.

Advantages and Disadvantages of First-Person POV

First person is the most intimate POV and would work best in romance for a story that focuses on one character's struggle or flaws while the other character provides the catalyst for change. The spiritual life of this character and his or her worldview is more dynamic because readers can understand the spiritual motivation or struggle behind the actions and thoughts. It allows readers to climb beneath the skin of a character, to get to know him intimately, to hear every thought, to understand motivation at the time of the event, to see, hear, touch, taste, and smell everything the character does. Readers will see how the first-person POV character changes from what he learns.

On the other hand, Christian romance is the story of a man and woman falling in love; therefore, first-person POV is limited in use because it saturates readers with either the hero or heroine but not both, forging a close, emotional relationship with either the hero or heroine while giving a limited perspective of the other. If the novel is told from the heroine's first-person POV only, readers will never know the thoughts or see the action of the hero without the first-person character, the heroine, being in the scene. This means that the hero would have a difficult time to explain his deep fears or feelings without speaking them aloud to the heroine, because you can never be inside his head. Another difficulty is the first-person character must be in each scene since the story is told only through that character's eyes and emotions. Obviously, an advanced writer may devise techniques to overcome this occasional disadvantage.

The single POV character, whether the hero or heroine, must be dynamic and interesting enough to hold readers' interests without getting into the head of the other romantic character, and the character must be truthful to the readers. Holding back secrets does not work in first-person POV.

Multiple First Person in Christian Romance

Multiple-first-person POV is more common in Christian romance than secular romance because it provides a more intimate and unlimited view of the characters and of the romantic and spiritual struggle of both the hero and heroine. It also provides a way to get around the limited perspective in first-person POV, since both the hero and heroine will bring the story to life through his or her first-person POV within different scenes belonging to that character. Hero's POV: *I walked into the room and saw Susan, frowning, as usual.* Heroine's POV: *I was sitting in the recliner when Paul strode into the room and startled me. I studied his face, as I do so often, trying to understand why he always looks at me with such question.*

Depending on which character owns the scene and has the first-person POV, readers can see the questions and motivation of the character. In the sample above, the conflict of both characters is evident, but if readers were only seeing this scene from a single POV, they would not have the opportunity to understand the other character's thoughts and maturation. An advantage of using multiple-first-person POV in Christian romance is that it allows the intimacy of first person with an unlimited scope.

As you develop your story idea, begin to define characters, and establish the story's mood, decide on the type of POV that is best for your story, as well as whether it should be written in present or past tense. Most Christian romance is written in past tense from the POV of the hero and heroine, but occasionally the story can benefit from adding other characters' points of view, as found in Cindy Martinusen's *The Salt Garden*.

When Martinusen began brainstorming her novel, she believed the love stories would be best told from three viewpoints in first person because the three stories overlap and create an unique look at loss, love, and secrets. Martinusen says:

> There are discoveries made about the three women by seeing them from another viewpoint. And from that, a larger picture is discovered beyond each single life and perspective. With a tight view of each woman, the immediacy of present tense, the past voice, and vein of past, present, and future, *The Salt Garden* grows from small details and opens into a wider view of character, town, history, and the inner lives of even the participating reader.

She goes on to describe the process she used in this way:

> Though there's an old unsolved shipwreck, the antics of a small coastal town, and other elements to the novel, *The Salt Garden* is ultimately about the

weaving of three lives from three different generations—as in the past, present, and future—and how the women are shaped, changed, and healed by the connection of one another.

The reader needed to see and hear these women from the closest proximity. The reader gets closest to the characters in first person and can only know and feel what that character knows and feels. Also, nothing is more immediate than present tense. For two of the characters, I used present tense so the reader was along for every experience, not hearing a story already told. My voice from the past—Josephine—told her story in past tense through her written memoir, which slowed the pace and gave a more thoughtful structure connecting the more immediate other voices.

Although using three first-person POVs is unusual, in this story, readers experience the love and lives of three amazing women from three different generations in an intimate and dramatic way.

Omniscient in Christian Romance

Omniscient point of view is well known in classic literature. This POV style is not as much telling the characters' feelings but you, as the author, entering the story to explain what's happening and why. You might comment that if the heroine knew what was behind the door, she would never open it. In most Christian romance, this is considered author intrusion and is not accepted by editors for popular romance fiction.

The omniscient POV, through the "all-knowing" narrator, provides readers with backstory, information about the setting, and access to all characters' thoughts, feelings, and actions, even scenes in which no characters are present. To get a feel for this style, read the following paragraph about milking the cows and notice how it differs from the previous examples, told from different POVs:

Beside the barn, built a hundred years early by the present owner's ancestors, cows wagged their tails and lowed, contented that they had been milked and fed. A young woman who stood nearby turned toward them, her ponytail flicking like an old Dobbin whacking flies from his flank. She smiled at the cows, knowing they were satisfied.

Through whose eyes are we seeing this scene? Can we picture the speaker? Do you feel a sense of place and time? The answer is probably not as much as you did with the same scene presented by Alice or Chip earlier in this chapter. We witnessed the scene through each of their eyes, but now we've viewed the same scene through the eyes of an omniscient narrator.

Because of the lack of intimacy with the POV characters, omniscient POV is limited in Christian romance. When it is found in a romance, it will usually appear in a Christian historical romance novel, which lends itself more readily to the omniscient narration style and is usually blended with third-person POV. In Louise Gouge's *Ahab's Bride*, readers are introduced to the town and its people in these combination omniscient narrative excerpts.

> Sunday morning services at the Trinitarian Congregational Church of New Bedford were always well attended. The popularity of the new assistant pastor brought this day's crowd to overflowing when word was circulated that he would deliver the message. However, it was not only Jeremiah's sermon that increased the assemblage. A number of the men in the church had signed on as crew members of the *Sharona*, and it was considered advantageous for them and their families to attend services just before a voyage.

Later in *Ahab's Bride*, the internal struggle of the women of the town is presented using the omniscient POV. Notice that the emotional impact is not as powerful as if it had been told directly from the POV of the heroine.

> Despite these outward signs that all could see, everyone involved with each ship hungered for details. Married to the bravest of seafaring men, a Nantucket woman displayed her own fortitude by patiently waiting for her husband to finish his duties, to visit the bathhouse for a bath and shave, and to walk through the door of their home. For the ship captain's wife, news would be brought by young boys not yet old enough to sail. The first one to deliver the news to her earned a silver dollar.

Writing the Christian Romance

Advantages and Disadvantages of Omniscient POV

An advantage of using omniscient POV is your freedom to provide a multitude of information, from any POV, and not be limited by the presence or absence of the characters.

In Christian romance, omniscient POV works well for historical romance. In Regency or other historical novels, modesty hinders the heroine from describing her clothing, for example, so using the omniscient POV in some scenes adds to the readers' understanding of physical description.

To expedite scene transition, you can use omniscient POV to tell readers rather than show them. For example, *The traffic was heavy, and it took them twenty minutes rather than ten to reach the office building.* This statement doesn't seem to come from a character in the book, but instead from a narrator who's moving readers to the next scene.

Occasionally, omniscient POV works in a short paragraphs to provide setting information or description, but the preferred method is having a character describe the setting through his or her eyes. But sometimes, too much description can be distracting to readers so omniscient POV could work more efficiently.

Read the following paragraph and notice how the description is not from a character's POV but from an omniscient narrator:

> A warm breeze blew across the deck, and along the sandy path to the lake, tall grass and the myriad of wildflowers—oxeye daisies, orange hawkweed, and bladder campion—flanked the beach. The bright colors stood out among the spikes of timothy, wild oats, and oxtail. The day would prove to be as bright for Marsha.

Using this style, readers know how the setting looks, but they gain nothing that moves the story forward or provides insight from Marsha's POV. In contrast, see how effective the description is delivered in third-person POV through a character's eyes.

> Marsha slid open the screen and stepped onto the deck as a warm breeze wrapped around her. She descended the three steps to the sand, then ambled

down the path to the lake, her gaze drifted to the tall grass and the myriad of wildflowers—oxeye daisies, orange hawkweed, and bladder campion—that flanked her trek to the beach. The bright colors stood out among the spikes of timothy, wild oats, and oxtail. Sometimes amid life's weeds, she'd found a few bright spots in her life. Today seemed one of them.

Not only do readers see Marsha in action as she descends the steps and feels the warm breeze, but they also gain information about Marsha when the description serves as a metaphor for her life.

Omniscient POV is rarely used in contemporary Christian romance because it pulls readers outside the character rather than allowing them to spend time in the minds and hearts of the hero and heroine, and it doesn't offer an emotional outlet for the faith and romance journey.

Combining First- and Third-Person POV Styles

POV can be handled in amazing ways to create unique story-telling styles, but it takes an experienced writer to handle this. Newer writers are wise to stick to traditional POV styles, but they can benefit from knowing the many creative ways to present characters as confidence and experience grows.

When planning your Christian romance plot and characters, you may discover that you want your heroine to be in the more intimate POV of first person but would prefer your hero to be in third person. Using first- or third-person POV in Christian romance can work in a variety of situations.

Using First Person for the Focal Character Only

While very common in Christian fiction, combining first- and third-person POV is not as common in Christian romance. Combining first person with third-person POV can be used when your heroine or hero needs a more intimate exploration or has the most serious problems that can be more understood by seeing life through first-person POV.

In the historical novel *The Immortal*, Christian author Angela Hunt presents the heroine, Claudia, in first person and all other characters, including the hero, in third. Explaining why she would mix two POV styles, Hunt says,

> I wanted readers to have access to Claudia's emotions and see her thought processes because she's an intellectual protagonist. On the other hand, Ash-

er has secrets, and if I'd written him in first person and yet hidden his secrets, that would have been cheating the reader. By using mixed first/third, I was able to reveal Asher's secret slowly and let the reader experience Claudia's emotional and intellectual reactions to Asher's unusual story.

As I mentioned earlier, secrets cannot be kept in first person, so when there is backstory information or secrets that are important to the plot, it may be preferable to keep that character in third person.

Blending first and third works in Christian romance if you have, as Hunt does, a valid reason for using this technique, but creating two different POVs for characters without a meaningful purpose might confuse readers or pull them from the story. If you feel this will work for your characters, make sure that you keep each POV distinct.

Using First Person to Reflect Flashback

Christy Award-winning author Kristen Heitzmann uses an original style of POV, mixing first and third person between past and present tense. She does this to show a dramatic difference between the flashback scenes of the heroine's youth to the present day. To show an immediacy of the past, Heitzmann uses first person present tense and third person past tense for the present scenes. Notice how the POV changes with Antonia's character in this excerpt from *Unforgotten*. In this scene, Antonia, recovering from a stroke, has been carried downstairs to join her family dinner party, including her granddaughter Monica and her grandson Lance, who will introduce his new lady friend, Rese, whom Antonia believes he will marry.

> He [Lance] tried to take the seat to her left, but Monica wedged in, bossy as always. "I haven't gotten to know her yet. Go around the other side."
>
> The communication between Rese and her grandson's eyes told Nonna what she'd already guessed. This one was more to Lance than the others.
>
> Monica stuffed her napkin in her lap. "So tell me about this inn you and Lance have."
>
> And Antonia grew still, listening to her home described in such detail she found herself once again in its comforting arms …

The porch is dark as a light rain falls and only the lamplight through the living room window spills out. Marco has called regularly over the past weeks, yet made no advance. I am unsure what to make of that. Is he more serious than the suitors who press their luck, or less interested than he seems?

He leans against the plastered pillar, playing softly on the mandolin. It is only the second time he's brought it, and he doesn't sing along this time, merely studies me with a serious mien.

"What is it?" I whisper.

He shakes himself as though only realizing how he's been, and it's as though he puts on a mask, a smile as flimsy as cellophane. "You're beautiful in the lamplight."

"That's not what you were thinking."

"Bella Antonia, if a man shared everything he was thinking, he'd have his face slapped too often."

The scene begins in the present and slips into the past. Antonia's reminiscence, and all the scenes that are told in the historical sections, are in first-person present tense, while the body of the book is in third person past tense. Heitzmann explains, "To Antonia, the past is more real to her in many ways than the happenings of the family she has around her. So I chose to tell her stories of the past in the most imminent form."

The uniqueness of this selection is not only the change of one character from first to third person, but also the change from past to present tense, which adds a totally different feeling to the sound and rhythm of the narration. The opening line of the backstory—the porch *is* dark (present tense), rather than *was* dark (past tense)—leaves readers in no doubt as to the moment the story changes from the present to the past.

The Christian romance genre opens doors for wonderful, creative ways to present a love story to readers. In the example above, the two POVs for one person allow readers to see the two sides of Antonia—her youth and her old age. The style makes a vivid impression on readers and enhances the romantic memory of the elderly woman's past while Heitzmann presents the newer romance of Lance and Rese.

Using First Person for Anonymity in Christian Romantic Suspense

Hiding a villain's identity in a Christian romantic suspense can be done effectively by using first person for his character and third person for the hero and heroine. In my novel *Adam's Promise,* I hid the villain behind a first-person exterior. Marlo Schalesky also uses this technique in her Christian romantic suspense *Veil of Fire.* While all other characters are in third person, the unidentified first-person POV antagonist provides a mysterious backdrop for the story.

Veil of Fire opens in 1894, Hinckley, Minnesota, after a huge firestorm swept through the town and destroyed the surrounding area. This scene occurs as the town begins to rebuild and deals with a cart, the only possession that Josef thinks he has left from the fire.

> "One more question, then I'll hand this in for you. What property do you have left? Was anything spared?"
>
> Josef grimaced. "Just a cart. Maggie's old gardening cart."
>
> "A cart? Are you certain?"
>
> "Saw it up at the farmstead yesterday. I know it ain't much."
>
> Nils placed a hand on Josef's shoulder. "I was up to your place just this morning." His hand dropped away. "I'm sorry, Josef. There was no cart."
>
> No cart. He should have known. Josef clenched his fists and glared into the sky.
>
> * * *
>
> Shame. It wells up in me, spilling over like bile. Shame, screaming at me in the form of this ramshackle cart that I have made my own. It is a small cart, one wheel broken, one side singed with flame. Still, for it I have sacrificed my last shreds of dignity.

In the scene after the asterisk break, the story switches to first person, and the person is not introduced. Schalesky explains her POV style:

> It was absolutely essential that I use first person for one character. After the fire, one character is terribly burned, so much so that the person is unrecognizable

and becomes a hermit in the hills. A major story question is who that person really is. I also wanted to explore life and the world through the eyes of a person who has lost everything—his home, family, friends, identity, and even gender. This person is completely stripped bare. First person provided both the anonymity with no gender nor name and also the intense intimacy that would allow the reader to live in the disfigured skin of the mystery character.

Blending first and third person creates an interesting method of presenting character, but each POV should be selected with a purpose in mind. While first person allows intimacy and can allow for hidden identify, third person gives you a broader scope for each of your characters, and it allows readers to get inside more than one head and see the characters from different perspectives.

PERFECTING POV TECHNIQUES IN CHRISTIAN ROMANCE

Defining POV and describing the various types does not solve the basic problem of using POV effectively in a novel. POV is the major cause of stress for beginning writers, and its misuse is often a key to rejection. You have heard that you must put yourself inside the head of the POV character so that you can write with realism. You have learned about first person, third person, and the blends of POVs available. You have learned that you must select the best POV character for the scene based on who has the most at stake. Your challenge is putting this into practice.

Seeing the Impossible

To help you understand problems that can occur when using POV, read the following example, written in third person from Jill's POV, and identify what's wrong:

Jill's pulse galloped when Brandon stepped through the doorway—muscular, assured, and handsome. His gaze trailed down the length of her windblown, golden-blond hair, then glided along her ivory skin, and rested on her full, coral lips. She winced as a red flush crept up her neck and covered her face.

What is the POV flaw in this paragraph? First, Jill can only describe what she sees. Can she see her windblown hair and the red flush? No. Only Brandon can see that. She can feel the flush and logic tells her that her hair is windblown. Have you ever said to someone, "Look at my messy golden-blond hair" or "I need to refresh my full coral lips"? I hope not. But Jill does this in the scene above. Avoid having characters describe how they look.

The scene is more realistic and far more effective through Brandon's eyes in third-person POV:

> Brandon came through the doorway into the sunlight and faltered. Jill. The wind ruffled her golden, sun-speckled hair. His gaze glided over her delicate, ivory skin to her full, coral-hued lips. He warmed, watching a rosy flush creep up her hairline and spread along her cheeks.

Not only can readers visualize Jill, but Brandon's characterization is enhanced because readers can sense his attraction.

How could the same paragraph come across through Jill's eyes? You would use proper POV techniques. Instead of having Jill focus on herself, she would focus on Brandon:

> Jill's pulse galloped when Brandon stepped through the doorway—muscular, assured, and handsome. His eyes shifted, drifting along her frame, and the fiery heat of embarrassment crept up her neck. She longed to counter with her own admiration of his bold, manly appearance.

In this version, readers experience only what Jill sees, feels, and thinks. This paragraph works if you want readers to experience Jill's embarrassment and her admiration of Brandon. Another benefit to this scene through Jill's eyes is that you can provide a visual description of Brandon that could not be presented in the paragraph through his eyes.

While emotional reactions belong to the POV character, physical description is most effective from another character. To make your writing believable, only describe what can be seen, heard, felt, and thought through the POV character's eyes.

Testing POV

POV errors ruin a story for seasoned readers and editors who are looking for well-written novels. As you write your scenes, make sure that what your characters see and hear is realistic. You cannot see through walls or read other people's minds. You don't describe yourself in your introspection. Look for the correct use of POV in this example and then look for the POV errors.

> Gina's feet were glued to the kitchen floor. She forced her gaze upward to look into Bill's eyes. "You kissed me."
>
> "I know." A deep flush rose from beneath his collar.
>
> She managed not to laugh. "I realize you would know, but why did you do it?"
>
> A bewildered look filled his face. "I couldn't help myself. I—I'm sorry. I should have asked." He turned and darted from the kitchen.
>
> Adhered to the spot, Gina watched as he swung open the front door, darted to his car, and drove away as if he were a fireman called to a house fire.

Although the last paragraph might make readers grin, picturing the embarrassing incident, most readers will catch the flaw and allow it to spoil the reality of the scene. You easily note that if Gina is glued to the kitchen floor, she hasn't followed Bill out of the kitchen, and logic tells you she is unable to see through walls to watch Bill dart from the house in the manner described.

As a reminder when writing scenes, you can be more accurate if you picture the event through your own eyes to make sure that the scene is realistic for the POV character. Readers might chuckle at the way the above scene is written, but not for the right reason.

Avoiding Head-Hopping

Head-hopping—shifts in POV from one character to another within a scene—signals the work of an amateur to an editor, who will toss the manuscript out without a second glance even if a good story might be hidden beneath the head-hopping POV. Since editors receive hundreds of manuscripts a week, writing pure POV scenes is vital to the possibility of a sale. Learning to use POV according to the "rules" is a necessity. The following example shows the problems of head-hopping. In this sample, Belle has interrupted a burglar:

> After the police ambled out the door, Belle's neighbor, Nancy, bustled from the kitchen and embraced her. Belle's tension eased away in the protection of Nancy's arms.
>
> "I'll stay here until Jim gets here," Nancy said, not wanting to leave her dear friend alone. She clung to the fragile woman, fearing she'd break in her arms.
>
> "Excuse me," Sgt. Smith said, coming through the doorway. "Don't—" He paused, seeing the lovely young woman smothered in the arms of the amply-built neighbor. He shoved his thought back to the business at hand. "Don't go anywhere. We'll have someone surveilling the place tonight. We hope the perp comes back."
>
> Come back? She sat with her mouth gaping. What kind of thing was that to say to someone already scared out of her mind?

Notice the problems created by the scenario above. The first three paragraphs are each through a different character's POV—Belle, Nancy, and the police sergeant. The fourth paragraph creates a new problem. "She" is not identified. With two women previously owning the preceding paragraph, the readers have no idea who's thoughts those are. The words fit either of the women. With the POV jumping from one character to another, readers cannot connect with any single character nor sense the depth of emotion Belle would feel finding a burglar or killer in her home.

Although some best-selling authors have "earned" the right to break the rules of good writing, an unpublished or newly published author cannot take the chance by writing scenes in which the POV skips from one character to another. Keep to only one POV within each scene. This allows readers to connect with the character and removes any confusion about who's experiencing what.

CREATING CLEAR CHANGES IN POV

To change POV from one character to another, you have three choices. The first is to make a scene break by leaving an extra double-space in the manuscript and opening the next scene with a clear transition. The blank space signals to readers that there is a change in time, place, or POV.

A second method is to use a symbol at the end of the scene on its own double-spaced line, and then begin with the next scene. A common scene marker is three asterisks in a row (* * *), with the second scene beginning on the next line. With one POV per scene and clear transitions, the reader will be content to return to the hero's POV to know what's on his mind. The method chosen to mark a scene break must remain consistent throughout the novel.

Third, chapter breaks can sometimes, though not always, change the POV character. When a chapter opens, you are wise to start the scene by using the POV character's name so readers have no question who owns the scene.

Though POV can seem complicated, keep the following tips mind. Once you accomplish them, you will have no trouble dealing with POV in your novels.

- The POV character can see, hear, taste, touch, smell, and know only what you would experience or know if you were in the same situation.
- To decide which POV character should own the scene, choose the one who has the most at stake or the most to lose.
- The POV should remain with one person throughout a scene to avoid head-hopping.
- POV changes are best when separated by a scene or chapter break and clarified by naming the next POV character early in the next scene.

EXERCISES

1. Read the following scene and identify the POV errors, then go back and correct them.

Sunlight danced on Jane's hair as she ambled toward the open field. She had problems to solve, and nature helped her think. In the middle of the field, she sank down on the warm grass, her skirt billowing out behind her like a parachute.

Between the Virginia bluebells and the oxeye daisies, Jane spotted a clump of dandelions. She plucked one and held it beneath her chin as she did when she was a child. The yellow reflection meant she liked butter, and she grinned, knowing she loved butter.

Her argument with Bill came back to her. Last night, he looked at her with a deep frown, thinking that she'd lied to him, but she'd told the truth. Now how could she prove it?

A breeze slid through the warm air and ruffled her long, silken hair, sending a few strands rising above her head like an Indian headdress. She closed her eyes. Today was too beautiful to be angry at Bill. Tonight they would talk, and even though he wouldn't say a word, he loved her.

2. Take a few paragraphs from an opening scene of one of your novels or from a novel you're reading, and rewrite it, changing it from third person to first, or first to third, depending on how it is presently written. Remember the rules of POV.

3. Using part of a conflict scene between the hero and heroine, rewrite the scene from the other character's POV. Again, make sure you check the rules for good POV. When you finish, ask yourself which works best and why. Has something new been revealed from this POV character's take on the scene's action? Which POV do you prefer? Why?

4. Write a scene from the hero's or heroine's POV that deals with their growing relationship in terms of his or her faith walk. This scene could be written in dialogue or the characters' thoughts between two believers who are unsure about the relationship or between a strong believer and a faltering believer.

CHAPTER 8

Writing Believable Dialogue

Chitchat is part of real-life conversation; we hear it daily at the coffee shop, on a bus, at a restaurant, or in our own homes. But dialogue in fiction must serve a greater purpose by moving the plot forward, filling in the story blanks, and making something happen.

When you listen to people talk, you will hear popular slang and mundane conversation. When you write dialogue, forget what life is like and ask yourself, *What would make me interested in this person's conversation?* When you talk with friends or family, you often "catch up" on what's happened in your life. You share things about your children, your pets, or your work. Dialogue in novels must be purposeful. The characters must get to the meat of what is important in their lives. Do a short lead-in to set the stage for the scene and then get to the important information you want to share with readers.

In a Christian romance, as in any fiction, dialogue serves four basic purposes: to move the storyline forward by providing backstory or new and pertinent information; to introduce goals and motivation and advance the conflict; to set the mood or establish a theme; and to reveal character through attitude, speech patterns, and word choice.

Writing good dialogue is an art, because it must sound natural, yet provide all the purposes listed above. When you listen to people talk, notice they do not speak in long, flowing sentences. As Randall Ingermanson says:

People talk in short responses or partial phrases. Others interrupt. Real people get sidetracked. They avoid answering by changing the subject, by asking a new question, or by their silence. Dialogue must sound real, but remember, in a novel, dialogue is not chitchat. Each conversation must move the story along by adding new information or insight into the characters or plot.

Dialogue in Christian romance also is key in showing signs of growth in the character, the romance, or the faith journey, and in creating unique personalities that make the characters believable.

The Danger of Making Your Dialogue "Real"

Randall Ingermanson, author and creator of *Advanced Fiction Writing E-Zine*, says this:

If you write fiction, then you have probably gone through a stage where you tried your best to make your dialogue like Real Conversation. The problem is that Real Conversation is boring! Go ahead. Test me on this. Next time you're in a subway or on the bus or in line at the supermarket eavesdrop on the conversation around you. Real conversation is rarely about conflict. Think about the real conversations you've had lately. You'll find they fall into various boring categories like these:

- people making small talk to pass the time
- people exchanging information
- people avoiding conflict
- people trying to solve a problem

Why are these boring? Simply look for the conflict in each one. Small talk has zero conflict. So what's a writer to do? It's obvious. Don't write Real Conversation. Write Dialogue!

MAKING THE HERO AND HEROINE SOUND REAL

In Christian romance, dialogue's purpose is to broaden characterization of the hero and heroine by not only providing information but by using a variety of verbal techniques, such as subtexting or double meanings, tonal attitudes, and speech patterns (repetition, hesitation, brevity, or verbosity) to develop characterization. These techniques show the hero or heroine's timidity, moodiness, precision, or a variety of traits depending on the verbal cue.

Dialogue captures the personalities of the hero and heroine, and it also provides information about education (by the character's use of, or failure to use, correct grammar), ethnic background (by the use of slang, grammar, and vocabulary), profession (by the use of jargon), and regional background (by the pace of speech—slower in the south, faster in the north, which could be reflected by another character's remarks—and slang). In Christian romantic suspense, you have an extra challenge to create the proper jargon for the cops as well as the "bad guys." If characters belong to a group—career, hobby, or interest—the group expressions and lingo must be mastered to make their dialogue sound realistic. Their language is a code to the readers, and in Christian fiction, dialogue is a key method of learning about the characters' depth of faith by the language they use in reference to their beliefs.

It's important to make these characters real by making their dialogue sound real. A character's personality is evidenced in the way she speaks. The introverted heroine will often be soft spoken, thoughtful in her responses, and serious in tone. The businesswoman will be organized and appear in control. She'll have ideas and want to express them. Her conversation will be well thought out, and she'll be willing to debate issues. A heroine with a purpose may be spunky, exuberant, or analytical in her dialogue. Well-educated characters will have a broader vocabulary, and those from a strong ethnic background may use words or phrases in their native language, or expressions stemming from their roots.

Though dialogue is different from real-life conversation, it is still important to have it sound as natural as real-life conversation, while being convincing and capturing the moods and attitudes of the characters' particular styles. Deborah Raney, author of *Over the Waters,* says:

> For me, the most important thing is to read the dialogue aloud. I have a good sense of what the female characters would say, but for my male characters, I

must imagine my husband or my father, my brother or my grown sons saying the words. Would the line ring true for them as I've written it?

Raney also aims to create realistic gestures and body language for her characters:

> I keep a mirror at my desk, and as I write dialogue, I often act out the body language, imagining how the men in my life would deliver the line. I watch myself say the words, noting my facial expression and body language. I take a lot of dialogue from real life, and my husband often recognizes himself in my hero's words and reactions.

Testing Realistic Dialogue

Hearing dialogue is an excellent method of testing its realism and making certain it sounds the way your character would speak. Software programs that offer text-to-voice capabilities are available on the Internet and in computer stores. They are inexpensive and provide an outstanding tool for any author. You can use it to hear the flow of the language and to find typos or missing words. It works very well for edits. If you can't afford a text-to-voice program, read the dialogue aloud, or even better, ask someone to read it to you.

If you are a female writing Christian romance, you will be more comfortable making women's dialogue sound authentic. Writing dialogue for the opposite sex can be more challenging. One technique I use is to listen to men's conversations on television and radio, then take notes of their vocabulary, their expressions, and their topics of interest. I pay attention to male friends and family, noting the dynamics of their conversation. This helps me understand how men speak.

Men don't usually want to talk about emotions and feelings, preferring instead action and plans. To use a food analogy, instead of a gourmet dinner, men want the meat and potatoes. They tend to relate to practical information rather than pretension or artsy ideas. They want to get to the nitty-gritty and not drag out a conversation that includes too many details. Most don't use words like *pretty* and *cute* unless they are talking to a child. Men don't generally note color other than main colors and black and white—if your dress color is lapis, to most men it is blue. By listening to masculine conversation and, if possible, having a man read the dialogue for critique purposes, you can write good dialogue for both genders. A male author can do the same to write realistic female characters.

An important side note: Readers like to read about the "perfect" man, the dream man who will meet their expectations. Therefore, in Christian romance, you may add some feminine elements—for example, a man who will state his feelings—to your male character in order to please your readers and allow emotion to be in the forefront of your story.

CHRISTIAN WORLDVIEW IN DIALOGUE

One thing that makes Christian romance different from secular is the characters' approach to life in attitude, values, and behavior. How often, when listening to conversation around you, are taken aback by the foul language, sexual references, and wishy-washy morals or values being expressed? Even Christians can easily slip into this kind of conversation. The phrase "I bet" is very common; yet, even if it's a cliché phrase, Christians are not supposed to wager. How often do you hear people say "You're so lucky"? Christians think of it as being blessed.

Because you are writing Christian romance, your book will rise from a Christian worldview, which will be reflected in the characters' conversations. They will discuss things that trouble them about themselves, or behaviors that concern them about their romantic interest, especially as it relates to their faith. The Christian morals and values in the dialogue of the characters should be appropriate to whether the character is a faithful Christian, a struggling or weak Christian, or a nonbeliever.

Christian beliefs fall easily into believers' conversation. The Lord is part of their lives, and speaking about him is as simple as talking about a neighbor. "God has blessed me" is a phrase that could easily appear in dialogue. "I need to see where the Lord leads me" is another. "I want to pray on it." All of these sentences could be part of Christian romance dialogue and would seem natural and believable.

Discussions of abortions, casual sex, homosexuality, and the use of drugs, alcohol, and tobacco are topics on which conservative and liberal Christians have attitudes that would be reflected in everyday conversations. Some of these are touchy because Christians have varied attitudes toward these topics, so you may need editor approval before including them in your book.

Some Christian publishers do not accept lying in a story plot, even little white lies. They believe a Christian should not lie, so if a heroine is trying to avoid admitting her romantic feelings toward the hero, she will have to work her way around the truth for an evasive answer that falls short of deceitfulness. Any kind of deception can be an issue, so be sure to study the publisher's guidelines. (One area in which most publishers will make allowances is in a romantic suspense, when falsehood is necessary to protect or hide the true identity of a character or as a part of his or her undercover role.)

Remember that the readers of your books are mainly Christian—some more conservative than others—so keep the readers in mind when dialogue revolves around sensitive topics or doctrinal beliefs. As you read through your dialogue, make sure you haven't included offensive words or topics. It is best to err on the side of caution.

Avoid Offending the Readers

When editing your work, make a list of possible situations or language that might offend readers and revise it to reflect the Christian worldview, or speak with your editor to make sure this will pass the publisher's scrutiny. By creating a list—for example, curse words and euphemisms, deception and lying, alcohol use, specific Christian religious traditions—you will have the key ideas to guide you on each book you write.

COMPONENTS OF DIALOGUE

Dialogue doesn't stand alone. In fiction, it is blended with action beats (body and facial movements the characters make while speaking) and introspection. Each of these components plays off the other to make the dialogue believable. Yet even with the help of introspection and action beats, the dialogue must be able to stand alone in terms of providing pertinent information to move the story forward or develop characterization. Readers and editors look for character growth and growing conflict. These are necessary elements to remember when creating a dynamic story.

Getting to the meat of your story is a must. Remove the typical set-up of everyday conversations—forget the mundane and ordinary "Hi" and "How are you." Dialogue must begin in the middle of a situation. To make this work, you can use narrative transitions, such as *After ten minutes of catching up, Jim got down to business*, or *Sue talked around the issue until she found the courage to tell him what she really had on her mind*. These transitional sentences take you to what's important in the discussion.

Good dialogue must be able to stand alone so that it provides emotion and allows readers to understand its purpose in the scene. For example, read only the dialogue (in bold below) from Denise Hunter's *Mending Places*. Notice how it gives insight into Hanna's character and a vivid view of her faith. Hanna has hired Micah to lead guests into the mountains near her lodge in Wyoming. Her business has declined, and Micah's arrival at her door appeared to be God's blessing at a time she needs help and at a time her heart needs help, too.

Twilight was falling like a sheer curtain, giving a sense of anonymity she found comforting. Wouldn't she rather confront him about it now when he could barely see her than in the stark light of day?

"I've been wanting to talk to you about something." *Oh boy, there's no turning back now.*

He continued to dig. **"What's that?"**

The moment was here, and she didn't know what to say. Words flew frantically around her mind.

The odd silence drew his attention.

Help me, God.

He quirked a brow.

"I have a feeling about us."

He waited.

She took a deep breath. **"It might sound strange. In fact, I know it'll sound strange, but ... look, you're a Christian, too, so I'm just going to say it outright. God has impressed on me that He wants us together for some ... purpose."**

He stiffened, then thrust the shovel into the ground and left it standing upright. **"You're mistaken."**

Hanna let out the breath she'd been holding. She'd expected him to laugh. To roll his eyes. To tell her she was nuts. Anything but this. **"I thought so, too, at first but—"**

"It's a bad idea." He stabbed the pole into the ground.

"If you're already involved with someone—"

"There's no one else. I'm just not interested." His bass voice vibrated through the night air.

The dialogue's purpose and meaning is clear without the action and introspection. Hanna feels that God has bound her and Micah together for a reason, but when in the next line, readers realize Hanna is proposing far more than working together. She's initiating a romance. The excerpt is from Hanna's point of view, so at this point, readers have no understanding why Micah reacts as he does. As the scenes continue, we learn that Micah has issues. He is a Christian with a past and with secrets he doesn't want to share.

Now go back and read the complete excerpt. Although the dialogue provides good information and moves the story forward, readers can learn much more about the character and the intonation of the dialogue when they read the entire scene. The actions and introspection help you to gain a fuller picture of Hanna's emotional struggle. Her silent prayer, her attempt to garner courage, her struggle to understand Micah's rejection, and the action beats and introspection offer readers a greater emotional impact.

At the same time, readers recognize Micah's determination to say no. He stiffens and thrusts the shovel into the ground. He stabs the pole into the soil. Readers can sense the impact of silence between them; silence is sometimes as important as the dialogue.

In a scene, dialogue must be the core, while the action and introspection broadens the scope of the dialogue and adds to its realism. Each piece of action and thought must enhance the dialogue.

TELEPHONE DIALOGUE

When writing a scene with characters talking on a telephone, you have two options: one-sided or two-sided conversations. The two-sided call is most popular in Christian romance because it is often between the hero and heroine, and what each says is significant. Remember that a telephone call allows the point of view character only to hear the other character's voice and inflection; it gives no insight into appearance or action.

In an excerpt from a telephone conversation in Hannah Alexander's romantic suspense *Grave Risk,* the hero is concerned about the well-being of the heroine and has added extra security to her home. The last sentence makes reference to a clue she has found. Notice how effective the dialogue is with only one tag and no actions beats. The point of view character is the heroine, and the first speaker is the hero.

"I told you, I don't like the thought of you alone in that house right now."

Great. "Greg and Tom already think I'm a neurotic female, and now they're going to think I put you up to this."

"Does it really matter what they think? I would just feel more comfortable if there's extra security for the next few days, until we find who's been so interested in your house. Or in you."

"Okay, look. I'm getting a little bit of a headache, and here I am trying to relax. Why don't we talk about this later?" she suggested. "Meanwhile, try to spend some quality time with Tyler."

"Yes, boss. Will do."

"And Rex?"

"Yes?"

"Thanks."

"For what?"

"For caring enough to humiliate me."

"You're welcome."

This partial conversation flows mainly in short, simple statements with only one dialogue tag, leaving lots of white space on the page—short sentences and paragraphs—but readers have no question about who is speaking. When writing a telephone scene, it is not necessary to use "he said/she said" tags unless the speaker is unclear.

One-sided conversations are used most often when the call is short and the person calling is not a major character. You can provide enough meaning for readers by listening to the main character. One-sided calls often serve as a transition to the new scene by stopping the preceding action and moving the character to a new scene.

DIALOGUE TAGS

Dialogue tags are the "he said/she said" used to keep readers attuned as to who is speaking. Although they serve a purpose, tags are not always needed if the speaker is obvious. There are much more effective ways to cue readers as to who the speaker is—which also alerts an editor to those who have mastered the craft of writing dialogue.

Character action beats—movements, gestures, and action—and thoughts, woven with dialogue, show the speaker without the intrusion of *said* or *asked* and, at the same time, provide insight into characterization, conflict, and mood.

Notice how this example from Robert Elmer's *The Duet* is effective despite the lack of dialogue tags. In this scene, Gerrit, an elderly farmer, and a new resident in the town, Joan Horton, a concert pianist who gives piano lessons to the town's children and to Gerrit, are discussing their differences. The point of view character is Joan.

"You don't get your hands dirty much, do you?" he asked.

"Is that something new you've just discovered?"

"Nope." He shook his head. "I knew you were different. But man, the more I find out about you, Joan Horton, the more I realize you're from a different planet."

"Oh, so now I'm an alien, am I?" She put her hands on her hips.

"Sorry." He almost looked serious as he studied her with those big blue Dutch eyes of his. "I guess it's just that you're going back home soon, so it don't matter."

His eyes widened as if he had just bit his tongue, then he did some very obvious backpedaling.

"I—I didn't mean that," he stammered. "Let's just say that I don't understand you very well, and you don't understand me."

"And I guess you would prefer to keep it that way?"

Though there are only two tags—the opening question, which establishes the speaker, Gerrit, and the one reference to his stammer—there is no difficulty knowing who said what.

When two characters of the same sex are talking, authors often use more dialogue tags with the character's name so that confusion doesn't occur for the readers as to who is speaking. Wherever you place your tags, make them as inconspicuous as possible, and leave them out entirely when other techniques can be used more effectively.

Improving Dialogue Tags

Dialogue tags can be improved by following two simple rules. First, *said* and *asked* are the two most acceptable dialogue tags. They are verbs that move past readers' eyes without stopping the story. Occasionally, you will find an exception—such as *whispered, murmured, screamed, bellowed,* and other words describing a tone of voice—but it is best to keep those options to a minimum. Use *he said/she said,* and avoid *said he/said she.*

Stephen King says in his book, *On Writing,* "The road to hell is paved with adverbs." Adding adverbs to anything in your work is shortchanging your writing; it's telling rather than showing. Instead of *he yelled loudly,* let words and action portray the drama.

"Stop it." He slammed his fist on the table.

Or use a verb that describes the emotion.

"Stop it," he bellowed.

PURPOSES OF DIALOGUE

As I said before, dialogue adds action to a Christian romance as well as information that moves the story forward. Dialogue serves as an outlet for faith, provides humor, presents backstory, shows goals and motivation, and presents conflict.

Outlet for Faith in Dialogue

Christian romance writers work hard to balance the growth in the characters, romance, and faith of the hero and heroine. Dialogue provides a natural, real-life way to share the spiritual struggles without being preachy.

In His Dreams is my story of widowed in-laws falling in love. Marsha had nursed her husband, the hero's brother, while he struggled with Lou Gehrig's disease, and the hero struggles with the tragic death of his wife and his lost faith. A conversation between the hero and heroine gives readers an in-depth understanding of where they are in their faith journeys.

> "Let me ask you a question," he said, tucking his hands back into his pockets and striding on again. "How did you keep your faith so strong during all that time?"
>
> His question surprised her, and she found herself fumbling through her thoughts for an answer. Finally she shook her head. "I guess I trusted God. I know each of us has a purpose, and God can see the big picture, so I had to accept that the Lord knew what He was doing."
>
> "That takes powerful faith, Marsha. I give you credit."
>
> "Don't give me credit. I probably can't remember the precise verse, but the Bible says something like hope doesn't disappoint us, because God has filled our hearts with his love through the Holy Spirit."
>
> "And you believe God is with you in all of this?"
>
> Marsha's chest tightened, hearing his disbelieving voice. "Absolutely."

It is easy to see the hero's curiosity about Marsha's strong faith and, most important, his questioning of his own ability to accept or deal with it.

You can provide this kind of realism to your novel's faith journey with an occasional discussion between two characters that allows readers to see the strong faith of the one character along with the deeper struggle of the other. If the dialogue is done well, the conversation is real, not preachy.

Dialogue about faith can also occur between characters with strong faith. The hero could express thankfulness that God has answered a need, or the heroine might mention a need to pray about a difficult situation. When faith issues come into dialogue, keep it real, with no more or no less than would occur in a discussion you might have with a believing friend or loved one. Refer to chapter six on spirituality for more advice on using scripture in dialogue.

Humor in Dialogue

Christian romances can revolve around humor by showing the playful nature of the hero or heroine in dialogue. Since Christian romance often deals with serious life and spiritual issues, humor is an excellent release for readers. It also provides insight into characterization and is even more humorous when it plays against a more serious character.

Humorous dialogue is created by stating the unexpected or underplaying a situation; for example, if a robber walks into a bank, and the hero looks at the heroine and says, "I think we have a slight problem." This works if the hero's playful attitude has been evident earlier in the book.

In this excerpt from the action-packed romance *A Kiss of Adventure* by awarding-winning author Catherine Palmer, the heroine, Tillie, is given a locket that contains a yellowed note. The man who had just saved her life and who wants the information in the note tricks her into getting involved in his adventurous journey. The heroine opens the scene.

"So how far is Timbuktu?"

Graeme let out a breath. "You're coming with me, then?"

"As long as you keep your distance. I don't fraternize with kidnappers."

He mused a moment. "Well, you might be useful in the long run."

"Useful?"

"Crocodile bait." He gave her quick wink.

The manipulating character of Graeme adds humor with his unexpected comment. The heroine probably thought she'd be useful cooking meals or providing some menial service, not as "crocodile bait."

Backstory in Dialogue

Dialogue provides a kind of action, as opposed to the more passive narration through the character's thoughts, so backstory in dialogue is a more dynamic way of bringing it to life than through the character's thoughts. It also has an emotional impact on the readers.

Revealing backstory in dialogue is brought about by a situation that forces the character to talk about the past. The compelling dialogue might be to defend himself, protect the innocent, open doors toward change, or explain a fear. In my novel *Upon a Midnight Clear*, Callie finally finds the courage to open the door of a secret that has riddled her dreams for years. She tells David about an event that happened during a choral audition.

> As if marching through her dream, she led David through the audition. "Then Jim McKee led me to the couch, and kept calling me his 'little meadowlark.' My poor mother called me that a few months ago, and I panicked. I can't hear that word without remembering."
>
> David leaned over to kiss her cheek. "It's okay, Callie. I love you."
>
> "How can you love me, David?" The sobs broke from her throat, and she buried her face in her hands. "I was a virgin. And he took the most precious gift I longed to share with a husband someday. He raped me, David."

With the hero's confession of love, the scene has set the stage for Callie to reveal her backstory secret in a natural way. Because the scene is near the end of the book, readers care about what happens, they know the characters' struggles and conflicts, and they have a stake in the outcome of the story. Emotion evolves from the dialogue, helping the book to be a page-turner for readers.

Goals and Motivation in Dialogue

Dialogue gives readers an opportunity to hear the goals and sometimes the motivation of characters. Each conflict or need in a character's life presents a new goal, and each goal is motivated by something in the past. If a character grew up in poverty (the motivation), his goal might be wealth, or it might be to help others who are poor. Although this information can be provided to readers through the character's introspection, the information is usually imparted more dramatically and effectively through dialogue.

Motivation and goals are not always stated in the dialogue, but they can be deduced by the readers when new facts are provided that add to what they already know about the character. The previous excerpt between Callie and David allows the deduction that Callie feels unlovable and has perhaps not forgiven herself for what happened. Her need is to be loved, but first she must feel forgiven.

Conflict in Dialogue

Conflict causes tension, and tension is what keeps readers glued to the pages of a book. Conflict in romance can arise in many forms: a simple misunderstanding, a conflict concocted by the hero or heroine to delay the romance or avoid attraction, a serious difference in Christian beliefs or values, or a dire consequence (an ended marriage, a broken engagement, a crisis with God, or even a murder). The greater the conflict, the greater the tension.

Conflict in dialogue can take different forms. To avoid dealing with a sensitive situation or topic, the character can use silence, answer with a question, use delay tactics, or change the subject. You can also use the technique of an interruption to delay the resolution of a conflict and thus prolong the tension.

The Conflict of Silence

Silence creates tension. It is used extensively in romance: those thoughtful and restrained moments between the hero and heroine that leave readers eager to hear what will happen next. (Some silence can be positive, as when the hero and heroine enjoy the quiet together, but usually silence indicates an uncomfortable or angry tension.) Triggering the lack of response can be a probing question about the past, an endearment unanswered, or even a proposal without a response. Negative silence is like a cold shoulder that leaves not only silence, but an emptiness, because the emotion comes to an abrupt halt.

The use of negative silence between the hero and heroine creates discomfort and adds to the tension. In this excerpt from my novel *And Baby Makes Five,* notice how the heroine's silence, brought on by her reverie, triggers a concerned response from the hero.

> Out of the corner of her eye, she watched Chad making gentle circles on Nate's back. The baby looked contented.
>
> "I fed him a short time ago so he shouldn't be hungry," she said.
>
> "He wants attention. We all need that sometimes."
>
> His words sounded melancholy, and her pulse tripped. Everyone needed to be loved and caressed. She'd been without that kind of relationship since she'd married Miguel. His love had become rough and his drunken words, vile.
>
> Silence settled over them until Chad turned toward her. "Do you understand what I'm saying?"

Chad's comment about attention demonstrates his personal need. It's not a general comment; he wants her to be motivated to give him that attention. Although he's only admitting his need indirectly, readers sense the conflict it creates when the heroine doesn't respond.

The Conflict of Avoidance

Christian romance is based on honesty and truth. These attributes are a priority before the hero and heroine can make a commitment. When a character becomes evasive or noncommittal, the approach creates concern for the readers. While silence is one means of avoidance, other types provide the same tension, such as answering a question with a question:

> "Would you like to take a walk and talk about us?"
>
> "About us?"

This technique, though not as dramatic as silence, leaves an incomplete feeling and creates tension. Similarly, delay tactics also leave an empty and incomplete feeling for readers.

"Would you like to take a walk and talk about us?"

"I—I don't know."

Interruptions that stop the dialogue or the action are a good technique when wanting to add tension to a scene. In Christian romance, halting the first kiss or the first admission of attraction is an excellent way to prolong the romantic tension. The interruption can be from outside—a telephone call, a knock on the door, another person entering the scene—or from the other character.

"Would you like to walk and—"

"No more walking for me. I walked three miles this morning before work."

Changing the subject or talking around a topic is an interesting technique that reflects characterization and adds tension. Reading a scene using this technique is like listening to two unconnected conversations in which neither person is listening. The dialogue's agenda never quite hits the mark.

Lisa Samson uses this method of avoidance in her novel *Tiger Lillie*. In this scene, Tacy is talking to her mother in her mother's freshly painted master bedroom.

"I asked Rawlins if I could work for the ad agency, Mom."

"I already know his answer. Do you think you could paint some murals here for us? It will be a while before we move in—until your father retires, which might be years from now."

"Rawlins said the ad world is too competitive. He doesn't want me to become jaded."

"I was thinking maybe a garden scene in the kitchen."

"Maybe I could sell my paintings."

"Or do trompe l'oeil. Here would be a good place to start."

"I really want to go to college."

Mom looked around. "Of course, the master bath has lots of potential, too."

The dialogue in this excerpt is a prime example of talking without listening, and this creates tension and conflict without presenting an argument or unpleasant situation. It is the way people talk in real life, only half listening while their minds deal with the next point they want to make. This type of battling dialogue vies for subject matter rather than to prove a point, yet it creates interesting tension. Use half sentences, incomplete words with an em dash (—), or simply ignore the statement or question, as the mother does in *Tiger Lillie*, and move on to a new topic.

The Conflict of Disagreement

The most obvious conflict is a disagreement—two people with opposing ideas. But to create real tension, the disagreements in dialogue must be more than arguing about which restaurant to visit or who should be invited to a party. The conflict should be based on one of the basic needs of the character.

In Athol Dickson's Christian romance *The Cure*, tension rises as the characters deal with a failing marriage. Riley has a drinking problem and abandoned his wife, Hope, and their daughter, Bree. Now his drinking is under control, and he has come back after three years. He assumed Hope had already divorced him, but upon arriving he learns she did not, as well as the reason why. As Hope peels potatoes to keep him from seeing her tears, she responds to Riley's statement that he'd assumed she had gotten divorced. Hope speaks first.

"Have you ever slept with another woman?"

"No."

"Then what did you expect?"

"So that's the only reason?"

Laughing bitterly, she wiped her eyes. "Did you come over here with romantic notions, Riley?"

"Well, I was kind of thinking maybe ..."

"Don't flatter yourself. When we got married I made a commitment. Not just to you, either. I believe in Jesus, Riley. I *really* believe. So I'm gonna try to do what Jesus wants me to do, even if it kills me. There's been a lot of people told me I should divorce you, but I'm not gonna weasel out by pretending alcoholism is adultery. It isn't. And neither is abandonment. Jesus meant what he said, plain and simple, and I'm not done believin' just be-cause life stinks. Commitments matter to *me*."

In this conflict, Riley has come home because he wants Hope, and though she is a very strong-willed person, she is unsure of what she ought to do. Athol Dickson explains the scene and how the blend of dialogue with ac-tion deepens the impact of the words for the readers:

> Hope stands at her kitchen counter, making dinner. Riley is behind her. She makes him speak to her back throughout this scene, turning away from him to focus on the food as he once turned from her to focus on drink. The work of her hands is more than a way to escape from him; it is an expression of what is happening to her heart.

Conflict in Subtext

Subtext is the implicit or underlying meaning behind our words, those indirect utterances used sometimes to avoid touchy subjects or to make a point while avoiding a direct statement, and it is a form of conflict. In real life, people often avoid saying what they mean, or they attempt to conceal their true meaning with other words that have an added mean-ing below the obvious one.

> "Do you like my dress?"
> "It's unbelievable."

The question isn't answered. Does he like the dress, or doesn't he? The comment could be a subtext sentence indicating he doesn't.

Angela Hunt, a popular Christian fiction author, says it this way:

> To counter dialogue that ping-pongs back and forth with never a missed beat, you can use subtext or implicit dialogue, as opposed to explicit dia-logue. You can have your characters say exactly the opposite of what they mean and clarify meaning by expression, action, and interior monologue.

Subtext has not only an underlying meaning, but also the speaker's ex-pectations that the true meaning is understood. This type of dialogue is subtle and not easily written, but it adds depth and a credible quality to dialogue. People don't talk in straight lines in real life. They are often evasive and avoid what they really want to say for fear of becoming vulnerable or of being rejected. Talking around an issue or making a joke about it covers their true feelings or concerns.

Tamara Alexander illustrates in *Revealed* that subtext in Christian romance does not always have to deal with a serious issue. In this historical romance, Annabelle Grayson, a former prostitute, now widowed, has hired Matthew Taylor as a trail guide to take her across Colorado territory to Idaho. In this scene, they are discussing the preparation for the trip.

> He motioned to stacks of crates and boxes near where they stood. "I already picked everything up from the mercantile and will go through it tonight, make sure the order's all accounted for."
>
> "That's not what I'm here about, but thank you." Determined to see this through, she held out a cup of coffee.
>
> He glanced at it, then back at her.
>
> His tentative expression coaxed a laugh. "It's safe, I promise you. I've already paid you a third of your salary, Mr. Taylor. It wouldn't do for me to try and poison you now." She nudged the cup a few inches closer to him. "I'd wait and do that once we're closer to Idaho. Makes more sense, don't you think?"
>
> That earned her a slight *humph* but not the half grin she'd hoped for. He took the coffee but didn't drink it.

The subtext of this dialogue is about trust, confidence, and opposing personalities. The humor causes readers to smile. The scene progresses with talk about the change Taylor still has from the money Annabelle gave him to buy the supplies and their preparations for the trip, but as they talk, the coffee remains beside him without being touched.

> She glanced at his untouched coffee. "Would you like me to taste it first? Show you it's safe?" A gleam lit his eyes, and she could well imagine the sharp replies running through his mind about drinking from the same cup as a woman like her.
>
> He took a sip, the gesture answering for him.

"I'm flattered. Seems you trust me too, Mr. Taylor."

"Not hardly, ma'am. I just figure you need me. For now, anyway."

She lifted a brow.

"Like you said, you've already paid me. I'm thinking I can enjoy coffee at least until we're—" he tilted his head as though in deep thought, "across Wyoming."

"And then what?"

"Then I might have to start brewing my own."

The coffee has become a test of trust. Though it gives readers a grin, it also offers a clear picture that the trust Annabelle refers to is truly no trust at all between either party. Yet the playful dialogue allows readers to enjoy the characters and gives a foreshadowing of the witty yet persistent conflict that continues to grow as they travel across the Colorado territory.

Using subtext in Christian romance is an excellent away to build romantic tension early in the story, using the dialogue as flirtation. For example, the hero says, "I'm thinking about going on a picnic tomorrow." The heroine responds, "Really? I hope you have a nice time." We know the heroine is hoping that the hero plans to ask her. Subtext in dialogue allows readers to enjoy the romance "game" along with the hero and heroine.

DIALOGUE SHOWS MOOD AND ATTITUDE

Through language, line rhythm, and content, dialogue helps create mood and reflects character attitude. Alexander's scene above reflects humor, but the readers also feel the attitude of distrust and the mood created by forced proximity. As much as the words spoken, the language and speaking style help to accentuate the mood.

Short lines of dialogue create a sense of excitement, anxiety, or confusion. During times of conflict and tension in real life, our words are clipped, strident, or punctuated by vocal pauses and interruptions. Quiet moments of romance or contemplation will produce longer sentences, woven with complex phrases and a lilting rhythm that flows with the words.

You can use hard sounds—consonants such as *p, t, k, b, q, d, g*—in scenes of tension or excitement while softer sounds—*m, n, l, f, h, w*—work best for the romantic and contemplative scenes. Sometimes these letters are used in an alliterative pattern to accentuate the mood. *Terrifying tapping* or *pistol pointed* doubles the hard sound, presenting a pounding accent to the words. The opposite would be *mellow moon* or *lilting lullaby*, which give a sing-song affect and soothing sounds.

Writing good dialogue that sounds real yet purposeful is a major key to a good novel. Enhance the dialogue with appropriate word selection and a variety of speaking styles, and allow the hero and heroine's personalities and beliefs to shine through.

Guidelines for Dialogue

- Dialogue is not conversation, it is a purposeful tool to deepen characterization, reflect characters' personalities, and move the story forward.
- The most appropriate dialogue tags are *he said* or *she said*; otherwise, intersperse dialogue with action and introspection without tags
- Dialogue is important to present information, characterization, backstory, mood, attitudes, goals, motivation, and conflict

EXERCISES

1. Read the following dialogue, written from Brad's point of view, and edit it with the information you learned in this chapter. Remember that men and women talk differently and the best way to show this is to use both tags and the action beats that can replace tags.

Brad's back stiffened when she sailed into the room late. She looked so innocent it made him sick. "I saw you in town," Brad said, suspiciously, " talking to a man."

"A man? In town? Where?" she said in astonishment.

"By the coffee shop," he stated. "Don't play dumb with me, Amy. I know it was you because you had on the skirt with the pink flowers that you like so much."

"I'm in a dress," she said. "Can't you see? What's wrong with you?" She studied his face, wondering if he'd even been in town.

"Who is he?" he boomed loudly.

Eyeing him, she replied, "I have no idea. I wasn't near the coffee shop."

"I'm not playing your game anymore. This isn't the first time. You're cheating on me. You've found someone new, and you're breaking my heart," said Brad.

"Let me explain," she rebutted. "I was talking with an acquaintance about a birthday gift I want to buy you. He told me he could get me a good deal."

"You were talking to someone about a birthday gift. I'm supposed to believe this?" He looked into her eyes and recognized the truth. "Oh, Amy, I'm so sorry. Forgive me. I should never doubt you," he begged.

Amy struggled with letting it go that easily. How could he doubt her? "You're forgiven, Brad. I love you," she cooed.

He took her in his arms. "I love you, too," he murmured.

2. Using the information from the backstory below, write a scene from Julie's point of view using all you've learned about dialogue as she tells Ben the truth about her past.

Julie and Ben are close to becoming engaged. Their love is strong, but Julie has a secret and telling Ben might destroy his trust. When they first began dating, she cheated on him with two other men. Now with Ben's example and her own realization of what's important, her faith has been strengthened and she's sorry for what she did. She decides to tell Ben the truth because she believes marriage is too important to hide behind her sinful past.

3. Rewrite the scene from exercise two using the same dialogue, but coming from Ben's POV. Let readers know his motivation, his fears, and his true emotions as he talks with Julie.

CHAPTER 9

Introspection

Introspection—also called self-talk or internal monologue—is head-talk, or the thought processes inside a character's head, and it is as important as spoken dialogue. These thoughts, which only come from the point of view character, reveal the hero's or heroine's real fears, what makes them vulnerable, and where their hearts are headed in terms of romance. Without introspection and the depth of emotions and true motivation it reveals, the reader has only two-dimensional characters. It is a time of reflection, often a quiet pondering, but also a time of soul-searching and anguish.

Introspection serves the same purpose as any scene in a book. The character with the most to share must be the point of view character in that scene. The introspection must move the plot forward by providing new information, deepening characterization, demonstrating the character's feelings and emotions, revealing internal conflict, reflecting the character's spiritual journey, or demonstrating the character's romantic growth.

Hearing the character's thoughts overrides any other action or dialogue because within the character's mind, the readers see the truth in all its darkness and light. As in real life, an individual can put up an artificial front, distort reality in dialogue, and be guarded in action and reaction so as to leave a false impression. The thoughts and reflections of the character provide the only real understanding of the individual's conflicts, goals, and motivation. Introspection can stand as a solid paragraph of thought or be dispersed through dialogue as the character reacts to what's been said or to an action of the other characters.

Your characters struggle with negative attitudes, fears, concerns, and questions that don't always come out in dialogue, yet they flavor the characters' actions and reactions. For example, when conversing with a person he doesn't respect or like, a character will treat the person civilly, but his mind is dealing with the discrepancy between his actions and his feelings. He knows what God expects him to do—forgive and love his enemy—but he can't seem to do that. This could create feelings of guilt.

Delving into the characters' thought processes shows the motivations behind their decisions and actions, the past experiences, fears, or assumptions that drive them. A character might know that God has forgiven him for a past action, but through introspection, readers learn that he has not forgiven himself, which affects his relationships and life. This gives readers greater insight into a character's truth, as he sees it, and his faith journey.

INTROSPECTION OFFERS INFORMATION AND CHARACTERIZATION

While providing information, introspection adds depth to a novel through multi-layering the characterization of the hero and heroine. The readers are given access to the complexity of their thought processes and shown first-hand the traumatic effect of their emotional or spiritual struggles.

Introspection provides two kinds of in-depth characterization: the hero's and heroine's own personal feelings and emotions and clues about, insights into, and descriptions of the other character. In Gayle Roper's novel *Winter Winds*, Dori sees her estranged husband after a six-year absence. The readers experience Dori's feelings and see Trev through her eyes.

> He looked wonderful. He'd always been a good-looking boy and a handsome if unfinished teenager, but now as a man, the skinniness that had followed him through his growing years had been replaced by a lean maturity. His black hair was thick and shiny, his shoulders broad, his blue eyes brilliant, and his jaw firm. He exuded strength.

Dori's introspection allows readers to see the Trev she loved. Each descriptive word provides not only a picture of Trev, but also an image of his character—his maturity, determination, and strength. This information allows readers to learn the truth: Dori still admires Trev and is still attracted to him.

The hero and heroine should not describe themselves, so present your characters' physical descriptions through introspection. The hero, for example, notices the heroine's bright smile, welcoming eyes, even teeth, bowed lips, and curly hair. In addition to creating a mental picture, word choice and the focus of the physical description can also give clues to the introspective character's feelings for the other person.

Introspection also presents the motivation and goals of the hero and heroine to the readers. Backstory, detailed in chapter two, is the backbone of motivation and goals. It provides information about what happened in the characters' pasts that make them who they are today. In my novel *Loving Care*, Patrick Hanuman, a widower, returns to his hometown with his young son, following the death of his second wife, to help his ailing father. When Christie Hanuman faces her former husband, her introspection provides a piece of backstory and also sets up conflict:

> Though Christie recognized disappointment in his face, she had no desire to appease him. She hadn't been able to please him years earlier. Why try now? She stepped backward, stretching the distance between them.

Notice how these few lines shed light on many areas of Christie's struggle. First you understand that Christie felt unable to please her former husband (her backstory), then you experience her determination to stay uninvolved when she says she has no desire to please him now, and the determination is accentuated by her stepping back, creating more distance between them. Yet within these four sentences, you recognize hope when she asks herself, *Why try now?* Though the three words are filled with doubt, the word *now* is a form of foreshadowing, showing that a hint of possibility exists in her mind.

Motivation and goals also create Christie's internal conflict as she deals with the situation. As a Christian, she knows she should forgive, and part of her internal struggle is being able to forgive Patrick for ending their marriage years earlier. Without being aware, Patrick struggles with his own problem, similar to Christie's, which is learned through his introspection. He has become a strong Christian since their divorce and knows he sinned by ending their marriage.

The Truth Within

Introspection reveals truth. The character's head-talk is honest and forthright, or honest as the character sees it. Since most people don't lie to themselves, readers learn the real feelings and struggles of the characters. Yet be aware of unintentional self-deception, which can lead the character astray. In real life, people cover their feelings and emotions and play down traits that bother them: Shy people push themselves to be more outgoing; impatient people monitor their irritation with someone who's dallying if they want to make a good impression. Readers learn the truth and gain understanding when those fears and problems are included in introspection.

The characterization of the hero and heroine is strengthened by digging into the fears and beliefs that might not be learned through dialogue. Introspection can be used to let readers in on the hero's or heroine's secrets that they hide from each other, which are usually the motivation for conflict and a factor that keeps the hero and heroine from admitting their love for each other.

As you create your characters, make sure you have developed internal struggles that influence the hero and heroine's behaviors, and introduce them through introspection. The struggles may be spiritual issues, personal weaknesses, incompetencies, or fears. For example, the hero asks the heroine on a date, and she hesitates. Through introspection, readers learn she's recently come from a bad relationship, or that she is attracted to the hero, but he's a strong believer and she is angry at God for not healing a loved one who died. Characters' lives influence their choices, and introspection provides readers with information they need to understand the characters' reactions and choices.

INTROSPECTION AND EMOTION

Emotion is the key to a heart-touching romance, and it affects readers' pulses and heart rates as if they were experiencing what the hero and heroine are going through. Introspection gives readers a look into the characters' hearts, their honest thoughts and emotions.

In this excerpt from *Loving Care*, readers again view Christie struggling with her feelings when she runs into Patrick in a pharmacy. He'd walked out on her early in their marriage with little explanation except to say that the marriage was a mistake:

> Christie hated the emotion that rushed through her. She stumbled backward and felt her heel sink into one of the plastic strip packages. "I hope your dad's doing better," she mumbled, wishing to sound sincere. Yet in reality, she didn't know how she felt as her heart fluttered and thudded like a captured bird."

When she walks away from Patrick, readers learn even more about her emotional struggle:

> She turned and headed for the checkout. No way would she continue shopping and run into Patrick again in another aisle. Seeing him today had reopened the wound she'd soothed and healed years ago. She looked at the packages of plastic strips in her basket and wondered which one she should use to cover the deep scar that ached within her.

When you create emotion, select words that reflect the character's feelings. Words and phrases like *stumbled, sink, captive bird, wound, deep scar,* and *ached* are triggers that arouse emotional images for the readers. Seeing Christie stumble over the plastic bandages that had fallen to the floor would have little meaning without the introspection to explain her emotion, and her last comment, wondering which bandage might cover her deep scar, adds to the depth of her feelings. Readers are drawn into the emotion with the language and the images created through the internal dialogue.

Characters' emotions can make readers laugh with and cry for and shout at the characters to avoid a dark room. To make a book compelling, recall the emotion that you have felt in your life, then bring them to your writing. Use the characters' memories of past hurts and fears, then relate them to their present actions. Swimming in the same lake that resulted in the drowning of a loved one can affect the character. Hearing an ambulance can trigger memories of a fateful day when the heroine nearly lost her life. An electrical storm can take the hero back to days in the military when he was barraged with gunfire.

INTROSPECTION AND THE SPIRITUAL JOURNEY

Through introspection, the readers can also follow the characters' faith journeys and view their faith struggles. Praying in silence, pondering Bible verses, and questioning what the Lord would have the character do when facing a crisis or decision is a clear way to show how God fits into a character's life.

As you learned in chapter six, the spiritual struggle in Christian romance is an important element of conflict because it affects not only the hero and heroine's relationship, but also the characters' relationships with God. Nothing is more important to a Christian than to be loved and forgiven by God, so sin or stumbling in the Christian walk results in a deep crisis for characters in Christian romance. Combining spiritual conflict and emotion packs a punch for the readers, who have often gone through those same human struggles.

To create a faith struggle, allow the readers to see through introspection where a character is in his faith journey. If the hero questions God, let the readers know. If he wonders if God even exists, say it in his thoughts, then explain why. Perhaps he had prayed fervently for the Lord to spare a younger sibling from a serious illness, but God did not answer his prayer with a yes. When his little sister died, his faith died, too. This kind of head-talk shows the spiritual struggle along with motivation.

Introspection shows not only faith struggles, but also faith maturation, the steps a character goes through to accept Jesus as Savior or to understand God's promises. In Deborah Raney's novel *A Nest of Sparrows*, readers can hear Wade's spiritual struggle as he mourns the loss of his fiancée, Starr:

He thought about the scripture that promised a day when God would wipe away every tear, when there would be no more death or mourning or crying or pain. How he longed for that day. Maybe it wasn't to be on this earth. But suddenly it didn't matter. Whether on this side of heaven or the other, it was a promise he could grasp, a promise to live by.

Wade's introspection demonstrates a real-life struggle with a promise of God that seems to have failed; yet he begins to understand, and the process moves him from one plane to another.

INTROSPECTION AND ROMANTIC GROWTH

Through well-written dialogue, the hero and heroine get to know each other, and readers hear the couple's expressions of love and learn about their hopes, dreams, and plans. Through introspection, however, the readers see the hero and heroine's internal struggles as they try to resolve conflicts, lean on God for help in making choices, and relay their motivation for those choices.

Introspection guides the romantic journey of the hero and heroine. Since the awareness, interest, and attraction stages are not always expressed in dialogue, the growth of the relationship can be presented through their head-talk. Each admires the other and expresses what qualities they admire and what aspects cause them conflict.

While the emotion might be a feeling of excitement or discovery, it could also be one of concern or discomfort. For example, the heroine finds the hero handsome, but in introspection readers learn that he reminds her of someone from her past who caused her problems. This describes the hero's appearance and also initiates a possible conflict if the heroine compares him to the person who hurt her.

Because you are writing Christian romance, physical appearance is not the only source of attraction. As you learned earlier, spiritual attributes and traits of the hero and heroine are significant and rank as important as the physical characteristics. Introspection must also reflect the qualities the hero and heroine admire in each other.

INTROSPECTION AND CONFLICTS

Internal conflict can occur within the character; for example, not what is actually said in a conversation, but what the conversation triggers in the mind of the character. The struggle between heart and head can begin early in a romance. Since Christian romance moves slowly through the process of awareness, getting to know each other, finding points of interest, and finally being attracted, the novel would move too slowly without romantic conflict. The best way to resolve this is to deal with the conflict issues within one or both of the characters.

You can do this by having the hero or heroine pose questions to him- or herself about the problems in the relationship. For example, *How can our love grow when I live in California and he lives in Maine?* Or, *How can I fall in love with a man fifteen years older than I am?* You can also have the character review the issue that is causing the conflict, such as, *I'm fifteen years older than Carrie. Could she love a man my age? I'm not ready to be hurt, and I refuse to be called a cradle-snatcher. I have no choice but to forget my feelings.*

Introspection deepens characterization by revealing the emotional and spiritual struggle, showing the growth of the hero and heroine, and enhancing their romantic conflict.

EXERCISES

1. Read the following dialogue and enhance it by adding the introspection of the woman in the scene. Make sure that the thoughts help to expand the meaning of the words spoken. Allow the readers to know the heroine's true feelings along with her internal conflict.

She sank beside him.

"Let's be honest. I feel like you do, Marsha."

"What are you talking about?"

"Uncomfortable. Uneasy in a way."

She winced. "I don't feel—"

"Yes, you do. For years, we spent time together with each other and our mates. They're gone, and it's different. We feel guilty."

"Guilty? But we're not doing anything wrong."

"No, but we're alive and they aren't."

Marsha lowered her head. "You're right."

"I know, so let's get rid of the guilt stuff. We're alive. Life goes on."

She nodded. "You've always been a good friend, Jeff."

"And there's no reason why we can't be good friends, is there?"

Her heart gave a kick. "No."

"Okay then," he said, resting his hand on her shoulder.

2. Rewrite the example from exercise one from the point of view of the hero, Jeff, including his motivation, his fears, and his true emotions about Marsha. Make sure to delete information Jeff wouldn't know.

3. Create a paragraph of introspection showing a hero or heroine reflecting on his or her growing romantic feelings and emotional struggle. For example, the hero is rooted to his career and not ready for love despite his feelings; or the heroine with two children fears the impact on herself and her children of falling in love and being rejected.

4. Write a paragraph of introspection on a spiritual issue for the hero in the dialogue below. Following the last line of dialogue, show Bill looking into his recent past. Does he see what God has done for him? Is this a turning point? Does it open his eyes?

"Bill, I can never marry a man who's angry at God."

"Why? I'm not asking you to forget your faith. I respect it. I just don't think God cares."

"But he does." She closed her eyes as tears rimmed her lashes.

"How can you be so sure?"

She shook her head. "If you can't see it, then I can't tell you. Just think."

CHAPTER 10

Plotting the Christian Romance

According to *The American Heritage Dictionary of the English Language*, a plot is a plan of events or the main story in a narrative drama. Sounds simple, doesn't it? Yet plotting is one of the most complicated skills in writing. A good plot encompasses believable characters, a memorable setting, meaningful dialogue, realistic goals and motivation, clear points of view, emotional situations, and compelling conflicts, written in a style that results in the readers' inability to put down the book. Good plotting is the engine of a good story. No matter how beguiling the premise, how delightful the characters, how alluring the setting, without a dynamic plot, a story falls on its face.

In all romance, the plot includes the action of the story and growth of the characters and their romance, but what sets Christian romance apart is the growth of the characters' spirituality. The faith element cannot be separated from the romantic situation; it must be woven into the plot.

When embarking on a new novel, creating the plot can become tangled in all of the writing techniques you face. The simple boy meets girl, boy dates girl, girl rejects boy, boy persists, girl gives in, and happy ending isn't quite enough to create a page-turner. When I begin to plot a Christian romance, I often think of this simple system I call the *Five Cs of Plotting*:

Commanding Characters: appealing, yet flawed, hero and heroine, plus a valiant opponent

Clear Cause: understandable motivation and goals

Compelling Conflicts: growing problems, dissension, strife, and crisis

Comprehensive Commitment: growth in both romantic relationship and Christian faith

Captivating Conclusion: end that ties all the plot threads together and creates emotion

(To simplify this even more, drop the adjectives: characters, Cause, Conflicts, Commitment, and Conclusion.)

Readers' Plot Expectations

To add to your plotting challenges, readers have expectations. They look for certain elements that make a novel gratifying and memorable. Christian romance does not escape this scrutiny, so you will want to meet the readers' expectations, which include:

- Loss of something important—love, health, mental health, career, life, pride, hope. For example: *You've Got Mail, The Grapes of Wrath, To Kill a Mockingbird.* Christian novel examples include: Maureen Lang's *The Oak Leaves,* Yvonne Lehman'a *Coffee Rings.*

- Challenging an opponent—a person, group, health, nature, or inner struggle. For example: Hannibal Lecter from *The Silence of the Lambs,* nature in *The Call of the Wild,* or any other formidable foe, such as Al Qaeda or Alzheimer's disease. Christian novels that do an excellent job of demonstrating challenging an opponent include: Stephanie Whitson's *Secrets on the Wind,* Gayle Roper's *Spring Rain,* Neta Jackson's *Yada Yada Prayer Group.*

- Building tension that develops each scene with action, dialogue, introspection, and emotion. For example: Charlotte Brontë's *Jane Eyre,* or Christian novel examples like Francine Rivers's *Redeeming Love,* Deborah Raney's *Beneath a Southern Sky,* Terri Blackstock's *Last Light.*

How plots come to a writer is as different as the authors themselves. Sometimes the plot begins with a small idea—often a "what if"—or a compelling character that arouses a story idea. Sometimes it's a romantic setting or even a personal experience that you can fictionalize to be the bud of a new story. Other times it might be a faith-based issue, problem, or principle that can serve as stimulus for a plot idea. No matter where the idea comes from, the five Cs are needed to begin to plot.

STYLES OF PLOTTING

Plotting styles are as different as plot ideas, and no style is right or wrong. Your approach depends on what works for you. When I'm going on vacation, I love to sit with maps and travel brochures and plan my course. What do I want to see? How will I get there? Some people know where they're going but have no idea of their route, while other adventurous souls enjoy hopping into their vehicles and pulling onto the highway with no thought of where they're going. They'll know when they get there!

Plotting styles work the same way. The typical styles are synopsis, chapter outline, index cards, or the infamous seat-of-the-pants (SOTP) approach, in which authors take the trip without a map. Each style has its weaknesses and strengths. Too much plotting can destroy the creative process of keeping the door open for a story twist or a plot adventure. Too little plotting can hinder a story's flow and realistic character growth. Experiment until you find the best method of supplying all of the needed story points while still stimulating the greatest creativity.

Synopsis

The most popular style used for plotting a Christian romance is a synopsis format, similar to what you would send to an editor or agent, written in narrative, omniscient point of view in present tense. A synopsis allows creativity while still providing you with direction. Like the vacationer heading for parts unknown, you can travel from beginning to end in the shortest time, or you can make an occasional side trip that enhances the plot yet brings the journey to its designated conclusion.

Before beginning your story, you probably have given thought to characterization, as well as the story's opening, ending, and the major conflicts experienced by the character on his journey toward his goal. A synopsis should also capture the story's theme, which in Christian romance is often based on a Bible verse. Although this is not a requirement, most authors use a Bible verse as a focus point to keep the faith message woven throughout the novel.

Using a Synopsis for Plotting

From an Internet writing tip Web site, young adult author Victoria J. Coe says, "The first thing I do when writing a synopsis is sum up the whole story in one paragraph."

- Begin by telling the entire plot in one sentence.
- Next, explain the main character's motivation in one or two sentences.
- Then summarize the "middle" of the story and climax in one or two sentences.
- Finally, tell how the main character grows or what he learns as a result of his experiences.

Here's an example of this type of summary using *Charlie and the Chocolate Factory*: Charlie wants to visit Mr. Willy Wonka's top-secret candy factory. After he and four other lucky children win a tour of the factory, misfortune befalls the selfish, misbehaving four, while amiable Charlie earns Mr. Wonka's trust and inherits the factory.

Using Coe's method of summarizing the story as if writing the back-cover blurb for the book, you can abstract the theme, goals, and conflict while providing the tone of the novel. Then, to deepen the substance of the book, expand the ideas by including motivation and conflicts to provide a clear plotting plan. (Remember, for the purposes of plotting, you're telling, not showing—it's just a summary.)

With these points in mind, a synopsis can open with the first "C," the introduction of the hero and heroine and their first meeting. The first few chapters should provide a solid picture of the first Compelling Conflict coupled with Clear Cause, which sets the tone of the novel—lighthearted, dramatic, suspenseful, or thoughtful. The middle of the synopsis touches on major *plot points*, the important movement forward that leaves the character no turning back. These plot points provide growing conflicts stemming from the character's motivation, goals, and the Comprehensive Commitment, which is how the conflicts stimulate the hero or heroine to grow both emotionally and spiritually. Finally, the synopsis will present the Captivating Conclusion that pulls together all loose ends of the main plot and subplots and shows the culmination of a happily-ever-after ending.

More examples of synopsis styles can be found in chapter eleven, but here's a summary of my synopsis format. I begin with a Bible verse quote, followed by a short one- or two-sentence summary, a hook list, a brief backstory characterization of the hero and heroine, and the basic plot with growing conflicts. A brief character backstory can provide a clear picture of the motivation and goals for the two main characters and make the conflicts realistic as they are presented in the narrative synopsis. The synopsis beginning of *Loving Feelings* illustrates my synopsis style:

Loving Feelings Synopsis

"Your beauty should not come from outward adornment ... Instead, it should be that of your inner self, the unfading beauty of a gentle and quiet spirit, which is of great worth in God's sight." (1 Peter 3:3a, 4).

A homemade candy enterprise brings two people together who can open the doors for love and healing, but secrets from their pasts keep them from facing the truth and realizing it will take more than kisses, or chocolate to heal their wounds. Only God can offer them a sweet, loving ending.

The Hooks

Repeated characters and setting from previous novel, breast cancer survivor, secrets, raising sister's troubled child, hidden agenda, workplace romance.

> ## The Characters
>
> **Jennifer (Jenni) Anderson**, 33, grew up in a stable Christian home with an older sister, Kris. After her mother died from breast cancer, the stability crumbled when their father settled into a relationship neither daughter could tolerate. Rebelling, Kris became wild and ...
>
> ## The Story
>
> Jenni hears strange sounds coming from her nephew's bedroom late one evening. When she investigates, he's playing pinball on a laptop computer. She's startled and asks him where he got the computer, and he says he found it. After interrogation, Cory admits he stole the computer. She finds no identification in the case, but when opening a word-processing program, she ...

Writing a synopsis in narrative style allows you to present the information using the novel's tone and your own writing voice, both of which add a unique presentation of the story. This style also allows easy revisions. No matter how carefully you plan the story, occasionally a new plot point or new conflict will arise. This style of synopsis leaves room to develop this fresh idea without major revisions to your original idea, as long as the incident or conflict is in keeping with the characterization developed at this point in the story.

The negative side of a short synopsis is grasping what should be included and what details are not needed. The key is to ask yourself if the information is absolutely necessary to understanding your basic plot. The time of day, the characters' dress, setting descriptions, and detailed subplots, unless they hinge dramatically upon the romantic commitment, can be left out of the details, leaving you the opportunity to make those decisions when you arrive at that point in the story. Go through with a sharp pencil and question each sentence in a synopsis to make sure it has a specific purpose that moves the story forward by explaining goals and motivation, conflicts, or character growth. If it doesn't, then cut the detail.

Chapter Outline

A chapter outline is a descriptive paragraph of each chapter in a scene-by-scene breakdown. The information will include the mood of the scene and what's to be accomplished. The focus of each scene description is not the story details, but rather a focus on the goals, motivation, and conflict of each character. This ensures that the story moves forward in a realistic manner and that the plot shows the growth of the characters and their relationship and faith. Remember to keep the faith message woven through the book along with the romance.

Using the five Cs of plotting works in similar fashion to the synopsis plotting style. The first scenes will introduce the Character and the Cause for change, then will be followed by Conflicts. The scenes will continue to develop Cause and Conflicts as well as showing the Commitment growth of the romance and faith. The last few scenes will present the Captivating Conclusion.

This narrative outline sample from my novel *Out on a Limb* illustrates the sketchy details of each scene that leads to the biblical theme "love your enemy."

Chapter 1

Scene 1: Humorous. Introducing characters establishing the two-family feud. Karen Chapman, 28, visits her grandfather's farm in northern Michigan to find solace from her stressful job and to support her newly widowed, ailing grandfather. Sitting in a tree in the woods, she is teased by Eric Kendall, 29, the grandson of the next-door neighbor. Recalling a long-time feud between the Chapman and Kendall men, and determined not to get involved, Karen tries to escape, nearly falling out of the tree, to Eric's amusement.

Scene 2: Humorous. Eric asks about the feud's origin with no success. He recalls his and Karen's childhood friendship and now understands Karen's attitude. He figures she is following the long-time two-family feud, whose origin is unknown to him. He recalls at age seven giving her his first kiss.

Outlining is effective because it provides a concise view of each scene without details that are unnecessary to understanding the motivation, goals, and conflicts, both internal and external. You can indicate the mood you've chosen for this scene, and you can check each scene to make certain that something purposeful happens and moves the story forward. For example, while having the hero and heroine grow in familiarity is significant, the scene must also present a situation or past incident that affects the growing conflict. If nothing in the scene moves the story forward, it should be cut. This style of outlining allows creativity as you present the scene, and with less specific details, editors have less to question when you present the submission.

The negative side of this outline comes when writing the book. You have already structured your story, and sometimes you realize that a scene proves more effective in an earlier or later chapter or that an element of the plot isn't moving the story forward as well as you thought. This could mean revising of the outline to fit the rearranged plot points.

Index-Card Plotting

Index cards are a familiar tool for research. Once the research is gathered and quotes, facts, statistics, and ideas are noted on the cards, they can be shuffled and moved around to provide the clearest and most logical organization.

In the same manner, index cards are an excellent means of recording plot ideas, creating dialogue, developing themes, defining symbolism, and entering characterization notes. These cards then become the resource by which you can sort and shift the information into categories and into chapters and scenes. Review the five Cs of plotting and expand upon any of the ideas, develop deeper characterization, or provide a more dynamic conclusion; make notes on character growth, both spiritual and emotional, and measure if the faith element or message has been fully developed. The index cards can help you decide what is missing and in what order these ideas or scenes should play out.

Index cards allow you to see if plot turning points are balanced throughout the story in a way that will draw the greatest emotion and keep the readers' interest. Additionally, index cards will help ensure that subplot scenes provide a hook by shifting the focus of the novel for a time or by adding to the conflict. (Remember, a subplot in romance must always affect the outcome of the relationship between the hero and heroine in a direct way.)

Index Card Plotting

Think of index card plotting as similar to storyboarding. This process is a graphic, sequential organization, first developed by Walt Disney to create cartoons but now used by the motion picture industry because it provides the most effective way to follow a storyline and organize it into an exciting and meaningful presentation.

Though index cards are not visually graphic, they do break the story down into key scenes and ideas that can be organized in the same manner as a storyboard. An advantage of index card plotting is the opportunity to shift the cards around to evoke a more powerful story. It allows brainstorming revision by rearranging the cards to test the emotional impact of the storyline with the changes.

The cards may be categorized by purpose—characterization, plot idea, theme, setting—or they may be organized by where they will fall in the story—beginning, middle, end. If you know a scene must occur but are not sure where it fits in the story, title it by setting or purpose.

As you begin to organize these cards, you will want to add the chapters and scene numbers and whose point of view will present the scene. Again, these can be shifted and moved, then retagged with chapter, scene, and point of view.

Chapter 3—Scene 1   Bill's POV

Bill realizes Sally is curious about his evasiveness, but he cannot tell her the truth and he can't lie, because that's a sin. He talks his way around the subject.

While index plotting allows you to write your ideas and details in note fashion and then build a story, a problem can arise when you're overwhelmed by your data and unable to put the pieces together in a logical, dynamic order. You have to decide what information to include and what to exclude for a concise yet sufficiently descriptive synopsis. Even with that minor problem, the index cards will make that an easier job by providing the synopsis information in an orderly fashion.

ROWBOAT—Confrontation Scene   Sally's POV

Sally suspects Bill has been evasive. While in a rowboat in the middle of the lake, she confronts him. He has nowhere to go and he can no longer evade her question. Bill tells the truth. Sally wishes she could get away from him to think, but she's now faced with the truth and must deal with it. Show confusion and dismay.

Seat-of-the-Pants Plotting

A vague comparison can be made between the index-card-plotting writers and the seat-of-the-pants (SOTP) plotters. Both produce pieces of work that must eventually be put together almost like a puzzle: Which piece goes here, and which one works better there? The major difference is the SOTP writer is working with large pieces of writing, scenes, or dialogue, while the index-card plotter is working with ideas and scene sketches.

Most SOTP plotters can't imagine writing any other way. They can start at the beginning, in the middle, or even the ending. They think of an interesting scene, or perhaps have an insight into characterization that provides compelling dialogue, then jot down these snippets of plot without concern for logic. They enjoy the eventual task of fitting the pieces together until it forms a picture—or in the novelist's case, a story. They smooth the rough edges in the editing process and find transitional scenes needed to connect parts of the story; as this happens, their characters become clearer and their theme appears.

Plotting the Christian Romance

A concern for the SOTP plotter is making sure the spiritual message is fully fleshed out and that the characters' growth and change is woven into the plot in a smooth, logical manner, not just slipped in as another piece of the puzzle.

SOTP style allows you spontaneous creativity. You are free to let plot ideas spark in your mind and let the characters find themselves. Nothing bars the writer from going in any direction or taking any detour that strikes your fancy. While this process works for some, even proponents of the SOTP plotting style admit their stories often require massive rewrites. They can easily lose time taking detours that lead nowhere and sometimes face writer's block, which results in wasted writing time while they try to decide what happens next. Sometimes after finding themselves many pages into the story, they realize they have no story direction or no turning point for the characters.

Yet those who use this plotting method successfully have learned how to structure the story in an effective way, in the same way a puzzle seems impossible to solve until moving one piece makes everything else clear.

CONFLICT

To understand plotting, you must have a good understanding of conflict. Without conflict you have no story. Conflict creates the action, drama, focus, and emotion for the readers. Readers expect conflict that moves them, touches them, and excites them, and they don't want to be disappointed.

Conflict is naturally found in suspense and mystery novels, but it is necessary in all forms of fiction. In Christian romance, it is often based on a spiritual truth. Because conflict is enhanced when readers can relate to the issue, universal struggles—problems that confront Christian people in real life—work well for sources of conflict.

The deepest conflict arises from believable motivation and goals, often based on information gleaned from the characters' pasts. Though two people might be in conflict to head a committee, for example, the reason each wants to head the committee is the deeper issue. One character might have a humanitarian project that he knows he can bring to fruition by being in charge. The other may want the position only because his family demands that he wins every contest.

As characters face conflicts, they must search their abilities and intelligence for answers, garner strength and confidence to solve the issues, and call on God for help. But remember that characters must solve their own problems and conflicts; the resolution shouldn't come from another character or a miracle from God. Certainly God can be praised in the story for giving the character wisdom and strength, but it's the character's efforts that bring the story to a conclusion.

Backstory Provides Needs, Fears, and Conflict

In Christian romance, conflict usually arises from behaviors and situations that occurred before the story began. This can include failures, successes, relationships, health, education, Christian upbringing and nurturing, romantic experiences, or dysfunctional childhoods. These details mold characters into individuals with specific needs, fears, and attitudes.

Driven by such past experiences, each individual is motivated to reach a particular goal—to be forgiven, find true love, locate a lost child, uncover the buried treasure, or save the world. The goals come in all shapes and sizes, and the character's conflict can be within himself, or between himself and another person, nature, ideas, or even God. Conflict is dramatized by obstacles getting in the way of reaching a goal, sometimes in the form of life-threatening or life-changing events, such as loss of self-worth, loss of a career, or loss of the love interest.

External and Internal Conflict

Conflict is both external (having to do with physical action or outward needs) and internal (a mental, emotional, or faith struggle). Conflict is not squabbling and arguments. It is two people reaching to obtain something that affects the other or reaching for something that goes against one of the character's beliefs, whether faith-based or personal.

External Conflict

External conflict can come from nature, illness, disability, or other forces that affect the lives of the characters and their romantic relationship. In

Christian romance, conflict is often between the hero and heroine, whose needs are in competition. Sometimes a man wants freedom while a woman wants equality in a career, but the relationship blossoms and both begin to weigh their goals. Is freedom really what he wants? Is her career that important? They find that perhaps it is the relationship that brings happiness.

Internal Conflict

Internal conflict is the characters' struggles with personal issues, flaws, mistakes, or sins that have motivated their needs. Internal conflict most often stems from the characters' backstories. The issues with which the characters struggle most often deal with Christian behavior toward themes such as trust, honesty, self-centeredness, forgiveness, shame, guilt, conceit, imperfection, promiscuity, hatred, and anger. In Christian romance, the internal struggle will often be the major conflict because it affects not only the characters' goals but also their relationships with God. Still, for a compelling story, the characters should have both external and internal conflicts that hinder their relationships and cause deep emotions.

Presenting Conflict

Your story should open with a few chapters of introduction to the characters and their goals and motivations. The opening also provides the initial conflict of the story, something that keeps the characters from achieving the goal. The middle of your plot deals with growing problems between the hero and heroine. The ending encompasses the "black moment," the direst conflict that causes readers to wonder if the problem can be solved and if the characters will ever come together.

In addition to the internal and external struggle, other issues can involve subplots connected to the original journey—a parent issue, an old flame, a job crisis, or any other problem or distraction.

In an outline of my Christian romance *Secrets of the Heart*, notice how conflicts continue to build as the story moves ahead.

- Kate and Scott meet, and though attracted to him, Kate notices something about him that reminds her of a negative past experience.

- The story moves along, and you learn the heroine had a child when she was fifteen, fathered by a high school football player. The baby was put up for adoption.
- Conflict deepens as Kate learns the hero was an adopted child. Her guilt grows, as does the struggle when Scott reveals his strong belief in chastity until marriage.
- Conflict deepens when Scott, a doctor volunteering his time for worthy causes, invites Kate to a party at Madonna House, which is the facility where Kate gave birth to her child.
- The black moment occurs when Kate tells Scott the truth, and he walks away.

Notice how each conflict worsens the situation, creating empathy and stimulating readers emotions. By the time the conflicts occur, readers have a bond with the characters and are rooting for their happiness together. By arranging conflict from the smallest problem to the most serious struggle, a story gains momentum for readers and becomes a book they can't put down.

STORY STRUCTURE

One of the most popular methods of devising a plot is patterning after a three-act play. Act I is the beginning of the novel, when you present the characters, introduce motivation and goals, and initiate conflict. The first act answers the questions of what the characters want and why and what stands in the way of their goals. Act II is the middle, the longest part of a novel, which presents growing conflicts. Once a character overcomes the initiating conflict, a new one arises. This pattern continues through the middle. Finally, Act III, the end of the book, opens with the final struggle seemingly solved. Before readers can breathe, however, a new conflict, the black moment, arises and must be resolved and have all loose ends pulled together before the happily-ever-after conclusion.

Within the three acts, fiction is made up of chapters and scenes. In Christian romance, especially category romance, the chapters normally range from twelve to twenty pages and are usually broken into one to four scenes. Single-title romances can be more varied as to length of chapters and scenes.

A scene is a moment in time presented in one character's POV. The scene must accomplish a purpose; it should move the story forward by providing new information, deepening characterization, or foreshadowing an upcoming event. Conflict is a must in each scene, adding tension in the pursuit of the goal and arousing emotions.

Because Christian romance scenes are written in one point of view and you want both the hero and heroine to discuss and react to the various issues confronting them, you can use a sequel, which allows the action in one scene to span to the next scene. This gives the non-point-of-view character of the previous scene his or her own scene to address feelings in dialogue or introspection. Whether scene or sequel, this moment in time needs to move the story forward by deepening conflict, providing new insights from the point-of-view character, providing new information, presenting a new character, foreshadowing an event, or showing character or faith growth.

Testing Each Scene

To test each scene, you should ask the following questions to see what it has accomplished and what its value is in moving the story forward:

- What's important about this scene?
- What new information has been presented?
- What have I foreshadowed?
- Have I heightened a conflict?
- How have I deepened characterization?
- What have I accomplished?

If you find only one piece of worthy information in the scene, consider deleting the scene and adding the important information to another scene.

ACT I—THE BEGINNING

Act I, which involves the first three to four chapters, is expected to include:

- An event that causes change: a letter, an illness, a new character, a phone call, a discovery

- Introduction of the hero and heroine, making them likeable, vulnerable, sympathetic, or facing jeopardy/hardship so readers can bond with them
- An objective: What is the goal or need of the characters, and why?
- Introduction of external and internal conflict
- Setting, including location and time of year

Additionally, there should be a hook in the beginning pages to arouse the readers' interests.

Most readers agree that the first two paragraphs are critical in the decision to purchase a book. You have only a few seconds to capture the readers' interests. Unwilling to spend time with long narrations popular in the old classics, readers now prefer openings that leave them with questions or wanting more, so be sure your opening has action found in dialogue, active events, or narrative that fascinates, surprises, or shocks.

Keys to Writing a Page-Turner

To write a page-turner, the opening of a novel should:

- Include action or dialogue that is unique or unexpected and sets up a conflict
- Begin at the point of change—a new day, a character's arrival, a new problem
- Present a sense of urgency, characters in conflict, something unique or unexpected
- Provide a captivating character or a delightful or dreadful situation
- Introduce a hook that puzzles the mind, arouses curiosity, or raises questions

Theme Hooks

Christian romance offers many fiction topics, not necessarily popular in secular romances, that hook readers. These topics deal with Christians following their beliefs in a world that doesn't always have the same values on issues such as sex, alcohol, dishonesty, cheating, faithfulness, and family. Readers are interested by and relate to these topics because they are the same issues that they must deal with in their lives.

Opening Line Hooks

Hooks are sentences or topics that arouse curiosity and make readers want to know more, so opening with a hook is an excellent technique. Hooks include action or dialogue with a sense of urgency, captivating characters, or a humorous or unique situation, and they are always at the point of change. Notice the effect of these opening lines from well-known Christian authors.

> Two things had been on Cat Simmons's mind. Gage Farrell's handsome face. And a dirty undershirt. (*Hope's Garden*, Lynn Cote)
>
> Keryn Wills was in the shower when she figured out how to kill Josh Trenton. (*Double Vision*, Randy Ingermanson)
>
> Kate O'Malley had been in the dungeon since dawn. (*The Negotiator*, Dee Henderson)
>
> Leo Simmons had made good on his mumbled threats. (*The Perfect Match*, Susan May Warren)
>
> It isn't possible. (*Bookends*, Liz Curtis Higgs)
>
> Not again, I can't let it all start over again. (*Last Resort*, Hannah Alexander)
>
> "I'm just saying he's not everything you think he is, that's all." (*Blameless*, Thom Lemmons)
>
> Something was up. (*An Undivided Heart*, Vonette Bright and Nancy Moser)

As you study these opening lines, you notice key similarities. First, they leave readers with questions: Why had a dirty undershirt been on Cat Simmons's mind? Why did Keryn Wills want to kill Josh Trenton? Why was Kate O'Malley in a dungeon? What were the mumbled threats? What wasn't possible? What was starting over again? What about him is troubling? What was up? Opening line hooks capture readers from page one, and curiosity can carry them through to the end.

A story can open with dialogue, action, introspection, or narration, but the lines must draw readers in by presenting information that raises questions, stimulates emotion, creates an amazing setting, or sets the stage for a uniquely told story.

Ending Act I

When I think about the end of Act I, I'm reminded of Robert Frost's poem about making choices, "The Road Not Taken":

> Two roads diverged in a yellow wood
> And sorry I could not travel both
> And be one traveler, long I stood
> And looked down one as far as I could
> To where it bent in the undergrowth.
>
> Then took the other, as just as fair.
>
>   * * *
>
> Two roads diverged in a wood, and I—
> I took the one less traveled by,
> And that has made all the difference.

At the end of Act I, you should have your characters—or at least one character—facing choices: two paths with no turning back, and the choice makes all the difference. The choices can be based on faith, love, or conviction, or the choices can be made without thought. Whatever a character chooses, it will change his life. Placing one or more characters in this position keeps readers emotionally invested in the hero and heroine. Readers will be on the edge of their seats, waiting to know which road the characters will take, how they will reach their goals, and how their choices will lead them to the Lord.

ACT II—THE MIDDLE

The middle of the book, which includes the bulk of the story, is a series of escalating conflicts for both characters. As each conflict comes close to resolution, new and greater conflicts are introduced. (The most serious situation—the black moment—is left for Act III, the last few chapters of the book.)

While first chapters are filled with new information, character development, and set-up for conflict, the longer middle will often be your greatest challenge. It is about 60 percent of your book, and you must keep readers engrossed while showing growth of the characters, the romance, and the characters' faith by balancing action and introspection.

Understanding Pacing

Pacing deals with the emotional ebb and flow of the story, and it involves a balance of action scenes and reflective scenes. In the same way waves roll in a large swell, dash against the shore, and then pull back to ripples, Christian romance needs fast-paced scenes to drive the plot forward to a climax, balanced by reflective scenes that create quiet awareness, develop romantic growth, and create gentle emotion. The fast-paced scenes continue to show action through physical motion and build excitement as the characters become increasingly aware of one another, make decisions, heighten the romance, and provide emotional stimulus for readers. Each moves the story forward to show growth in the character, romance, and spiritual journey, but each in a different way. The shorter scenes offer time for reflection, often deepening characterization through introspection, and heightening the growing romance and spiritual theme. You can also include a paragraph of introspection within an action scene when it helps readers understand a character's action or reaction.

In Christian romantic suspense, the action scenes build the intensity of plot as you present the rising conflicts and create reader anxiety, while the slower-paced scenes give readers time to breathe, and allow them to be involved in the emotion of the characters as they weigh the suspect information and deal with what has happened, and see how it affects their relationships with God. In this way, the author deepens the love story.

While pacing is vital to a good story, it is also a difficult technique to learn. The best approach is to observe pacing in books you read and experiment with the balance between action and calm as you write. When a story feels too slow or bogged down, you know it is time to crank up the action. If there is a breathless feeling—so much going on that there is no time for the characters to regroup or for the readers to understand what is happening—then it's time to slow the pace. Each story will vary with the amount of action and contemplation needed to keep the story moving so that it hooks the readers and hangs on.

Enhance Pacing With Strategic Positioning

Good pacing is created by positioning plot details with the pacing balance in mind. With your story pacing divided by the ebb and flow of action and emotion, look for the best place to provide information or add a new crisis that will keep the story moving forward while enticing readers to follow along. Three pacing techniques that work well to draw readers into the story are conflict, restraint, and foreshadowing.

Conflict: Conflicts can be physical, mental, or spiritual. They must be purposeful and relate to the character's major goal or need. As one is conflict is resolved or near resolution, which slows the pace, introduce a new, worse conflict. Make certain every scene has a conflict, whether small or large. It can be waking with a migraine on the day of an important job presentation, a flat tire when picking up the heroine for a first date, or wondering why God doesn't answer a prayer. As the story progresses, the conflict becomes more serious. The character might fall down a staircase, be caught in a web of lies that affects her reputation, or allow herself to commit an act that goes against God's Word.

Restraint: Feed backstory or other information into the story only when it is needed to enhance a scene. Heavy backstory overburdens readers with unnecessary details and can affect pacing by slowing the immediacy of the story. Let the readers know the character is withholding information until later by providing a line such as *If she knew the whole truth, she would never forgive me.* This arouses curiosity and provides readers with incentive to keep reading.

Foreshadowing: Alert the readers to an impending new conflict that could affect the hero and heroine's relationship, such as hearing an old boyfriend has arrived in town or that Grandma is sick and needs care. The readers will wonder how the event will change the plot. The old boyfriend might try to cause a problem in the blossoming romance, or Grandma's illness might necessitate the hero or heroine becoming a caregiver, affecting their future together. Foreshadowing is also a seemingly insignificant piece of information that becomes more vital later. Readers take note of the information and begin to look for an upcoming crisis or dramatic turn in the story. Jim can't swim. Sue is afraid of heights. These informative details will arouse the readers' interests and be an "a-ha" moment when Jim must swim to save a friend from drowning or Sue must climb a ladder to hide from an intruder. While the foreshadowing is presented in quieter moments, it causes readers to look for excitement in the future.

By positioning plot details with strategy in mind and balancing a story's rhythm between active and reflective scenes, you can create excitement by promising upcoming action.

Enhance Pacing by Stretching Tension

Stretching the tension is another technique to improve pacing in the middle of the book. Imagine you are facing a person pulling back on a rubber slingshot. The shooter can release the rubber quickly and let the shot fly, or he can pull it back slowly, leaving you in anticipation and fear, knowing you will be hit, but not knowing when. This is stretching the tension.

Stretching tension has to do with content (action or thought) and time. Time shouldn't drag. Instead, like the slowly extracted sling, it can create exciting—sometimes fearful—anticipation for readers. A scene is the framework of life impacting the characters. You can stretch tension in your writing in a variety of ways by slowing the action while deepening the impact. Using techniques of delay, interruption, or extended emotional senses or responses are some techniques that can help to enhance pacing.

Action scenes can create tension by presenting the motion as a director does in a movie. Think of John Wayne Westerns. The camera focuses on Wayne's eyes, then the enemy's. The focus moves to Wayne's hand on his gun, then the enemy's. Each piece of action is presented in a dynamic way to draw out the excitement. In romance, you can frame the action of a kiss in the same manner. Moving from the eyes of the hero, then to the heroine, then to their body positions, then to the eyes again, then to their lips, then to the emotional responses of anticipation, and finally to the action—the kiss itself.

Tension can be stretched by interrupting the action. The hero leans toward the heroine, her lips ready to receive the expected kiss, and someone enters the room or the telephone rings. Sounds and sights in the scene can be used to make the story more realistic and to create an interruption of the heightening drama. For example, if a couple is having a serious talk on the front porch, the hero might be distracted by a barking dog or car lights passing by. These distractions can be used as metaphors to reflect the hero's discomfort at sharing his feelings or distracting him from his purpose or from God's will. These delays cause tension to increase as readers wait to know what will happen next.

In an emotional scene between the hero and heroine, you can delay the event by delving into the inner turmoil of a character while leaving the action hanging a moment to help build tension and deepen characterization.

Stretching tension allows readers to delve more deeply into the action and emotion by providing more time for them to anticipate the next step in the romantic journey.

Act II Hooks

Plotting hooks arouse the readers' interests in the same way opening line hooks do. Plotting hooks move readers from the end of a chapter or scene into the next without realizing it. Five well-known plotting hooks are: Time Bomb, Jack-in-the-Box, the Scare, Unanswered Questions, and the Cliff-Hanger.

Time Bomb

The Time Bomb technique brings with it a measure of built-in excitement, providing an explosive situation with a time limit for the goal to be reached, like a bomb-in-the-closet story. Time is running out and the solution must be found. This works extremely well in Christian romantic suspense when the killer has given his last clue and it's evident that he plans to murder the victim, or the kidnapped child must have his medication or he will die.

In romance, this technique escalates conflict, pulling readers more deeply into the story. For example, the heroine and hero argue and break up. When the hero later calls the heroine to ask for forgiveness, he learns she is on the way to the airport to catch a plane to Europe. The excitement mounts as readers wait to see if the hero will arrive at the airport in time, and if she will accept his apology.

Jack-in-the-Box

Jack-in-the-Box almost explains itself. You know when you turn the handle on the box that, somewhere in the midst of the song, the little jester or clown will pop up and scare you. This same technique can be used to create tension by foreshadowing what is to come. Readers expect something to happen, but they don't know when it will occur. Think of the movie *Jaws*. The viewers know a shark is nearby, but they don't know when he will strike again.

This technique is prevalent in romantic suspense, but it can be effective in romance, too. For example, the heroine has a secret that she's foreshadowed, and tension builds as readers wonder about the secret and when she will tell the hero. Or when the hero visits a jewelry store, readers want to know if he purchased an engagement ring, and if so, when he will propose.

The Scare

The Scare is a great movie technique that also works in Christian romance. It sets up a situation that puts readers on edge but does not necessarily affect the outcome of the story. This can include a dark house, noises coming from an attic, a dank basement, a stormy night, a news report of an escaped killer in the area, or any other plot element that makes readers look for the worst.

When using this technique, the scare must make sense. For example, the heroine hears the news that an escaped killer is in the area. She is walking through her house, thinking she's alone, but as she rounds a corner, someone steps in front of her. She screams, then focuses on the hero who came through the back door to surprise her with a bouquet of flowers. The real escaped killer might play a part in the story, but at this point, just knowing he's out there adds the extra scare for the readers.

Unanswered Questions

Most readers want to end their reading sessions at the end of a chapter. Unanswered questions cause them to turn pages, drawing them into the next chapter before they realize it. These unanswered questions are more important than what's for dinner; they are questions about values, morals, flaws, and deep character or spiritual issues, as well as questions about purpose, situation, or actions. If the heroine avoids kissing the hero, readers want to know why. The unanswered question will draw them into the next scene until they find the answer. If the heroine questions the hero about where he'd been and he diverts the conversation, readers will continue reading to find out where the hero had been and why he was being evasive.

Cliff-Hanger

Think about where commercial breaks are placed in most TV programs. They halt the storyline at the most exciting moment and leave the viewers hanging. Authors can do this, too, by stopping the action at the moment of maximum suspense and moving to the next scene or chapter in another character's point of view. When shifting point of view, you can delve into a subplot, then return to the story action. It hooks readers and pulls them along.

Avoiding the Sagging Middle

Despite your greatest efforts, the long middle of the book can begin to sag unless you are conscientious and use techniques to deepen the plot. When you consider that the middle of the book is about three or four times longer than the beginning and ending, you can understand your task to keep the story from dragging and going nowhere.

You cannot pad scenes with empty words and cute situations unless they are purposeful to reaching the hero and heroine's goals. Instead, you can use a variety of tried-and-true methods that will keep a story exciting and on a forward thrust. Familiarity with these methods can help you in a variety of story situations.

Add Subplots

Subplots can boost a sagging middle. Remember, a subplot in romance must always affect the outcome of the relationship between the hero and heroine in a direct way. A subplot can echo a character's struggle and provide another view of what might happen to the hero or heroine, or it can help teach the character a lesson. (In category Christian romance, subplots are limited because the story is shorter and the time needs to be focused on the hero and heroine. Single-title romances allow you to broaden the scope of subplots.)

In Christian romance, you can add a suspense subplot to make the story more dynamic. Perhaps the heroine's neighbor begins to act strangely and the situation causes her to pry into the neighbor's business, which goes against the hero's beliefs. You can introduce the subplot of a friend whose problem parallels the main character's; a career issue, such as a promotion that causes a transfer; or a proposition, such as investing in a company or running for a political office, that affects the main plot. The important element is that the main story belongs to the hero and heroine, and a subplot only enhances the main plot and is connected in a realistic way.

Replace Motivation/Raise the Stakes

Two techniques to avoid a thin story are replacing the motivation of a main character for reaching his or her goal and raising the stakes. Replacing motivation works this way: A man's goal is to double the amount of money raised last year for an Alzheimer's charity. His goal is humanitarian, though impersonal. But when the illness affects his own family, it has greater meaning to him, and thus changes his motivation. This also adds more story conflict and deeper emotion.

The second method to keep your story going is raising the stakes, which refers to a more intense plot that changes someone's life or turns into a life-and-death situation. For example, Julie works at a crisis center and deals with unfaithful husbands and wives. When she hears from a friend who suspects her husband is having an affair, her advice becomes more personal, and she approaches her job with greater concern. Her motivation changes further when she witnesses similar symptoms in her own relationship. Finally, the stakes are deepened when she receives anonymous notes threatening her life if she tells anyone about her suspicions.

Deborah Raney deepened the stakes in her novel *Beneath a Southern Sky*. Raney describes the story:

> The heroine, Daria Camfield, thinks her husband, Nate, has died in Colombia. She returns to the States to mourn and to give birth to Nate's baby. Later in the story, Daria marries Cole Hunter, only to have Nate turn up alive months after the marriage. Now she's married to two men, both of whom she loves ... I realized it weighted things heavily toward her first husband, since he was the father of her child, so I 'evened things up' and deepened the stakes by not having her find out about her first husband until after she's pregnant with Cole's child. Judging by reader response, it was very effective in making readers feel equal empathy for Nate and Cole.

Ask "What If ..."

One of the most common, yet effective, tools you can use for a sagging middle is the question "What if?" What if the hero's home burns? What if he misses the train and loses the account? What if a neighbor moves in who creates new fear for the heroine? What if a trustworthy character becomes untrustworthy, or a friend becomes an enemy? What if the situation has a time constraint? You can create events through new characters or twists of fate.

In his book *Writing the Breakout Novel*, author and agent Donald Maass suggests another technique using "what if." Each character has a personality—things they do and things they don't do, things they believe in and things they are against. By using "what if," you can put characters into a turmoil by causing them to do something they would ordinarily never do. For example, Susan is always a loyal friend but must turn against a friend to defend herself. Joe would never go alone to find a suspect, but his partner is wounded and he has no choice. Each of these "what if" methods add to an exciting middle.

Complicate the Situation

Another powerful way to strengthen the middle of the book is to add levels of complication to your novel. Don't make everything easy for the hero or heroine. In Christian romance, you don't want to be dishonest, but you can give the heroine a good reason for saying no when the hero asks her out. If he drops by, don't always have her home or dressed to greet company. Add complications to her life. When they go on a romantic picnic, create a rainstorm. Perhaps they drive an hour to a special restaurant and it's closed.

Don't forget to use people's phobias as part of their characterization. People have all kinds of fears, both rational and irrational: heights, enclosed places, crowds, being in public, thunderstorms, and everything in between. Some fear sounding stupid or speaking in public; others fear snakes, spiders, or mice. By adding one of these elements to an occasional character—and notice I said occasional—that fear can add drama by placing the character in a situation in which he or she must overcome the fear.

Christian author Colleen Coble describes her use of a phobia to add excitement to her novel set in Hawaii:

> In *Black Sand*, Annie was terrified of falling into lava again after being badly burned when a shelf gave way. When her sister is in mortal danger out on the lava field, Annie first lets the man she loves go to the rescue without her. But after he's gone, she realizes she has to face her fear—that Mano and Leilani need her. When she arrives at the scene, she has to face a volcano eruptions—her worst fear—in order to help save Leilani.

Using fear as a technique to add drama and tension to the story is an excellent method of keeping the middle of the book devoid of slumps.

Complicate the scenes even more by adding a situation that creates a dire element to the story. For example, to remain in his position at the firm, the hero must do something illegal, or to remain with the woman he loves, he must confess his father's recent crime. Put people in jeopardy, even in Christian romance. You are not perfect, and neither are your characters. Allow them to make mistakes and misjudgments. Doing so adds more excitement to your novel and allows readers to relate to the characters.

Remove a Character or Flesh Out a Secondary Character

A story can be changed by removing a character who affects the hero and heroine's relationship and adds conflict and drama to the plot. Kill off the main suspect. Have the babysitter move. Give the friend who always supports the hero or heroine a job promotion that requires a geographical move.

Sometimes an insignificant character can add to the plot and give it a twist, as Deborah Raney explains:

> In writing *After the Rains*, I added a character, a new love interest for my heroine, Natalie, after her childhood sweetheart chose Natalie's sister over her. A few chapters later, as I struggled to flesh out this man, I realized I had another character who had all but dropped out of the story, and it worked perfectly to have *him* become the new love interest. They had a history together, and thus his backstory was much less complicated to write, plus it achieved a second purpose of tying up loose ends with this character.

Another technique Donald Maass suggests from *Writing the Breakout Novel* is to cut a character from the story and give that character's role to one of the main characters. For example, Julie and her mother have a volatile relationship. When her mother becomes ill, Julie finds a caregiver to meet her mother's needs. To apply the cut-a-character technique, give the caregiver's role to Julie. This will provide two excellent additions to the plot: First, caregiving will add more stress and complication to Julie's romantic life; and second, this new role will force Julie to make amends with her mother and allow forgiveness to occur. As in this scenario, the technique works well in Christian romance when the removal of a character forces the hero or heroine to deal with a character flaw or a spiritual issues when taking over a new role.

Christian author Colleen Coble uses this technique in her novel *Abomination*. She says:

> I realized I had too many characters for the readers to keep track of, so I sent the sheriff on vacation and gave his role to the deputy. I also deleted a love interest for a secondary antagonist and had him switch his attention to my heroine. I think it worked and made the story stronger and more interwoven."

Give the Story a Twist

Perhaps you have heard it said that there are only a limited number of plots to be written. While the speculative number varies, the point is that many people believe there is nothing new to write about. Still, you can make the story your own by giving the plot a twist to make it different or special. You can twist the premise (the logical assumptions you make about a story) by creating what readers assume to be true different than expected—a doting husband is in love with his beautiful and happy wife, a successful businessman is confident, an engaged couple is planning a wedding. The wife could be miserable, the businessman could be floundering, and the couple could be uncertain about their engagement. You can twist a plot by not following the tried-and-true formulas.

When you provide hints early in the story that things aren't what they seem, the readers' curiosity is nabbed. The trick is to give your characters enough depth to have something to work with, then take the obvious and make it not so obvious. Take those universal plot ideas and surprise the readers; for example:

- Twist the fairy tale into a story where the *hero* is Cinderella.
- Twist the "secret baby" into a secret from the mother who thinks her child is dead.
- Twist a character who despises his father with the discovery that the man isn't his father.
- Twist the marriage of convenience into one of inconvenience.
- Twist the matchmaker story into one where the matchmaker finds love.

Remember to follow the Christian worldview as you twist your way through the story. Deceit is not acceptable to the readers or the Lord, so you must provide the truth but avoid giving every detail that might reveal the twist. This is not deceit, but a plotting technique that provides an unexpected and dynamic story.

To understand the twisted premise even more clearly, think of movies like *The Sixth Sense, Secret Window,* and *The Village*—all stories with amazing hooks. When you begin your romance with a twist in mind, you have many avenues from which to choose and investigate to the end. This not only provides a full, exciting Act II, but it also offers readers a memorable ending.

The Promise to the Readers

When readers begin a Christian romance, they conclude the author is making a promise, and they expect that promise to be fulfilled. They expect:

- A journey from beginning to end as characters reach their goals
- An ending in which all loose ends are tied
- Spiritual struggle and growth
- An emotional journey that relates to their own lives or dreams
- A "happily-ever-after" conclusion

ACT III—THE ENDING

Act III usually includes the last three or four chapters of your novel. When the ending nears, bring the story to a satisfactory close with excitement and emotion while pulling together the loose ends of any plot themes, issues, and subplots. In all romance, readers look forward to the happily-ever-after conclusion.

At the end of a Christian romantic suspense, solve the crime first by finding the killer, kidnap victim, or buried treasure. The criminal is taken away by the police, the heroine is safe and falls into the hero's arms. Also, resolve subplots before the conclusion of the romance quest.

Before the happy ending, you should view the full scope of the book's conclusion. At the end of Act II, leave your hero and heroine in near readiness for the romantic commitment. Many Christian romances end with a marriage proposal, and some even end with the wedding scene because readers often request it. You have brought both characters to faith or heightened spiritual awareness. You have deepened their characterization by adding to and defining who they are, as enhanced by their new relationship. Yet readers know and expect that something devastating can still happen, and you don't want to disappoint them. It is that black moment that makes the happy ending seem impossible.

Sometimes the black moment deals with the revelation of the hero or heroine's final secret. The character pulls away fearing the reaction and rejection, or just fearing the truth being known. Perhaps another character steps into the plot with a horrible conflict that pulls the hero and heroine apart, fearing for each other's safety. Sometimes the black moment is an illness or a long-awaited dream falling into place that doesn't encourage the romance.

I used this technique in my novel *With Christmas in His Heart*. Accepting the hero's love meant the heroine had to either give up her work or force the hero to leave his stained glass store on Mackinac Island and follow her to the big city. When she decides to give up her career, a career that means everything to her, she receives news of the long-awaited promotion to the position she'd long sought.

Readers realize these things happen and try to decide if they would leave a lifelong career for a relationship that had been on shaky ground for most of 235 pages. In this novel, the heroine leaves Mackinac Island, but while on the airplane to return home, she realizes that her career means nothing without the hero in her life. She can add to his career with her marketing experience, and she's learned to love the island. She returns to the hero, who is now confident she is everything and more that he'd dreamed and that the Lord had truly guided their love.

Don't make the ending easy. Love means more when you fight for it and win with God's blessing. Keep the tension high and leave the readers with questions right up to the final kiss and commitment. Keep note of your word count so that you don't rush the ending. Allow enough time to explore the full scope of the relationship, add those final touching moments that are filled with emotion, and bring the theme to a close. In Christian romance, the story seems rounded when you are able to end with faith's impact on the characters and how it changed them and moved them to trust and love.

GOOD PLOTTING

Plotting is complicated and complex. It can become frustrating to keep the romantic tension and character dynamics moving forward and showing growth and change. Remember that plotting is a journey on winding roads, never direct and easy. You take the readers up mountainsides and into valleys. You make short detours before bringing the characters back to the dilemmas they face and the faith issues with which they struggle.

This chapter has covered many steps and techniques to help you create an emotional journey for your readers. Remember that good plotting includes:

- a strong need or goal that can destroy or change a character or his purpose
- powerful opposition that deepens conflict
- a compelling situation or duty that binds the hero and heroine in their struggle
- building tension through situation, emotion, and action
- pacing enhanced with a blend of action, dialogue, and introspection
- hooks in theme, opening lines, or scenes that grab readers and hold them

With these steps, you can write novels that capture an editor's or agent's interest, provide reviewers with a story they love, and offer hours of pleasure to your faithful readers.

EXERCISES

1. Look at your work in progress and summarize the plot in fifty words or less. Then narrow it down to one sentence to help clarify your story's meaning and purpose.

2. Study the opening lines of your work in progress, then analyze the paragraph and answer these questions:

- Will the first line grab readers?
- Does it leave readers with questions?
- Is there unnecessary backstory?
- Is the first paragraph through the eyes of a character?

- Can readers sense a need or goal?
- Can readers anticipate a conflict?

If you find any problems, rewrite the opening paragraph to improve it.

3. Review the plot of your latest work or work in progress and make sure it is clearly divided into three acts and meets the purpose of each act.

4. Theme and conflicts are vital to your novel; make sure they are clear, focused, and purposeful in your story. What is your novel's theme? Is it a biblical or spiritual issue? Have you used a Bible verse as a focal statement as you write your novel? If not, consider using one. Do you use a theme to enhance your internal conflict? Review your story for character growth, including spiritual growth. Does it relate to the theme? Is it realistic?

5. Print three or four pages of work in progress. With colored pencils, underline all dialogue, action, emotion, introspection, and spiritual content, using different colors for each. Make sure you have a good balance between all of them. If you are missing introspection, dig into the point of view character's thoughts and decide what he or she may be thinking and feeling, then work introspection into the scene. Some scenes will have more action, some more dialogue, but each must provide introspection because it is through the character's thoughts that you find the scene's major elements of emotion. If the spiritual message is lacking, review your theme and make sure that your message is woven into each chapter in a realistic way.

CHAPTER 11

How to Sell a Christian Romance Novel

Even if you do everything right in your writing process, selling a book depends on its readiness for publication—a neat presentation, free of typos—and being sent to the right agent or publisher at the right time. Good stories are rejected if, for example, your storyline is too similar to one they just published, if the story doesn't have the right ingredients for the publisher's readership, or if they need to buy a completed manuscript and yours is incomplete or still needs some work.

Selling a book takes patience, commitment, and perseverance. You must present quality writing that follows the rules of the genre and the publisher's guidelines. Some Christian authors sell on their first try; others write for twenty years before selling their first novel, but you have a better chance if you scrutinize this chapter and use the tips to help you reach that "impossible" dream.

IS YOUR NOVEL READY FOR SUBMISSION?

You've probably had family and friends read your books and tell you they are great, but family and friends love you and don't always know what is currently selling and what an editor accepts. Many options—such as how-to books on writing, writers' organizations, Christian writing conferences, and critique groups—are available to help you learn the craft, test your work with those who know the genre, and discover the elements of a saleable novel *before* you send it to an agent or publisher.

How-To Books on Writing

Books on writing are an excellent source of information. These books are available in libraries or can be purchased at most bookstores or through publishers, such as Writer's Digest Books. Though only a few books are available on writing Christian fiction, writing books in general can teach the basics of good writing, including dialogue, emotion, characterization, point of view, plotting, and conflict.

Most how-to-write books provide excellent illustrations and numerous exercises to guide you in creating a well-written novel. By studying the examples and completing the exercises, you will have a better grasp of good writing techniques, which will carry over into your own work.

The two books I use the most are Strunk and White's *The Elements of Style* and *Self-Editing for the Fiction Writer* by Renni Browne and Dave King. These books are amazing sources of general information about good writing that will guide you as you prepare your book for submission. A book specifically for writing a synopsis, and which uses one of my synopses as an example, is *Give 'Em What They Want* by Blythe Camenson and Marshall J. Cook.

Writers' Organizations

Writers' organizations can be found locally and on the Internet. As a Christian romance writer, finding an organization that has a major focus on the romance genre and on the specialty genre of Christian romance is a boon to your writing. The two organizations detailed below can answer that need because they not only focus on writing romance fiction, but in an online writers' loop, they also cover writing and marketing information, offer critique groups, provide a newsletter, and host a national conference.

American Christian Fiction Writers (ACFW)

ACFW, founded as American Christian Romance Writers in 2000 and now a national organization that includes all Christian fiction genres, meets both stipulations—Christian and romance. You can learn more about ACFW and the benefits of membership at www.acfw.com. This organization provides a group e-mail correspondence loop—a group e-mail to all members so they can share ideas and information—on the business of writing, including group discussions on writing topics, topics of the week, marketing and publishing information, support, and spiritual strengthening. The Web site provides members-only forum groups with discussion on various writing topics and genre interest groups, research archives, and free online classes. Other benefits are critique groups, contests, and an annual conference. ACFW has also formed regional zones and local chapters in many states where members can meet locally to hold workshops, critique each other's work, and join in fellowship.

Romance Writers of America (RWA) and the FHL Christian Chapter

RWA is a national organization totally devoted to romance genres of both secular and inspirational (Christian) fiction with local chapters in many cities in the United States. While these chapters do not focus on the Christian genre, they are open to workshops and discussions on this topic and can provide excellent information and training in the craft of writing.

Its Internet Christian genre chapter, *Faith, Hope and Love, Inc.* (FHL) at www.faithhopelove-rwa.org, offers similar benefits to ACFW, including an online e-mail loop, marketing and publishing updates, guest speakers, critique groups, contests, and participation in RWA's national conference. An FHL mini-conference is held annually before the official RWA conference opening. To be a member of FHL, you must join the parent organization, RWA.

Other Christian Writers' Organizations

Having membership in Christian writing organizations is another form of invaluable networking that will provide you with the latest trends, publishing information, and guidance in writing in a variety of genres.

Besides ACFW and RWA and their local chapters and zones, other Christian writers' organizations are scattered across the U.S. Although these groups do not focus on Christian romance, they do offer writing information on fiction and nonfiction, and most offer newsletters, publishing information, mentoring, and some form of conference.

The Jerry Jenkins Christian Writers Guild at www.christianwriters guild.com offers an annual conference hosted by best-selling Christian author Jerry Jenkins and staffed by talented Christian authors, editors, and publishers of Christian works. Other benefits are a newsletter, contests, discounts on books, conferences, critiques, and members-only Web site access.

Christian Writers Fellowship International at www.cwfi-online.org publishes a well-known newsletter, *Cross and Quill*, as well as offering critique services, book promotion, e-mail conferences, agent information, contact guidance, and connections to other authors.

A Canadian writers' organization, InScribe Christian Writers' Fellowship, can be found at www.inscribe.org. It provides members with an annual conference, retreat, and a newsletter.

An organization with conferences throughout the year all over the United States is American Christian Writers. It is found at http://watkins .gospelcom.net/americanchristianwriters, and it includes an annual cruise-ship conference. It provides a monthly magazine, *The Christian Communicator*, and offer discounts on workshop tapes and books.

By using an Internet search engine, you can locate other local, regional, and national Christian writers' groups, such as Oregon Christian Writers at www.oregonchristianwriters.org and Northwest Christian Writers' Association at www.nwchristianwriters.org. Sally Stuart's *Christian Writers' Market Guide*, detailed on page 209, also includes a list of Christian writers' organizations by state.

Christian Writers Conferences

Each year across the United States, as well as in foreign countries, a variety of Christian writers conferences are held, allowing you to choose those that best match your interest. Most conferences offer workshops for beginners as well as more experienced writers. Large, more popular conferences bring in well-known speakers, agents, and editors, while the local conferences will offer fewer options but will be less expensive. These conferences provide workshops to help you hone your craft on a variety of writing topics, as well as an excellent opportunity to network with fellow writers, editors, and agents.

Two of the top conferences for Christian romance are American Christian Fiction Writers (ACFW) and Romance Writers of America (RWA). ACFW is the best for a focus on Christian fiction, including romance, while RWA's total focus is on romance and its various subgenres.

ACFW holds its conferences each September in a selected location. This conference is attended by Christian agents and editors representing many publishers of Christian romance. Besides full-day workshop schedules, the conference offers night-owl mini-workshops in a casual setting, as well as time for worship and praise, prayer, and spiritual inspiration.

RWA, held in July, is a national conference also located in a different U.S. city each year. Its emphasis is secular romance. Since the conference focuses on all genres of romance, it provides excellent workshops on craft, career, publishing, the writer's life, and research. *Faith, Hope and Love, Inc.*'s mini-conference, the day before the official RWA conference opening, is totally focused on Christian romance.

While romance is a primary focus of ACFW and RWA, numerous Christian conferences across the country provide excellent classes on writing Christian fiction. Though romantic fiction is not their primary focus, they offer a full conference schedule of worthwhile workshops covering topics on various genres of fiction and nonfiction writing, time management, getting published, and spiritual growth. Like the ACFW conference, these conferences offer times for worship and praise, prayer, and spiritual inspiration.

The Internet has countless Web sites that list Christian conferences. One helpful site is www.christianwritersinfo.net/conferences.htm, which offers an updated list of conferences with dates and Web sites. Use a search engine to locate other conferences that may be available.

Christian Conferences

Here are some of the largest, most well-known Christian writers conferences.

Spring Conferences

Blue Ridge Mountains Christian Writers Conference in Ridgecrest, North Carolina (www.lifeway.com/christianwriters)

Florida Christian Writers Conference in late February/early March in Sarasota/Bradenton, Florida (www.flwriters.org/index.html)

Christian Writers Conference in Mount Hermon, California (www.mount hermon.org/writers)

Write His Answer Colorado Christian Writers Conference in Estes Park, Colorado (www.writehisanswer.com/conference_(colorado).htm)

Summer Conferences

Write His Answer Greater Philadelphia Christian Writers Conference in August (www.writehisanswer.com/conference_(philly).htm)

Write-to-Publish Conference in Wheaton, Illinois (www.writetopublish.com)

Fall Conferences

Glorieta Christian Writers Conference in Santa Fe, New Mexico (www.classervices.com/CS_Glorieta_Conf.htm)

Sandy Cove Christian Writers Conference near North East, Maryland (http://watkins.gospelcom.net/sandycove.htm)

Winter Conferences

Glen Eyrie Christian Writers Conference in Colorado Springs, Colorado (www.navigators.org/us/ministries/gleneyrie/programs/programs)

The Jerry Jenkins Christian Writers Conference in Colorado Springs, Colorado (www.christianwritersguild.com/conferences)

Year Round Conferences

American Christian Writers conferences offer over twenty-one two-day conferences across the United States. (http://watkins.gospelcom.net/americanchristianwriters/acwconferences.htm)

Most conferences provide appointment times to meet with agents and editors, but many also offer opportunities to meet with published authors for one-on-one visits. Published authors sometimes provide paid critiques, which can be invaluable. For a small fee, they will read ten pages to a full chapter of your work ahead of time, then meet with you at the conference to talk about your strengths and weaknesses as a writer. If this author writes for a publisher you'd like to publish with, by meeting with the author you can learn a great deal the publisher's expectations.

Another benefit is the fellowship of meeting other writers and sharing in their ups and downs. Knowing you're not alone with rejections or long waits from an editor can boost your spirit. You might also learn about other critique groups, online or in person, that you can join, and find a host of other information to help you become a professional Christian romance author.

Critique Groups

Obtaining unbiased feedback about your writing is vital to improving your writing skills. Family and friends are not the best judges of what makes a good story, and although you like to hear them compliment your work, it may not stand up under the rigorous examination of an agent or editor. To be the best writer possible, use all resources available to you, one of which is critique groups.

Critique groups are for serious writers who can take the criticism of others writing in the same or similar genre. You benefit from having your work scrutinized for your writing strengths and weaknesses, but you also learn by studying other writers' work to see their techniques in creating a compelling story.

A critique group will look for all of the techniques covered in this book: believable characters, compelling plot with growing conflicts, strong goals and motivation, clear point of view, fresh dialogue, strong emotion and use of senses, appropriate sexuality for a Christian publisher, and a solid spiritual thread woven through the story. If two people identify the same problem in your work, take it into serious consideration and work to perfect any areas of weakness. If one person offers an idea that doesn't mesh with your good sense, you can make your own decision about whether to change it.

Critique groups are only as effective as their members. When looking for a group, find people who understand your genre and have been writing and pursuing publication, and make sure the group includes at least one or more published authors. When three or four people, none of whom have knowledge of good writing, form a group, the critique progress can lead you astray, so remember to weigh the critiques with common sense. Also, make sure the group is cohesive. Can each person accept criticism without becoming angry or give criticism without being overbearing in his or her suggestions? Cooperation and respect are major elements of critique groups.

You can find or form critique groups through your local writing organizations. These groups usually meet face to face once a month or bimonthly. Some organizations, such as ACFW, organize critique groups where you can work with published and unpublished authors on the Internet through e-mail or a chat room.

Critique groups provide the opportunity to take your work to the next level and make it the best it can be so you can present a positive picture to agents and editors when you submit a proposal.

PREPARING FOR SUBMISSION

The critique group members can't do all the work. You must continue to grow and polish your work in terms of format, punctuation, spelling, paragraphing, and cleaning up the typos to present a professional submission to agents and editors. When you have a completed manuscript and believe it is ready for submission, then you can proceed to the next step toward selling your book for publication. Nothing guarantees a sale, even if you've followed every rule of writing. Books are rejected for many reasons, as I mentioned earlier, but if you have done your homework—studying books on honing your craft, joining writers' organizations, attending conferences, and participating in critique groups—then you are showing you are a writer who wants to be a published author. Your next step is to make sure that your manuscript formatting and presentation looks as professional as possible. Then, once you're confident that it's as good as it can be, move your writing career to the next level by looking for a publishing house or an agent.

Make Your Submission Professional

To give your manuscript or proposal a positive appearance to an agent or editor, study these tips that address common mistakes of writers.

Formatting

All manuscripts should have at least one-inch margins using a standard 12-point font (Times New Roman is the most popular). Author and manuscript information—name, address, e-mail address, telephone number, and word count—should appear on the first page. Thereafter, a header—including the author's name, book title, and page number—should appear on each page.

Submission Presentation

Agents and editors dislike "cute" submissions on colorful paper or that include confetti or any other non-professional content. Use white paper for your proposal submission and bind with a rubber band before mailing.

Punctuation

Writers should spend time studying the punctuation chapter of a good grammar book, such as Strunk and White's *The Elements of Style*. Learn the proper use of commas, exclamation points, quote marks (single and double), em and en dashes, and ellipses. To an editor, the misuse of these is a sure sign of an inexperienced writer.

Paragraphing

White space on the page is good in fiction, so use shorter paragraphs. In fiction, a paragraph break is used to separate one speaker and his action from another or to separate a new idea from the previous thought. Avoid putting one character's action into the same paragraph with a different character's dialogue.

WAYS TO SUBMIT YOUR MANUSCRIPT

Authors have three basic ways to submit their manuscripts for publication: finding a publisher who accepts unsolicited material, meeting an editor at a conference appointment with the offer to submit an author's work, or finding an agent.

Publisher

Some writers prefer not to work with an agent, and some have been unable to secure one, so finding a publisher on their own is the first step.

The benefit of publishing without an agent is you are your own boss and your royalty earnings belong totally to you. You do not have to pay a percentage to an agent. Working directly with the publisher allows more personal contact to negotiate your own contract and to work at your own pace without advice from an agent. On the other hand, submitting on your own means your publisher options are limited. Besides Steeple Hill and Barbour Publishing, the only publishers who work directly with authors are mainly small presses and print-on-demand (POD) publishers, who usually do not pay royalty advances or provide good marketing and distribution, resulting in low sales numbers. An advance on royalties is money that the publisher anticipates you will earn and so is paid up front, but you must earn that money in actual book sales before you receive any future royalty payments. Another disadvantage of submitting on your own is understanding the contract lingo and butting heads with an editor without agent support. The tension might affect your future sales, and unless you have the tact for problem solving and the know-how to work with contracts, this may not be your best choice.

Another option is self-publishing, which has the same problems as the POD publishers but also costs out-of-pocket money to publish the book, with no guarantee of sales.

Conference Invitation to Submit

Another option for submitting your novel is through appointments with editors at conferences where you can pitch a novel and receive an invitation to submit. You are given only a few minutes to pitch your book, so you will want to prepare a one- or two-sentence summary of your book and leave time to ask questions and answer any questions the editor might have. If the book has won a contest, share that information, but never tell them that all your friends and family love the story. Let the short, well-prepared synopsis speak for itself.

Editors at conferences will usually not accept paper other than a business card, so unless they ask, do not request they carry home your proposal and manuscript. The benefit of having an editor request your proposal or manuscript is that it opens the door for you to submit without an agent. Their request to see your novel or partial novel is a solicitation, so be sure to identify where and when the manuscript was requested in your cover letter, and also place a notation that reads "Requested Manuscript" on the mailing envelope. This will make sure that the manuscript is not returned to you before the editor sees it. Be sure to include a self-addressed stamped envelope (SASE) with the proper postage so the manuscript can be returned to you. You can submit to more than one publishing house as long as you indicate in your cover letter that it is a simultaneous submission and if it does not go against the publisher's guidelines.

The only negative side of the editor appointment is that they often ask for submissions from many of those with whom they talk, so it's not an accurate picture of how well your manuscript will do. If they do not invite you to submit, your next step will be to find an agent to represent your work.

Agent

Many authors prefer to work with an agent, and most conferences offer agent appointments. Since working with an agent is often a more personal relationship than working directly with an editor, you will have a chance to speak with an agent and decide if his or her personality and work ethic match your own. Submitting to an agent is not dissimilar from submitting to an editor, although most agents will require a full, completed manuscript. If an agent offers to look at your work when you meet at a conference, write "Requested Manuscript" on your mailing envelope. If you are submitting to more than one agent, indicate this information in your cover letter.

The benefit of having an agent is that it opens more publishing house doors than trying to submit on your own. An agent will work on your behalf to find appropriate publishers and to obtain the best contract for you with the highest advance and royalty rates. He will also be your liaison when dealing with any publication problems so that you can concentrate on your writing and not create friction between you and your editors. On the other hand, you pay the agent for his work, and if your agent is not as excited about future manuscripts as about the first submission, or you find he doesn't meet your needs, you may find it necessary to sever your relationship.

FINDING A PUBLISHER

Each writer has her own voice and each story has its own flavor and nuances. You want to match your manuscript to the best possible publisher for success in selling your work, so the first step is to do market research. For any author, with or without an agent, familiarity with what kinds of books a publishing house is looking for is a major step in preparing for submission.

Read and Study Christian Romance

To write Christian romance, you must understand the genre. Study Christian romance authors you admire, who write the kind of stories you write. Read their books. Notice the plotlines. Are they pure romance? Are they in your style—not too literary or not too chick-lit, for example? Look at the names of the publishers. If two or three of your favorite authors, who publish the kinds of books you write, have the same publisher, put a star beside the publisher's name when you add it to your list.

Besides the books in your personal library, you will want to purchase a few newly released Christian romances to see what type of plotlines and story styles are currently selling. Publishers' needs shift year by year, meeting the demands of their readership as readers' tastes and interests change. Publishers look for themes that will attract readers, as evidenced in the new interest in publishing novels with a NASCAR plot, or that involve terrorists. By reading current Christian romance, you will also have a better idea of how the growing attraction between characters is depicted in the books of varying publishers, enabling you to find the publisher with your storytelling style.

Visit Bookstores

Take a trip to your local Christian bookstore and study the romances available. Check the copyright dates to make sure that the books you study are current. Read the back-cover blurbs and scan the openings. Look at the book length and compare it to yours. Some publishers have shorter romances; others prefer lengthier stories. If the publishers seem a good fit for your style and story, add them to your list. While you're there, look at the book covers. Covers attract readers. Were you attracted by the cover? Does it appear to capture the spirit and theme of the back-cover blurb? Your publisher's promotion and quality presentation can make or break a book, so keep that in mind while making decisions.

Use a Market Guide

Purchase a copy of Sally Stuart's *Christian Writers' Market Guide* or find the book at your local library. Stuart's book lists traditional and subsidy publishers for all Christian genres, including romance. Subsidy means you must also pay part of the cost to have your book published, which can be very expensive, so you may prefer to look for royalty-paying publishers. Again, make sure the book is current, since lines change and publishers' needs change also. The guide will often provide the names of editors, mailing addresses, specific needs and wants, page counts, royalty information, and a volume of information to help you make your choices.

Make a list of book publishers who accept Christian romance, then, before taking action, study the publisher's guidelines. You can write a letter and send it with an SASE requesting publisher's guidelines using the addresses found in Stuart's market guide or on the Internet; you can also locate many of the guidelines on publishers' Web sites. Christian author Lyn Cote has a yearly up-to-date page of Christian publishing houses and their acquiring editors on her Web site at www.booksby lyncote.com. Publishers' guidelines provide detailed information about what type of romances they publish (romantic suspense, for example, or medical or office romances), restrictions in content, preference for story themes or styles, detailed format and word count information, and much more that will help you prepare your manuscript for submission. You should obtain publisher's guidelines as soon as possible so you can follow them during the writing process.

Some publishers prefer a query letter while others prefer a proposal that includes a synopsis and one to three chapters. Still others want a full manuscript. Some allow electronic submission, but many require the manuscript to be mailed. So follow the submission requirements carefully to make the best impression as a serious writer who has done her homework on that publishing house.

Learn About a Publisher

Besides making sure the publisher is a royalty-paying house with an advance on royalties, you need to ask other questions to help decide if this is the publisher for you. What do they offer in book rights? Though they will have rights to your book for a contracted period of time, make sure the rights revert back to you once the book is out of print. What is their time for production and the expected release date after a sale? Do they provide line- and copyedits as part of your sale? What are the prices of their books? (If the novels are too pricey, new authors' novels are more difficult to sell since they have no following.) Where are the books sold? Does a major distributor handle their books and get them into the bookstores? (Books sold only on the Internet are hard sells.) Learn what you can about their marketing procedures. Do they promote authors' books, and if so, how?

When you have a list of publishers and their guidelines, and have identified which houses will best serve you and your book, you are ready to proceed. Your next step is getting your book in the hands of publishers by following their guidelines, submitting the most professional manuscript with the type of stories they accept or, if you prefer, finding the right agent for you.

AGENTS AND WHAT TO EXPECT

A literary agent is someone who represents your book to the publishers. He is the liaison between you and the publishers you hope will buy your book. Only a handful of large Christian publishers accept novels without an agent, so it is important that you look for an agent who will work best for you. Some specialize in certain genres, so it's important to take note of their specialties and find an agent who is looking for and selling the Christian romance genre. Remember, also, agents are not selling you. They are selling your work, so it's important that they love your novel as much as they like you.

What Does an Agent Do for You?

Agents earn their money by selling their clients' work, typically a commission of 15 percent for domestic rights and 20 percent for foreign or entertainment rights. Most reputable agents belong to the Association of Author Representatives (AAR), which provides guidelines for their relationship with a client. A good agent will not require money up front for reader fees, processing fees, or any other cost to you. Some agents ask authors to provide copies of their manuscripts; some have a duplication fee which they deduct from the author's advance or royalties. Agents should send you a copy of your royalty statements and checks in a timely manner. They should maintain an escrow account for clients' funds and provide you with copies of all correspondence received relating to your work. An agent should also provide you with accurate tax information at the end of the year, which includes a 1099 form and details listing all payments to you. The relationship between an agent and author is one of mutual trust: You believe the agent will sell your book, and the agent believes your book is saleable.

Agents have connections. They develop a good working relationship with editors and are known and trusted by the publishers, so when an agent submits a book, it has a better chance of being read by an acquisitions editor. Agents keep tuned to the latest trends and the needs of various publishing houses by making visits or phone calls. Most agents read your work and decide the best fit for your novel and a publisher, but they are usually happy to listen to your preferences. An agent may sometimes offer suggestions for revisions before submission if she spots a plot weakness or a subject that might prove offensive to a publisher.

An agent is your book's cheerleader. She is the person who loves your writing and guides your career with short- and long-range planning. She advises your next step, how to line up your projects, when to stay put and when to move on.

If you dislike the business part of writing and only want to write, an agent handles all the business details. She helps you keep track of delivery dates and your next royalty check. If a publisher proposes changes, your agent will notify you and discuss them with you. If problems or disagreements arise between you and your editor that you can't resolve alone, your agent will step in to mediate and help move the issue to a satisfactory conclusion.

An agent's job is to secure you the best possible contract. She reads it thoroughly, proposes changes, and negotiates to improve your benefits:, such as the amount of your advance, clauses regarding rights, timelines, better distribution, and promotion. She will also represent you when other offers are made on your books, such as movie or TV options.

Steer clear of agents who try to sell you other services such as paid editing or critiquing, Web site design, or self-publishing. Your agent's task is to sell your work to a traditional, royalty-paying publisher who will promote and market your book for you.

Finding a Literary Agent

Finding an agent can be as difficult as selling your book. Don't accept an agent's offer without checking out his track record and his clientele. Not every agent is a good one, and not every agent has your best interest at heart.

There are numerous ways to find the best agent for you. One is meeting agents at a conference. You'll know if you are on the same page in terms of your writing goals and talents, and you can ask questions. Is the agent a member of Association of Authors Representatives (AAR)? How many clients does the agent have, and how many are published?

Asking other writers about their agents and relationship satisfaction is another way to gather agent names. This approach also gives you the opportunity to ask questions: What are their agents' strengths and weaknesses? Do they communicate regularly on projects? If the agent doesn't keep in touch with the author, what makes you think the agent will keeping in touch with your editor? Are they fast with royalty statements and with answering their authors' questions?

If you'd like an online method to find an agent, the AAR has a database of member agents on their Web site at www.aar-online.org/mc/page.do, and they also have a Frequently Asked Questions section about agents. When you have any questions about the legitimacy of your agent or publisher, you can check out the Web site Editors and Predators at www.anotherealm.com/prededitors/ to find a list of agents and representatives as well as book publishers. The site warns of those who have been given questionable ratings. If you are a member of RWA, you can also contact their national offices for assistance. There is also excellent information on reputable agents in the book *Guide to Literary Agents*, which is updated annually.

Submitting to an Agent

Check the agent's guidelines in the market guide or on his Web site for her preference of submission. Most agents like a query letter that offers a brief description of your writing experience and a very short synopsis of your story, theme, and spiritual focus. If an agent is interested, she will request a full or partial manuscript. Another process is to send the agent a proposal, including a cover letter, short synopsis, and the first three chapters. These submissions take more time to prepare and have a longer waiting time to hear from the agent. If she is interested, you'll be asked to send the completed manuscript.

Agent and Author Agreement

Some agents provide a written contract while others have a verbal contractual agreement, usually submitted in letter form. The agreement states what the agent will do for you in terms of representation, commission, length of the agreement, and how works sold or initiated sales will be handled and for what time period, and how and when the agreement can be terminated.

All contracts should have an "out clause" for both author and agent. If the relationship is not working, a written notice can end the representation.

Though an agent accepts one of your projects, he may reject another if he doesn't believe it's up to your writing quality standard or doesn't believe the book will sell. Still, an agent hopes to follow your career and strives to sell your other work that he deems salable.

SUBMISSION PROCESS

Whether submitting to an agent or editor, follow the appropriate guidelines and prepare the most professional submission you can. Make sure you're clear about what an agent or editor is looking for in terms of genre (for example, literary fiction, multicultural fiction, or popular fiction), book length, and writing style.

Whether you begin with a query letter, a book proposal, or a full manuscript, keep your submission professional. While most publishers and agents prefer a query letter, be prepared to submit a proposal or full manuscript if it is requested. Authors occasionally begin the submission process before the manuscript is ready, but for a new author, this can be dangerous. While the process usually takes months, if you are blessed with an editor who reads your query immediately, you will be in a bind without a completed novel.

A Query/Cover Letter

A query or cover letter makes the first impression on an agent or editor. The purpose of a query or cover letter is to introduce you and your work. A query letter asks if the agent or editor would like to see more of a specific body of work. The cover letter is included when mailing a proposal or a full manuscript.

In your letter, be polite and professional. Use good quality paper in white, ivory, or buff color without borders or fancy design, and keep it to one page. Use a letterhead with your name and contact information. Be concise with your introduction, and though you want to make your novel sound intriguing, don't go to extremes.

The format for the two is very similar. Begin with the date and be precise with your salutation by including the editor's name. If you are sending the manuscript after having met the editor or agent at a conference or workshop, say so immediately in your letter. The first paragraph should indicate that you are sending your book for consideration and include the following information: the name of your novel, word count or page count, genre, and whether it is complete. You might also indicate if this book is part of a series and the progress you've made on future books: a completed novel and continued writing is a sign that you are a career writer.

Your next section should include a single-paragraph synopsis that gives a flavor of your novel, your story premise, and the major theme, conflict, and spiritual message. Write it as if it were a very short back-cover blurb with a hook. Use Victoria J. Coe's one-paragraph summary technique as described in chapter ten (on page 167).

The third paragraph is about you. You will include any previously published books, short fiction, or articles, and your professional work and education, especially if they relate to your writing skills. You can include awards, writing organizations to which you belong, writers conferences you've attended, and any expertise you have in writing this novel. You might even mention what motivated you to write the novel, but only if it relates to the novel itself; for example, *My grandfather was a lumberjack and I recall the stories he told about his experiences.* You can also give a one-line description of your life: *I am a Christian, married to my husband for twenty-one years, and the mother of three teenage boys.*

In the fourth paragraph, you thank them for considering your work, give the best times and methods of making contact, and express that you look forward to hearing from them. Sometimes I also include a statement about my willingness to make revisions and edits so that my book will be the best it can be. If you are including a proposal or manuscript, you should include an SASE with the proper amount of postage, or ask them to destroy your submission if they decide to decline your book.

New Christian novelist Missy Tippens's first novel, *Michael's Surrender*, released in February 2008, was submitted to an agent with the following cover letter:

Missy Tippens
Street Address
City and Sate
Telephone Contact
E-mail Contact
www.MissyTippens.com

Suzie Agent
Sell Your Book Literary Agency
Tall Building, Suite 10
Big City, Any State USA

Dear Suzie,

I enjoyed meeting with you at the ACFW conference in Dallas. I've enclosed the three chapters and synopsis you requested during our appointment.

Promises is an 88,000-word inspirational women's fiction written in two first-person points of view: a mother and the daughter she gave up for adoption. The manuscript is the winner of a Georgia Romance Writers Maggie Award and was a 2006 finalist in Romance Writers of America's Golden Heart contest.

Jessica Malone is going through a crisis. Years of infertility have put a strain on her marriage. The man who used to encourage her to excel at teaching now only encourages her to excel at ovulating. She's even begun to doubt she loves the stranger who sleeps on the other side of the bed. But when an eighteen-year-old girl named Angela e-mails her, her life is totally flipped upside down. Angela is the child Jessica secretly gave up for adoption. Now Angela is in trouble and is looking for answers. Maybe the woman who birthed her can help her decide whether to keep her own baby. Maybe, just maybe, Jessica will provide the extended family Angela craves. The problem is, Jessica's family is falling apart.

My writing credits include a short story published by BelleBooks in "Blessings of Mossy Creek" (June 2004). My other complete manuscripts have won and placed in multiple contests, including the Maggie, Molly, Finally a Bride, Jasmine, Lone Star, Toronto Golden Opportunity, Southern Heat, and Laurie.

I hope you enjoy reading this portion of *Promises*. I would be happy to send the complete manuscript if you would like to see more. I also want to let you know this manuscript was sent to another agent in August from a request I received at RWA's national conference, and it is still under consideration there. I look forward to hearing from you.

Sincerely,
Missy Tippens

Proposal

A novel proposal is your first opportunity to introduce an editor or agent to your writing style as well as your story. The proposal consists of a cover letter, summary/marketing sheet, synopsis, and three chapters of your novel. (In Christian romance, most editors prefer the first three chapters.)

Proposal Summary Sheet

A proposal summary sheet is not required by all publishers, but it would not be wrong to send one. It is basically a marketing tool for the publisher and provides the title, genre, back-cover-blurb-style synopsis, brief author bio, and anything significant that might prove successful in marketing your book (reader popularity, contacts with organizations, or speaking ministry). You can also indicate the novel's theme, Bible verse, spiritual take-away, and proposed author marketing (Web site, promotion groups, author newsletter, and any other method you would use to encourage readers to buy your book).

Synopsis

As described in chapter ten, a synopsis can be many lengths. Most editors and agents prefer one of the shorter styles, from a few paragraphs to one or two pages, usually with a five-page maximum. Format your synopsis as you would your novel manuscript, with headings but no cover page. A synopsis can be single-spaced with an easy-to-read font, such as 12-point Times New Roman. Begin with the novel title, author, and Bible verse that guides the story, and remember, the synopsis is written in summary style in present tense.

Short Synopsis. The short synopsis is a paragraph or two, similar to a back-cover blurb, that summarizes the story. The paragraph sets up the plot and stresses the conflict. End or begin with a hook, if possible. For example: *Will Perry and Laurie face their flaws and find true love?* Try to capture the tone of your story in the blurb. This means if your novel is a mystery, comedy, or pure romance, use language that will create that flavor.

Christian author Lenora Worth explains her approach:

> When it comes to writing a good synopsis, remember it's all about the conflict. Editors want to see the main conflict of the story right away. I always start a synopsis with 'This is a story about ...' Then I briefly mention the main characters and their main conflicts, the setting and set up the opening. This is not the time for long, drawn-out details. But an opening hook or question should be included in a brief synopsis.

Christian novelist Deborah Raney says she usually writes a one- to three-paragraph synopsis. Notice how this synopsis opens with a hook sentence, then follows with another hook that leads into a summary of her novel *Remember to Forget.*

> What if you could start all over again? What if you had a chance to walk away from past mistakes and reinvent yourself? That's exactly what graphic designer Maggie Anderson is offered when a terrifying carjacking leaves her alive and well, but stranded a hundred miles away from her New York apartment—and her abusive boyfriend. When a kind stranger offers Maggie a ride, she impulsively directs him west, away from her life in New York. After a grueling three-week journey, confused, heartbroken, and without a penny, she winds up in tiny Clayton, Kansas—and the beginning of a brand new life.

Without giving plot details, you have a clear picture of the plot points and understand Maggie's motivation for changing her life by running away.

This can easily arouse the interest of an editor who will ask to see a proposal or, in the case of a seasoned author, an editor who will buy the book. Notice that Raney does not tell us the name of the hero or her abusive boyfriend, nor does she provide details of the grueling three-week journey, but you know this is a time when you will see the hero and heroine tested and grow in character, familiarity, and faith as you watch them begin to fall in love.

In the following short synopsis from Lenora Worth's Christian romantic suspense *Deadly Texas Rose*, notice how Lenora structures her back-cover-blurb style to incorporate a hook.

SHORT SYNOPSIS

Deadly Texas Rose Synopsis
By Lenora Worth

This story is set in the small fictional town of Wildflower, Texas. When Deputy Sheriff Eric Butler goes across the street from the courthouse to eat lunch with some friends at a popular steakhouse, he notices the pretty new waitress who is serving his table. Her name tag tells him she is Julia Daniels. But before Eric can get to know her better, a robbery takes place in the restaurant and Julia is held at gunpoint.

Eric manages to distract the robber and winds up saving Julia's life. But Eric gets shot in the process. Julia goes to visit him in the hospital and thanks him for helping her.

As Eric gets to know Julia, he finds out she is a single mother with a sweet ten-year-old daughter. He also finds out Julia is hiding a troubled past and that the robber who nearly killed her might not be the only person who wishes Julia dead. It will be up to Eric to protect Julia and her child, and to finally tame this Texas wildflower.

Worth's hook is her final sentence. In a statement, she poses an open-ended comment that will arouse readers' interests. Eric must protect Julia and her child, but will he, and how? Enticing readers to buy the book and find out more or interesting an editor to learn more about this story is the purpose of a short synopsis.

One- or Two-Page Synopsis. The one- or two-page synopsis is the most popular because it provides more character and plot details, but still covers only the bare necessities—conflict, goals, and motivation, plus setting and a few plot points to set the tone of the book.

The first paragraph of the sample one-page synopsis of *Remember to Forget* (follows) is nearly the same as the back-cover blurb. It poses an opening question and a closing hook as well.

In the next paragraphs, Raney adds a few major plot points that provide realistic motivation and add conflict to the plot. You can sense the excitement of the plot as the ex-boyfriend closes the distance between himself and the heroine and her new life. Notice that the hero and heroine are not described physically, nor is the setting. When writing a synopsis, focus only on goals, motivation, and conflict with a few key plot points, usually giving a more descriptive opening and closing.

If you began with a shorter synopsis, you can flesh it out with more specific information to use as your writing guide. You do this by adding more plot points and details.

ONE-PAGE SYNOPSIS

Remember to Forget Synopsis

By Deborah Raney

Who hasn't dreamed of getting a chance to start life all over again? What if you could walk away from past mistakes, reinvent yourself, and begin a brand new life? That's exactly what graphic designer Maggie Anderson is offered when a terrifying carjacking leaves her alive and well, but stranded a hundred miles away from her New York apartment—and her boyfriend, whose verbal abuse has turned physical. When a kind stranger offers Maggie a ride, she impulsively directs him west, away from her life in New York. Confused and heartbroken, and after a grueling three-week journey, she finally winds up in tiny Clayton, Kansas.

Reinventing herself as Meg Anders, she is welcomed with open arms by the citizens of Clayton. Unable to use her bank account without giving away her

---

hiding place, Meg is forced to rely on her new friends' generosity. After staying for a week at the local bed-and-breakfast, she is offered a permanent room in exchange for cooking breakfast for the inn's rather infrequent guests. She soon finds an afternoon job in the town's small print shop. There, she works with a man who is the antithesis of her abusive ex-boyfriend, Kevin. Born and raised in Clayton, Trevor Fox has always been the town's favored son. But after his wife and son were killed in a car crash, Trevor went through a crisis of faith. He returned to the fold, but his once exuberant personality has been replaced by a cynicism that deeply concerns his large, extended family.

It takes awhile for Meg to learn to trust Trevor. But once she realizes he is for real, she falls hard for the man. But Trevor has trust issues of his own. If Meg reveals the truth about herself and her past, will she destroy everything she's worked so hard to build?

Meanwhile, Kevin Bryson isn't crazy about the fact that his girlfriend has disappeared, leaving him without access to the small inheritance from her parents—one he's become accustomed to dipping into. Unknown to Meg, he is conducting an all-out search for her, becoming more angry, irrational, broke, and desperate with each false lead and each mile that brings him closer to her safe haven.

Everything comes to a head when Kevin unearths a clue to Maggie's whereabouts. Now her life may depend on revealing the truth to Trevor.

Long Synopsis. While most editors or agents prefer the shorter synopsis, some novelists—especially those writing a complex plot—will need a few more pages to tell their story. Don't try to cover every story event or scene; only show the opening scene—how the hero and heroine meet—then how their relationship progresses by providing plot points that demonstrate conflicts, motivation, and change and growth, especially in terms of faith growth.

In your synopsis, make sure you follow the romance growth from curiosity, interest, attraction, to falling in love. Include only those secondary characters necessary for telling the main plot and avoid calling them by name if possible (the hero's mother, her sister, the neighbor).

This helps to focus on the two main characters. Avoid including detailed subplots unless they are vital to understanding a major plot element.

Tie all loose ends together. Don't leave the editor dangling in a mystery wondering how the story is resolved. Cover all the important bases to show that you can bring the story to a satisfying conclusion.

Once the synopsis is written, go through it again and ask yourself whether each fact, sentence, or phrase is important, and cut such descriptions as *the next morning, two days later, wearing a dark suit,* or *twiddling his thumbs.* What the editor wants is goals, motivation, and conflict, then resolution.

This style of synopsis also works well as a working plot plan for your novel. With greater detail, it stimulates scene ideas and allows you to follow the map, while still allowing you an occasional creative detour to add a plot twist or an additional conflict.

LONG SYNOPSIS

Surrender Bay Synopsis

By Denise Hunter

The Lord your God is with you,

He is mighty to save.

He will take great delight in you,

He will quiet you with his love,

He will rejoice over you with singing.

ZEPHANIAH 3:17

I will never leave you nor forsake you.

JOSHUA 1:5

Main Characters

Samantha Owens—Adventurous with everything but her heart, Sam has always been a risk-taker. Her independent streak has helped her overcome many obstacles, but others sometimes see her determination as stubborn-

---

ness. She's a tomboy, preferring the practical to the stylish, and most men see her as "one of the guys," though they are endeared by her klutziness. Because everyone she loves has abandoned her, becoming vulnerable is Sam's greatest fear, so she never lets anyone get too close.

Landon Reed—Cautious and contemplative, Landon is a man who gives careful thought to every action, but his prudence sometimes causes him to miss out on life's best surprises. His greatest fear is of water, the result of his brother's drowning. He is calm and steady, but his need for peace causes him to avoid confrontation. Landon has an inner strength and integrity that draws others, and when he loves, it is a deep and steadfast love. A born protector, Landon yearns to be a husband and father, but no one has ever compared to his childhood friend Sam.

The Story

Samantha Owens and her eleven-year-old daughter, **Caden**, live in Boston, where Sam works as a commercial cleaner. Independence and tenacity are the tools Sam has built her life with. She left Nantucket, the small, New England Island on which she grew up and single-handedly raised the child who was conceived after one night's indiscretion. When Sam sets her mind on a task, everything but the goal at hand is forgotten—sometimes even her daughter, whose preteen attitude coats every conversation with tension. Though she's thankful for her daughter and a paycheck that allows them to scrape by, Sam wonders why she feels so empty and lonely. Deep down, she longs for safety and love, but she runs from anything that promises those things.

Her loving father died when she was eight, then her mother remarried a year later, and she was adopted by her stepfather, **Emmett Owens**. Emmett was less than kind, but when her mother abandoned her two years later, her stepfather resented her even more and was often cruel. The events of Sam's life have left deep scars and taught Sam not to depend on others.

Sam wonders if everything is about to change when **Mrs. Biddle**, the widow who'd lived next door to her family on Nantucket, informs Sam that her stepfather passed away and that ownership of the cottage has fallen to her. She knows she must go back to her childhood home and prepare it for sale, but the thought of returning to the place of so many bad memories strikes a chord of fear in her. Perhaps Emmett, who'd once filled her life with uncertainty, could now, in his death, provide her and Caden with stability through the million dollars she could get from the sale of the waterfront cottage.

When the couple she works for agrees to a leave of absence, Sam returns to the island for the first time since she'd left eleven years ago. Part of Sam longs to see **Landon Reed**, her best friend, who grew up two cottages down on the Nantucket shoreline. Even Caden, who'd heard all her "Landon and me" stories, hopes to meet the boy who'd shared her mom's childhood. Sam doesn't know if Landon ever fulfilled his dream of becoming a Nantucket veterinarian on the island he'd always loved. He'd already left for college by the time Sam had found out she was pregnant. She'd taken her entire savings, and the small wad Mrs. Biddle had pressed in her hand, and left the island. Ashamed of her predicament, she'd told only Mrs. Biddle where she was going and had sworn her to secrecy. Sam remembers the deep feelings Landon had for her and the fire he stirred in her, but she also remembers the smothering fear that followed. What if the embers that had secretly burned for him in her heart have not yet grown cold?

Sam and Caden arrive in Nantucket and settle into her childhood home. The postcard-perfect island draws tourists like a hummingbird to nectar, but the churning blue waters and restless wind only send deep tremors of fear through Sam.

When Landon visits his parents, **Rick and Anna Reed**, who still live two doors down from Sam's childhood home, he can't believe his eyes when he sees who's pulling weeds outside her father's cottage. Sam. All grown up and as beautiful as ever. Seeing her again, priceless memories flood his mind bringing with it a tide of hope. She'd disappeared without a trace shortly after his brother, **Bailey,** drowned. For years, he'd tried to find Sam, to no avail. And now, here she was.

The awkwardness of time passed fades quickly as the two reminisce about their childhood adventures. Because of Sam's home life, she'd spent more time with Landon and his family than her own. As they catch up, Landon is reminded why no other woman has been able to capture his heart the way Sam had. Being with her again stirs up feelings he can't ignore.

Before they finish their first conversation, he already feels Sam pushing him away, like she had the summer before he left for college. Landon wants nothing more than to break through her barriers and rebuild their friendship. When a little miniature of Sam rumbles down the porch steps, Landon realizes it may be too late to ask forgiveness, too late for the kind of reunion he longs for.

As Sam begins to sort through her mom and stepfather's belongings, old wounds are reopened. Sam relives the death of her dear father, the disgrace of continually disappointing her mother, her mother's abandonment, and Emmett's unrelenting harshness. These resurfacing feelings only underscore her determination to keep others at arm's length. Overwhelmed by her deep wounds and by the fear Landon ignites in her heart, Sam frequently escapes reality by exercising or by hanging out at Cap'n Tully's Tavern. There, the numbing effects of alcohol and attention from men make her believe she can survive until she can leave the island and Landon's tempting presence.

Caden enjoys the setting Sam had grown up in, but it's clear the strain between Sam and her daughter has followed them to the island, and Sam wonders if the problem is more than just preteen challenges. She doesn't know how to handle Caden anymore, but at least she doesn't pick her to death the way her own mother had. And Sam would never think of abandoning Caden.

Landon comes over often with his dog, Max, threatening Sam's peace of mind. When he asks about Caden's age, Sam tells him. But since Caden is almost twelve, she knows Landon probably thinks she'd gotten got pregnant after she'd left the island. It would hurt him deeply to know she had slept with his brother that night, the same night Landon had told her he loved her.

As they talk, it's too easy for Sam to slip back into the same easy friendship she'd once enjoyed with Landon. He still knows her thoughts before she speaks, still has the same quiet strength that pulls her like a riptide, taking her to a place she's afraid to go, and the feelings still frighten Sam. In an effort to convince herself she doesn't need Landon, she agrees to a date with Tully, the owner of the tavern, and makes sure Landon knows about the upcoming date.

Sam's blatant rejection angers Landon. He can't believe she continues to push him away yet proceeds to go out with a notoriously unscrupulous man. Can't Sam see she's setting herself up for trouble? Worried for her safety, he reluctantly agrees to a double date—since Sam seems so eager to set him up with someone else. Watching her flirt with Tully all night is almost more than he can take, but at least Sam gets home safe and sound. Landon confides in his father, who has also known Sam all her life and has seen the pain that drives Sam. He convinces Landon to be patient.

Meanwhile, Caden's behavior perplexes Sam. Landon and his dog draw out Caden's warmth and playfulness, and even Mrs. Biddle connects with her daughter, but Sam only elicits her daughter's smart attitude. Between the stress of going through her parents' things, her guilt over Bailey, and fighting her feelings for Landon, it's almost more than she can take. The tension mounts when Landon expresses his feelings for her one night on the pier. After he leaves, Sam, feeling the familiar fear bubble up inside, escapes to Cap'n Tully's.

Landon receives a phone call from a friend who tells him that Sam is at the tavern and is drunk. By the time he arrives, she is leaving with a stranger, and Landon uses his fists to back up his right to take Sam home. When they get to her cottage, Sam, still under the influence, says and does things he knows she will regret the next morning. It takes everything in him to refuse her advances, but Landon loves her too much to take advantage of her. She deserves to be treated like a lady. He only wishes she could see that.

The next day, Sam remembers enough to be humiliated, and she dodges Landon for a few days. When would she learn to be more careful? It was exactly that situation that had gotten her Caden, and yet she still finds herself dancing with danger. Despite her efforts to push Landon away, he continues to show up at the cottage and help her sift though her parents' belongings.

Once she lives down her drunken behavior—and Landon's lecture about stranger danger—Sam finds her heart cautiously opening to her old friend.

One evening as they take a break from sorting out her parents' belongings, Landon tells her he loves her. When he kisses her, Sam intuitively responds, her heart catching fire at the contact. But soon, the old familiar fear rises up to suffocate her. Of all the men she'd ever cared for, none was more dangerous to her well-being than Landon.

Sensing a desperate need to push him away, she lets loose of the one secret she knows will drive him away. She admits that on the night of Landon's going away party, after he'd told her he loved her, she'd gone out with his brother in his boat. She told him how they'd drunk until they could hardly stand and how she'd slept with Bailey. She couldn't tell Landon why she'd done it: that Landon's confession of love terrified her and that his leaving for college left her feeling abandoned all over again. Sleeping with Bailey had been her pathetic way of proving to herself that she didn't need Landon.

Before Sam can stop herself, she admits the rest of her secret. That when Bailey had brought her back to the party, he'd stayed in the boat to sleep off the alcohol, not wanting his parents to find out he'd been drinking. He'd told her to tie off the boat, but her stomach had rolled as she exited the boat, and she'd scrambled to the edge of the pier to throw up. By the time she'd finished, she'd forgotten about tying off the boat.

The storm that had come up had been quick and fierce. Sam would never know if Bailey had even been aware of what was happening, but by the time his family had known where to look, his boat was capsized and Bailey was nowhere to be found.

As Sam tells her story, Landon's thoughts jet off to that August night. The party was over by the time his mom had asked where Bailey was. Rain began pelting the ground, and that's when Landon had noticed his brother's boat missing from the slip. He'd called for help then taken his dad's larger boat out on the tossing waves. The upturned boat was not far off shore, and when he neared it, Landon dived into the treacherous water screaming his brother's name. In his attempt to find Bailey, the roiling waves had nearly swallowed Landon, but he'd finally made it back to his boat. Bailey's body was found the next day.

Now, Sam was telling him about discovering she was pregnant, about how she'd feared everyone would find out she'd been responsible for Bailey's death. Sam's confession sends Landon's thoughts into a swirling whirlpool of emotions. Landon realizes Bailey is Caden's real father. He staggers under the weight of these revelations, but before he can respond, Caden comes in from playing outside, effectively stopping their conversation, and Sam practically pushes him out the door.

Sam knew Landon would despise her for sleeping with Bailey and for not admitting long ago to her part in Bailey's death. Now he would leave her alone forever. It was what she'd wanted, why she'd told him the truth. But why does her heart feel as heavy as an anchor now?

Landon takes time to digest Sam's news. His family had always wondered how Bailey had come to be on the water alone. He knows Sam would never have hurt Bailey intentionally and that she'd carried the guilt of her carelessness all these years. He wishes she had trusted him enough to come to him when she'd discovered her pregnancy. Did she really think he couldn't forgive her for the mistake that caused his brother's death? He would have married her and raised Caden as his own. Hadn't he always been there for her? And yet, here she was again, spilling her secrets only to scare him away, trying to drive a knife in his heart when he only wanted to love her. When would she learn that he was never going to leave her?

One evening when Sam and Caden go swimming off her pier, Caden drifts too far away and becomes caught in a riptide. With alarm surging through her, Sam goes in after her daughter. Sam reaches Caden and holds her tightly as she swims toward shore, but the riptide is too strong. Sam swims vigorously, pulling Caden farther down shore. Her daughter's eyes are wide with panic, her screams are growing weaker, and Sam is becoming too exhausted to swim. As they float slowly away from shore, Sam realizes the depths of love she has for Caden. Helpless, she clutches tightly to Caden. Sam's heart lies in shambles as she realizes that she's never allowed herself to love Caden the way her daughter deserved. She'd emotionally abandoned Caden because of her fear of loving again. As the realization sinks in, Sam confesses her failures to Caden and assures her daughter that she loves her more than life itself. Her daughter deserves all of her, and if they somehow live, Sam vows to do whatever it takes to be the kind of mother Caden needs.

When Landon stops by his parents' house, he knows it's just an excuse to check up on Sam and Caden. But when he exits his Jeep, the distant scream he hears sends chills up his spine. He jogs to the backyard and stares off into the wide expanse of the ocean. Then he sees the orange glow of Caden's swimming cap in the distance and knows she and Sam are in trouble. Shoving back his fear of the water, Landon grabs a life preserver and sets off into the ocean. The memories of the night Bailey drowned drive him through the water. He would save Sam and Caden or die trying.

When Sam hears Landon's voice, she thinks she's hallucinating. But she sees someone coming and calls for help. Before long, Landon's arms are around both of them, holding them tightly to the life preserver and drawing them to safety.

When Sam awakens, she's in the hospital and Landon is beside her bed. As she remembers what happened, her eyes search the room frantically for Caden, who is sleeping peacefully in the next bed. After a night at the hospital, Landon takes Sam and Caden home. Out on the pier, where Sam and Landon had shared so much of their childhood, Landon draws Sam to him again, knowing he'd nearly lost his two best girls. His throat choked with emotion, he tells Sam he loves her, had never stopped loving her. He admits it might not be easy. There would undoubtedly be misunderstandings and disappointments, but he would never leave her. If Sam let him, he'd hold on to her and Caden as tightly as he had in the ocean for the rest of his life.

In Landon's arms, Sam admits she learned a lot of things on the water: Loving is a risk, but life without love is empty and lonely. She could run, she could try and find substitutes, she could stay busy and try to forget, but there was still a hole in her life without Landon.

> Her father had unwillingly abandoned her by dying, her mother had deserted her in a way no child deserves, and her stepfather had never loved her. But Landon had never left her. She'd done nothing to deserve him. She'd done nothing but push him away and cause him pain, yet he'd never left her, never stopped loving her. He'd always been there for her when she'd needed him, even to the point of risking his life.
>
> Sam determines to open her heart to Landon the way she'd opened it to Caden on the water. She'd been running all her life ... running from Landon, running from the island, even running from motherhood in her own way. Running may have kept her heart safe, but it had also kept it empty.
>
> Landon whispers words that fill her heart again, telling her he wants to be her husband, that he wants Caden to be his daughter, that he wants them to be a family. Sam knows that she wants nothing more, and that Caden deserves nothing less.

After Submission

Once your query has been submitted—proposal or full manuscript with a cover letter sent to an agent or editor—you wait. An agent's or editor's first allegiance is to her present authors; your manuscript will be looked at as the agent or editor finds time.

After an agent or editor reads your book and sees its potential, she can take various steps. If she feels the book needs some revisions, she may send it back and ask you to change a few story elements so she might consider a sale. If this happens, you will choose between sticking to every detail of your story or possibly making a sale. Personally, I do revisions. If she likes the book as it is, she will take it to a committee, which usually includes the head editors and sometimes marketing personnel who will judge your book on story appeal and salability.

If your work receives a positive response, you will receive the longed-for "call" from an editor or agent with an offer to buy your book. When the book will be released depends on revisions and the publisher's schedule. Books are often scheduled one or two years in advance. Though the wait seems long, one day you'll open a box of author's-copy books and hold one in your hand. The long wait is worth every minute.

EXERCISES

1. Look at your work in progress or your completed novel and check to see that you have followed the guidelines for a professional-looking manuscript. Have you followed the proper format with margins, header, page numbers, and author identification? Have you reviewed your grammar and punctuation, such as commas, double and single quotations marks, exclamation points, em dashes, and ellipses? Are you taking advantage of "white space," making use of shorter paragraphs for eye appeal and easier reading for editors as well as readers? If any of these things aren't meeting the industry standard, be sure to change them.

2. If you belong to a critique group, evaluate your group according to the points in this chapter. Do they understand your genre? Do they provide positive as well as negative feedback? Is one of your critique partners published with a traditional royalty-paying publisher? Have you learned to weigh their comments, knowing that one person's comment might be wrong, but two means this is something you need to take seriously? If you don't have a critique group, think about people you might ask to critique with you from your local writers' group and contact them, or join an online organization that will match you up with a critique group.

3. Whatever stage your writing career is in, prepare a plan for selling your book. What should you do in the near future to guide you as you write your book? What steps must you take to find an agent or publisher? Planning for your novel's future will assure that you've done all you can to give your book the optimum chance for a sale.

Index